THE TERRIFICS

MEET THE TERRIFICS

VOL. 1

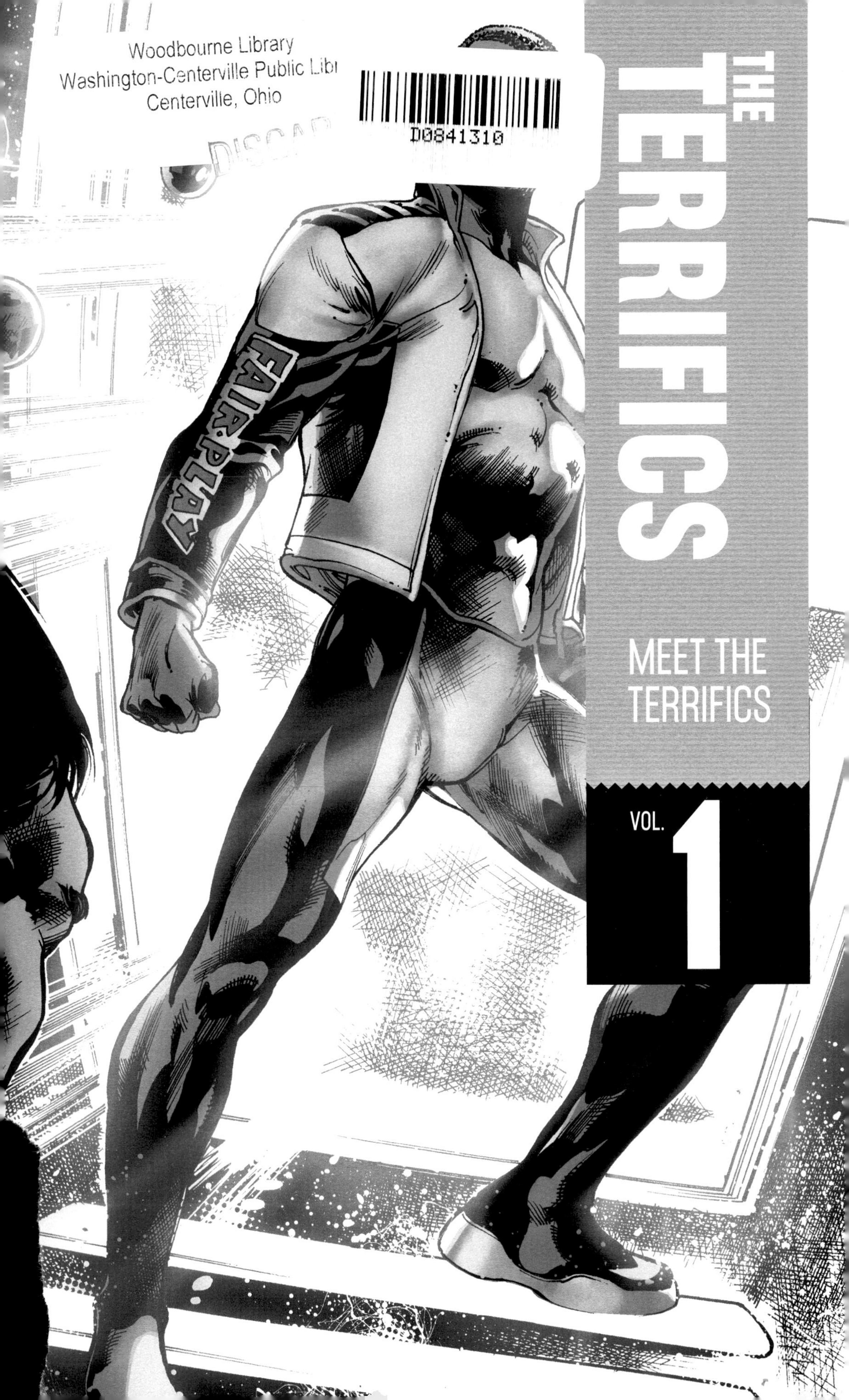
FAIR PLAY

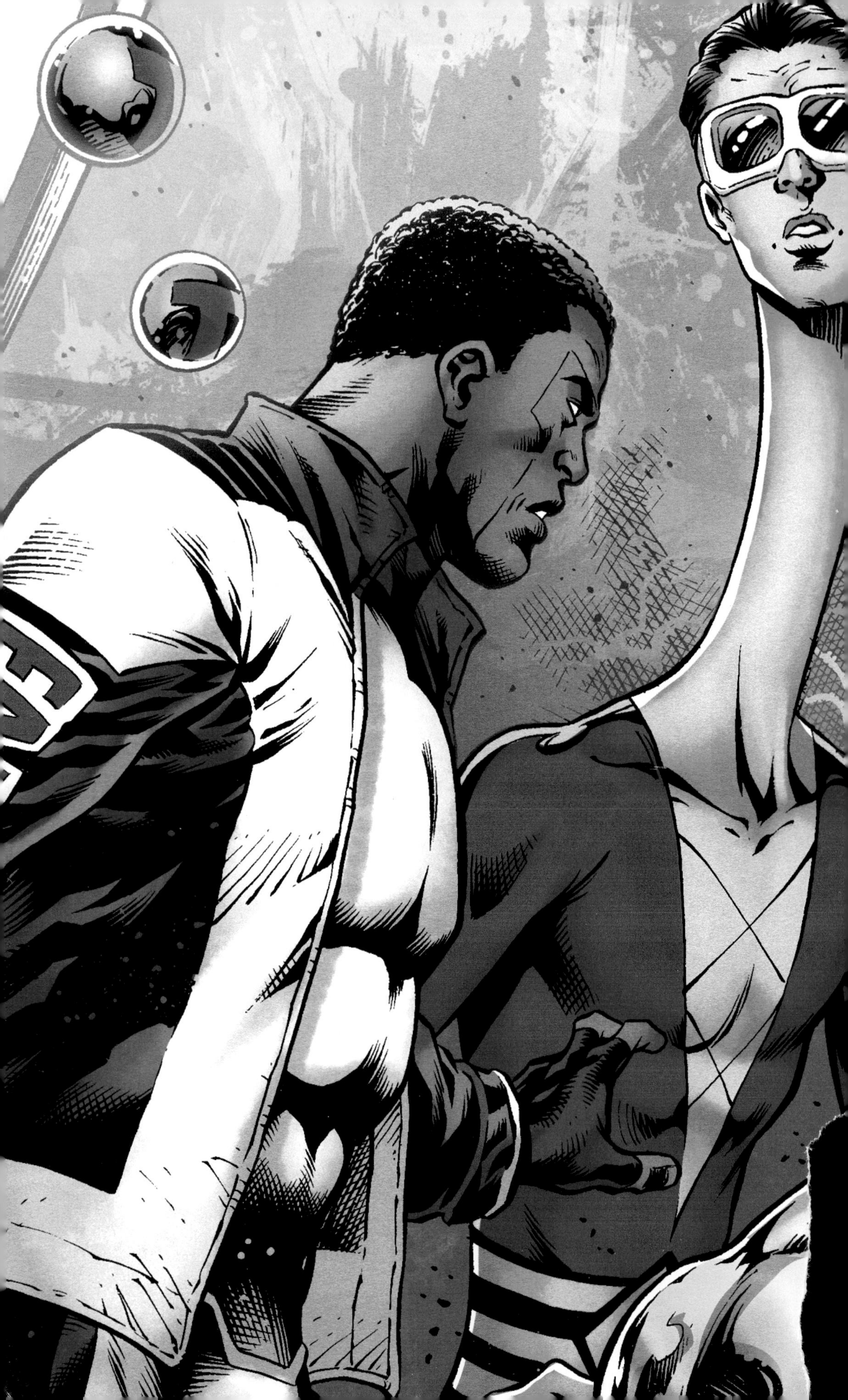

THE
TERRIFICS
MEET THE TERRIFICS

pencillers

IVAN REIS \ JOSÉ LUÍS
JOE BENNETT \ EVAN "DOC" SHANER

writer

JEFF LEMIRE

inkers

JOE PRADO \ VICENTE CIFUENTES
JORDI TARRAGONA \ SANDRA HOPE
JAIME MENDOZA \ ART THIBERT
MATT SANTORELLI
EVAN "DOC" SHANER

colorists

MARCELO MAIOLO
NATHAN FAIRBAIRN \ HI-FI

letterer

TOM NAPOLITANO

collection cover artists

IVAN REIS with MARCELO MAIOLO

VOL.
1

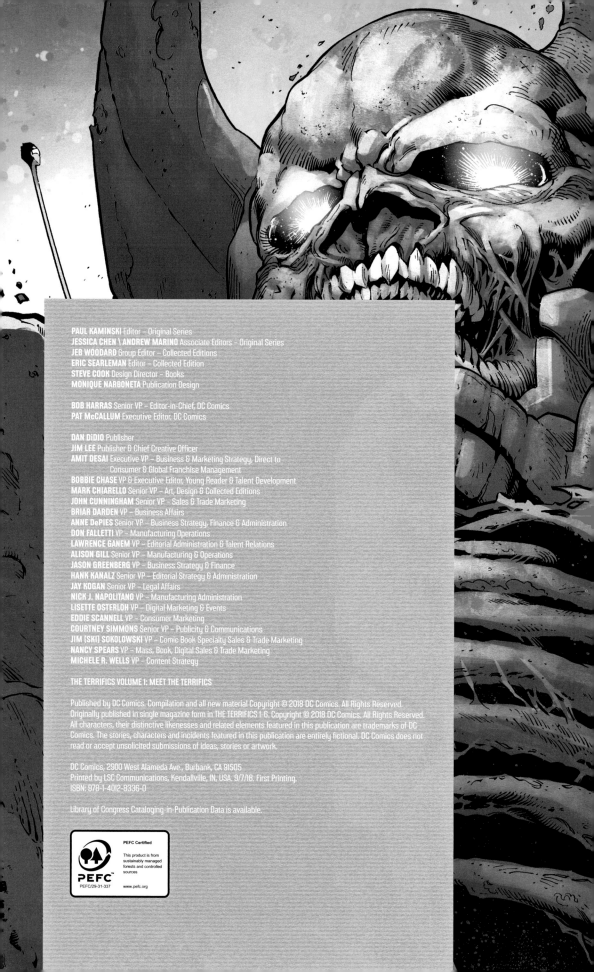

PAUL KAMINSKI Editor – Original Series
JESSICA CHEN \ ANDREW MARINO Associate Editors – Original Series
JEB WOODARD Group Editor – Collected Editions
ERIC SEARLEMAN Editor – Collected Edition
STEVE COOK Design Director – Books
MONIQUE NARBONETA Publication Design

BOB HARRAS Senior VP – Editor-in-Chief, DC Comics
PAT McCALLUM Executive Editor, DC Comics

DAN DiDIO Publisher
JIM LEE Publisher & Chief Creative Officer
AMIT DESAI Executive VP – Business & Marketing Strategy, Direct to Consumer & Global Franchise Management
BOBBIE CHASE VP & Executive Editor, Young Reader & Talent Development
MARK CHIARELLO Senior VP – Art, Design & Collected Editions
JOHN CUNNINGHAM Senior VP – Sales & Trade Marketing
BRIAR DARDEN VP – Business Affairs
ANNE DePIES Senior VP – Business Strategy, Finance & Administration
DON FALLETTI VP – Manufacturing Operations
LAWRENCE GANEM VP – Editorial Administration & Talent Relations
ALISON GILL Senior VP – Manufacturing & Operations
JASON GREENBERG VP – Business Strategy & Finance
HANK KANALZ Senior VP – Editorial Strategy & Administration
JAY KOGAN Senior VP – Legal Affairs
NICK J. NAPOLITANO VP – Manufacturing Administration
LISETTE OSTERLOH VP – Digital Marketing & Events
EDDIE SCANNELL VP – Consumer Marketing
COURTNEY SIMMONS Senior VP – Publicity & Communications
JIM (SKI) SOKOLOWSKI VP – Comic Book Specialty Sales & Trade Marketing
NANCY SPEARS VP – Mass, Book, Digital Sales & Trade Marketing
MICHELE R. WELLS VP – Content Strategy

THE TERRIFICS VOLUME 1: MEET THE TERRIFICS

DC Comics, 2900 West Alameda Ave., Burbank, CA 91505
Printed by LSC Communications, Kendallville, IN, USA. 9/7/18. First Printing.
ISBN: 978-1-4012-8336-0

Library of Congress Cataloging-in-Publication Data is available.

PEFC Certified
This product is from sustainably managed forests and controlled sources
PEFC
PEFC/29-31-337
www.pefc.org

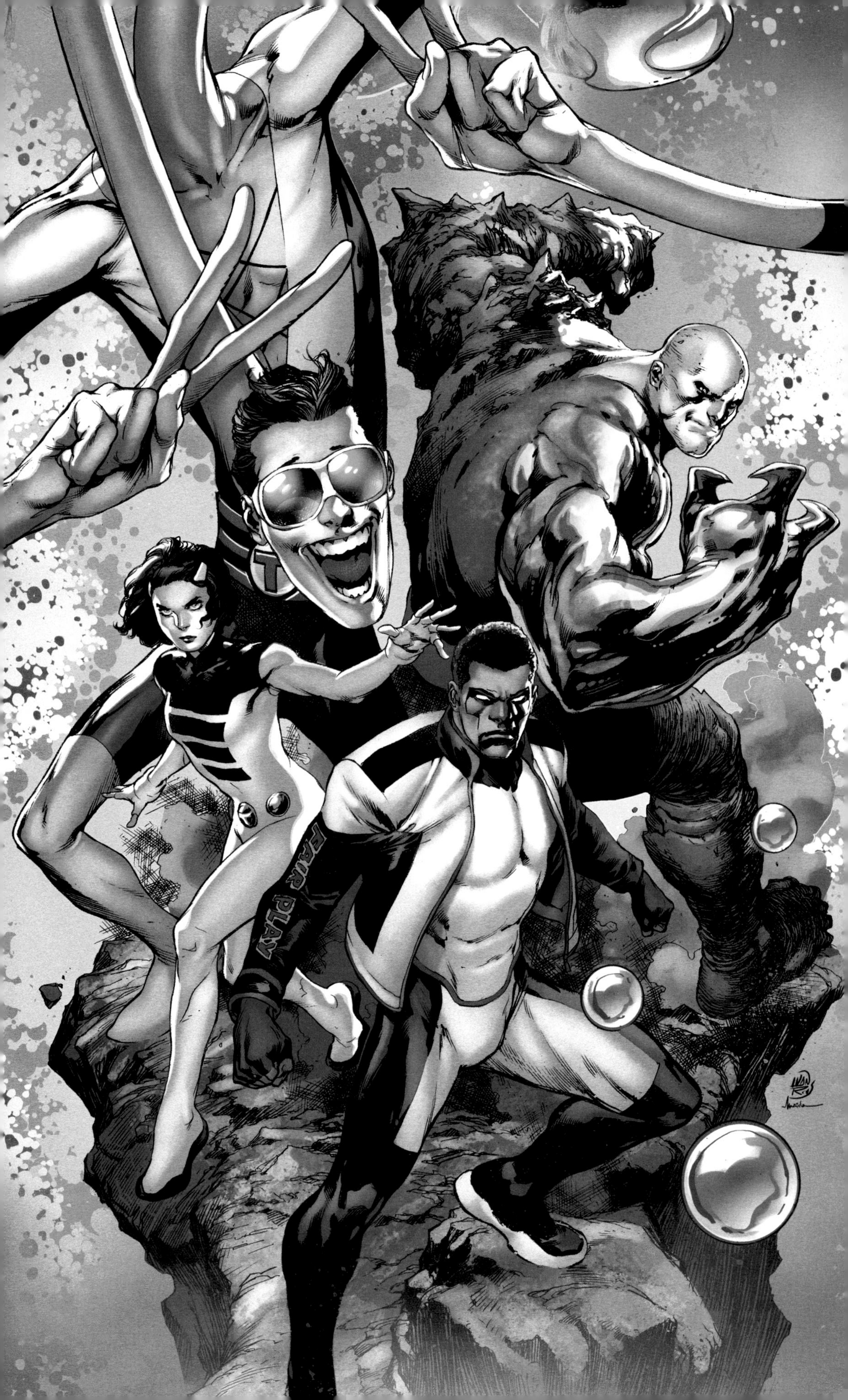
FAIR PLAY

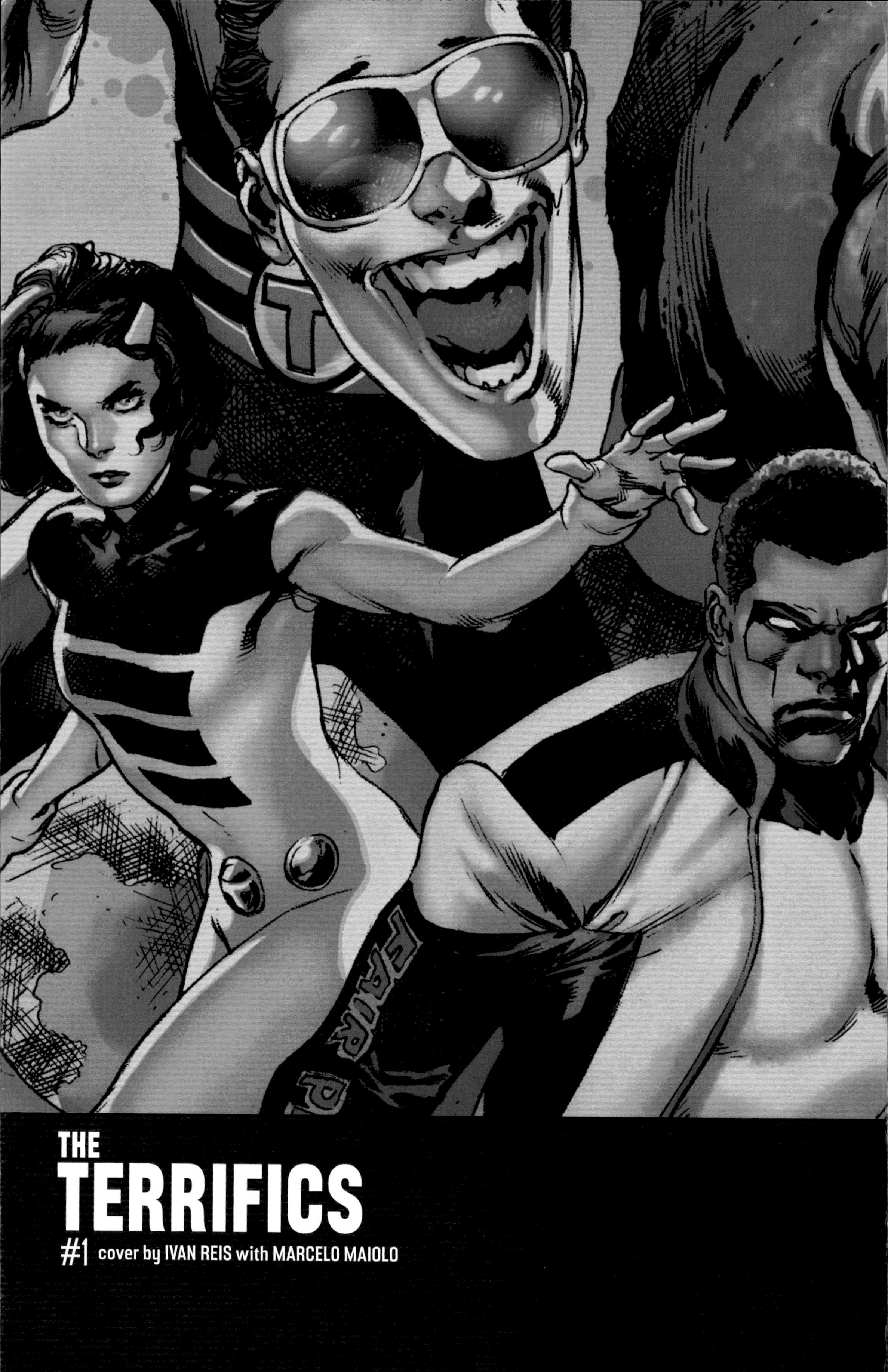

THE TERRIFICS

#1 cover by IVAN REIS with MARCELO MAIOLO

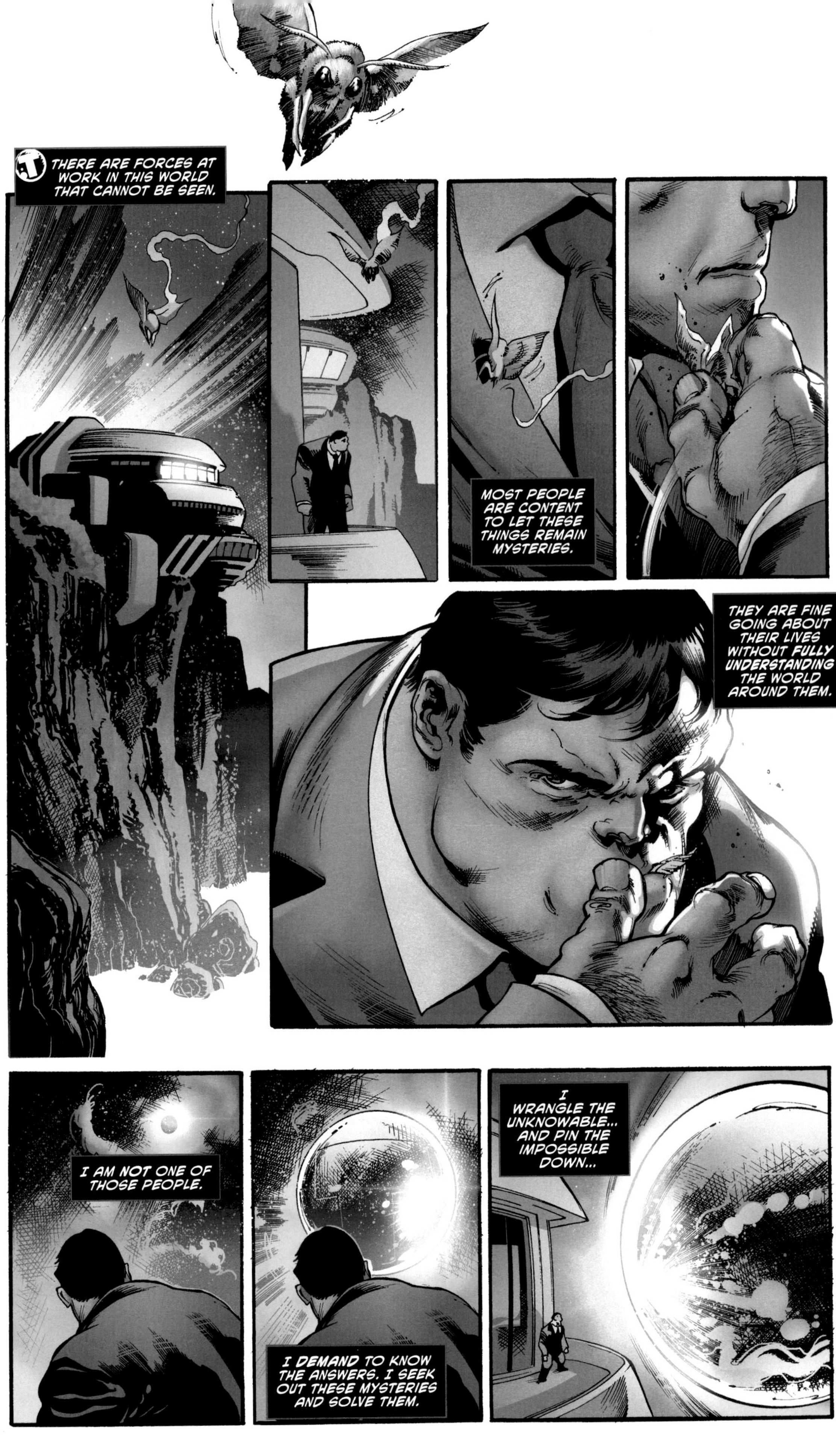
THERE ARE FORCES AT WORK IN THIS WORLD THAT CANNOT BE SEEN.
MOST PEOPLE ARE CONTENT TO LET THESE THINGS REMAIN MYSTERIES.
THEY ARE FINE GOING ABOUT THEIR LIVES WITHOUT FULLY UNDERSTANDING THE WORLD AROUND THEM.
I AM NOT ONE OF THOSE PEOPLE.
I DEMAND TO KNOW THE ANSWERS. I SEEK OUT THESE MYSTERIES AND SOLVE THEM.
I WRANGLE THE UNKNOWABLE... AND PIN THE IMPOSSIBLE DOWN...

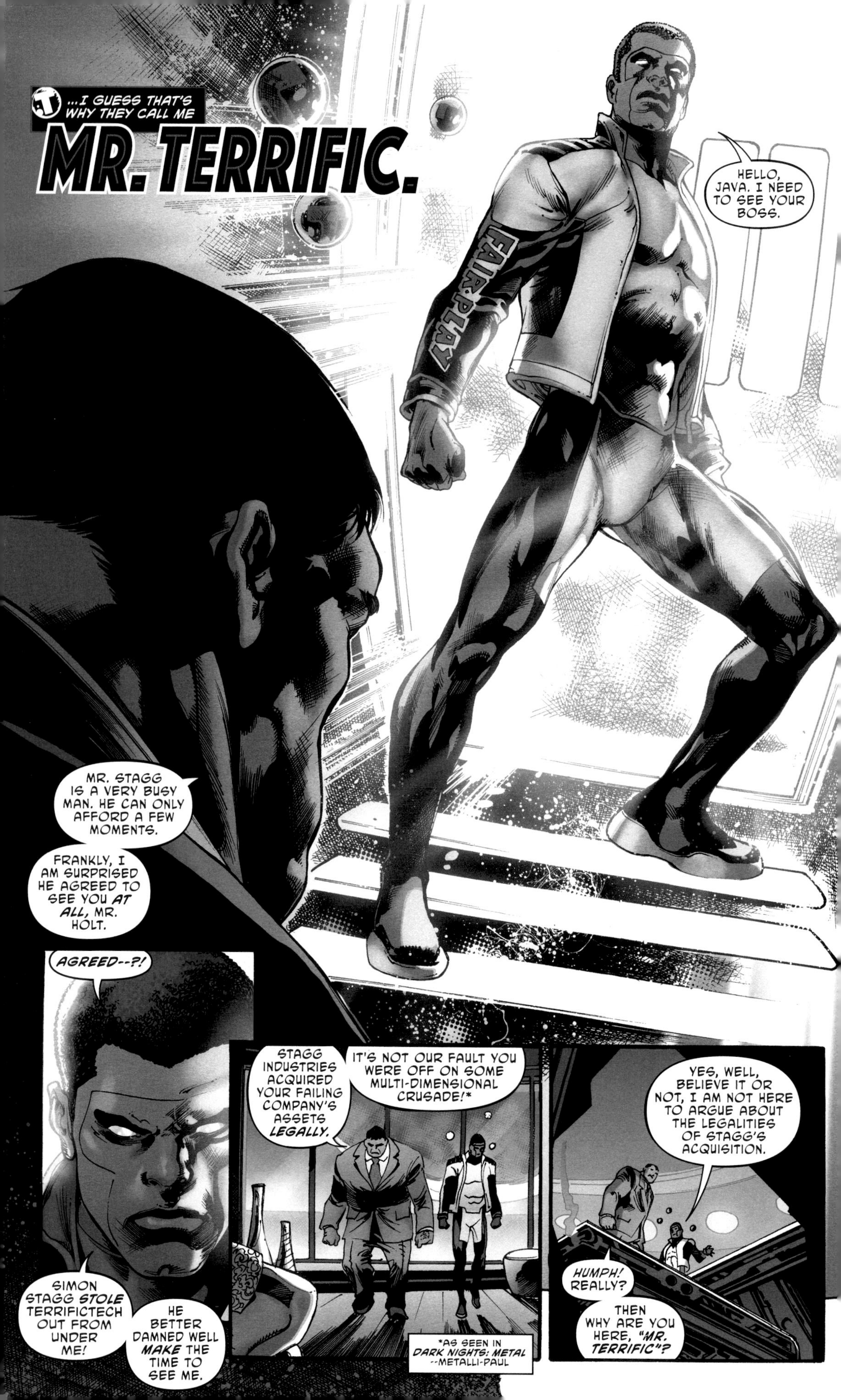

...I GUESS THAT'S WHY THEY CALL ME
MR. TERRIFIC.
HELLO, JAVA. I NEED TO SEE YOUR BOSS.
FAIRPLAY
MR. STAGG IS A VERY BUSY MAN. HE CAN ONLY AFFORD A FEW MOMENTS.
FRANKLY, I AM SURPRISED HE AGREED TO SEE YOU AT ALL, MR. HOLT.
AGREED--?!
SIMON STAGG STOLE TERRIFICTECH OUT FROM UNDER ME!
HE BETTER DAMNED WELL MAKE THE TIME TO SEE ME.
STAGG INDUSTRIES ACQUIRED YOUR FAILING COMPANY'S ASSETS LEGALLY.
IT'S NOT OUR FAULT YOU WERE OFF ON SOME MULTI-DIMENSIONAL CRUSADE!*
*AS SEEN IN DARK NIGHTS: METAL --METALLI-PAUL
YES, WELL, BELIEVE IT OR NOT, I AM NOT HERE TO ARGUE ABOUT THE LEGALITIES OF STAGG'S ACQUISITION.
HUMPH! REALLY?
THEN WHY ARE YOU HERE, "MR. TERRIFIC"?

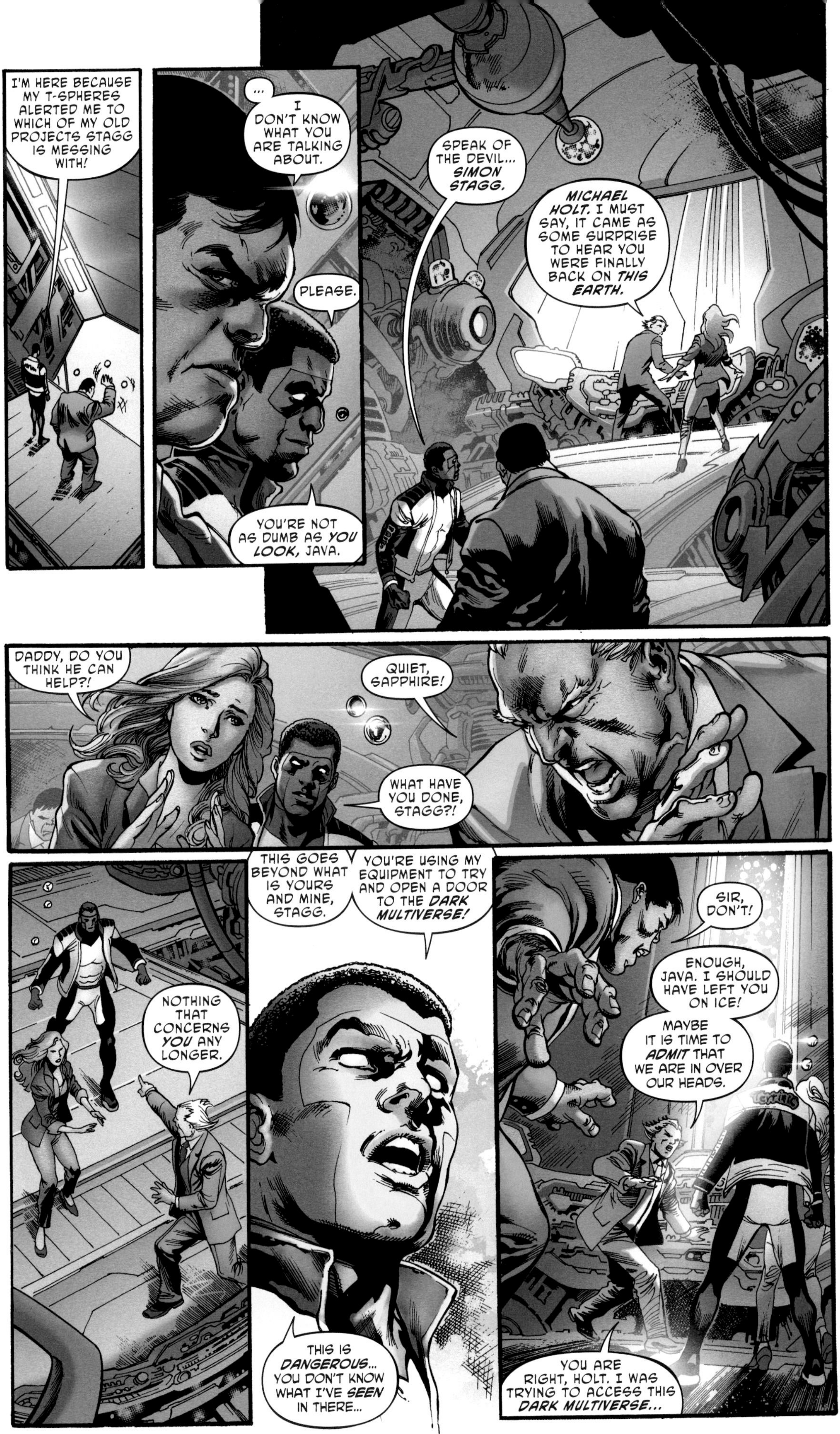
I'M HERE BECAUSE MY T-SPHERES ALERTED ME TO WHICH OF MY OLD PROJECTS STAGG IS MESSING WITH!
...
I DON'T KNOW WHAT YOU ARE TALKING ABOUT.
PLEASE.
YOU'RE NOT AS DUMB AS YOU LOOK, JAVA.
SPEAK OF THE DEVIL... SIMON STAGG.
MICHAEL HOLT. I MUST SAY, IT CAME AS SOME SURPRISE TO HEAR YOU WERE FINALLY BACK ON THIS EARTH.
DADDY, DO YOU THINK HE CAN HELP?!
QUIET, SAPPHIRE!
WHAT HAVE YOU DONE, STAGG?!
NOTHING THAT CONCERNS YOU ANY LONGER.
THIS GOES BEYOND WHAT IS YOURS AND MINE, STAGG.
YOU'RE USING MY EQUIPMENT TO TRY AND OPEN A DOOR TO THE DARK MULTIVERSE!
THIS IS DANGEROUS... YOU DON'T KNOW WHAT I'VE SEEN IN THERE...
SIR, DON'T!
ENOUGH, JAVA. I SHOULD HAVE LEFT YOU ON ICE!
MAYBE IT IS TIME TO ADMIT THAT WE ARE IN OVER OUR HEADS.
YOU ARE RIGHT, HOLT. I WAS TRYING TO ACCESS THIS DARK MULTIVERSE...

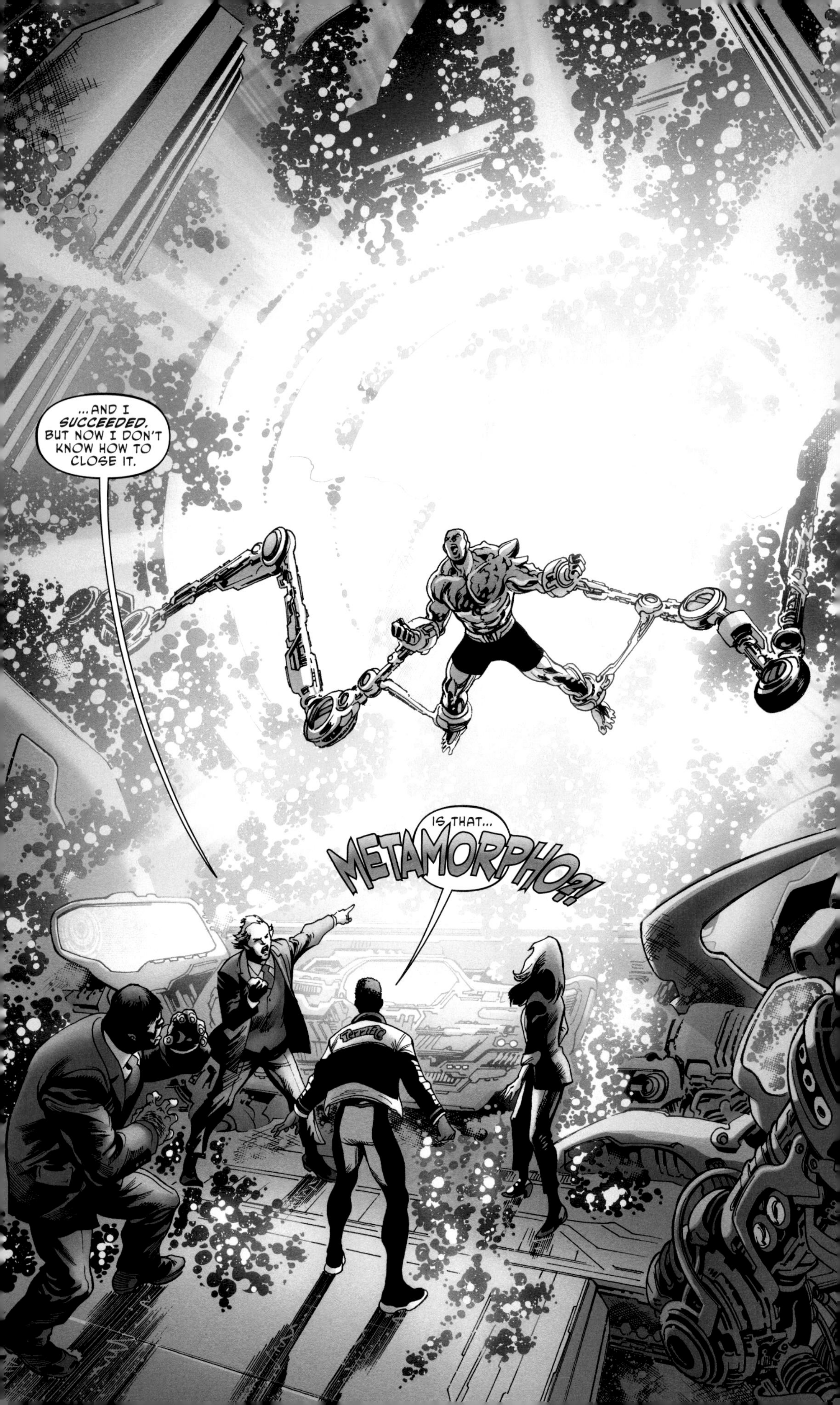
...AND I SUCCEEDED. BUT NOW I DON'T KNOW HOW TO CLOSE IT.
IS THAT... METAMORPHO?!
TERRIFIC

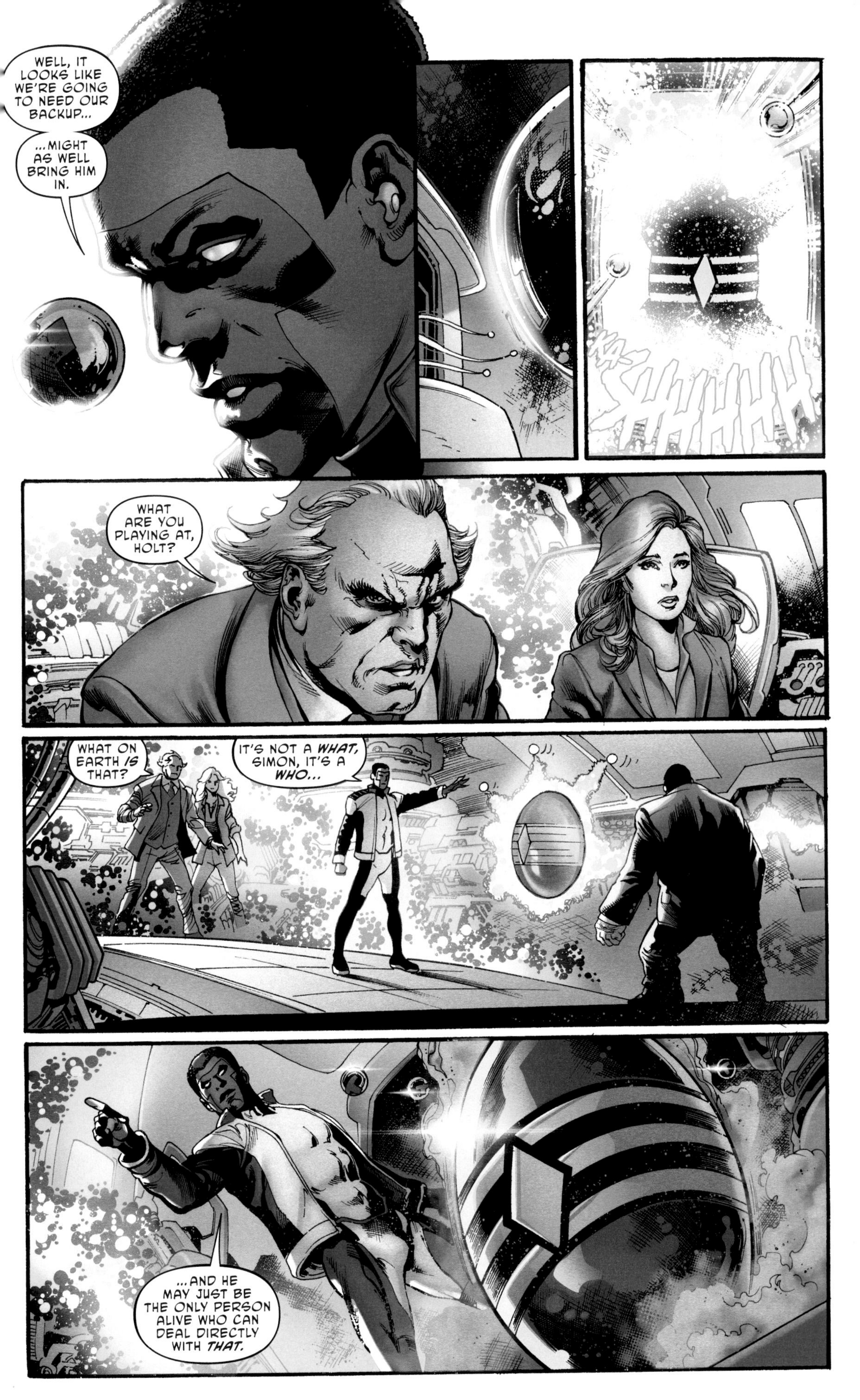
WELL, IT LOOKS LIKE WE'RE GOING TO NEED OUR BACKUP...
...MIGHT AS WELL BRING HIM IN.
KA-SHHHHH
WHAT ARE YOU PLAYING AT, HOLT?
WHAT ON EARTH *IS* THAT?
IT'S NOT A *WHAT*, SIMON, IT'S A *WHO*...
...AND HE MAY JUST BE THE ONLY PERSON ALIVE WHO CAN DEAL DIRECTLY WITH *THAT*.

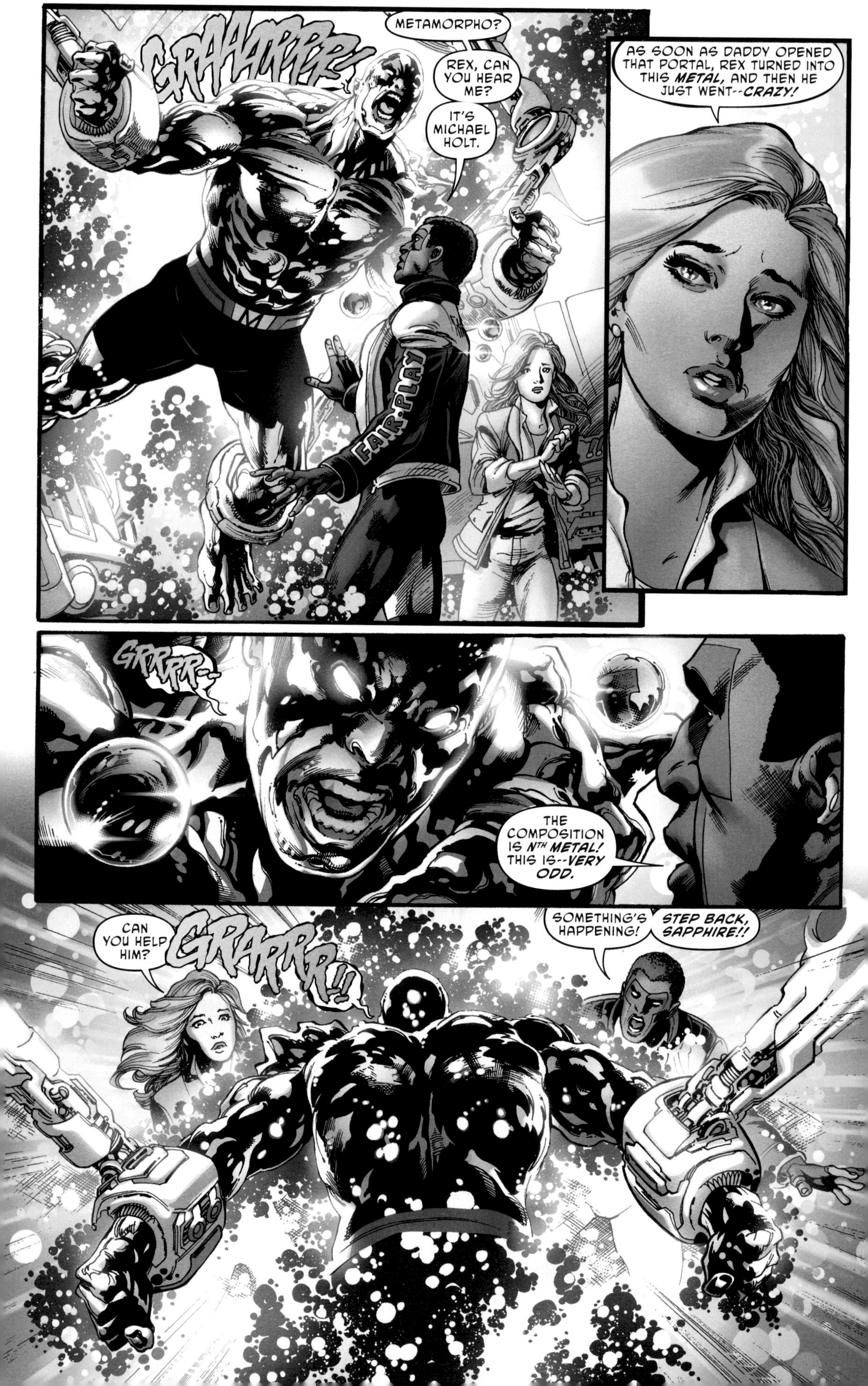
GRAAARRR!
METAMORPHO?
REX, CAN YOU HEAR ME?
IT'S MICHAEL HOLT.
AS SOON AS DADDY OPENED THAT PORTAL, REX TURNED INTO THIS METAL, AND THEN HE JUST WENT--CRAZY!
GRRRRR--
THE COMPOSITION IS NTH METAL! THIS IS--VERY ODD.
CAN YOU HELP HIM?
GRARRR!!
SOMETHING'S HAPPENING!
STEP BACK, SAPPHIRE!!

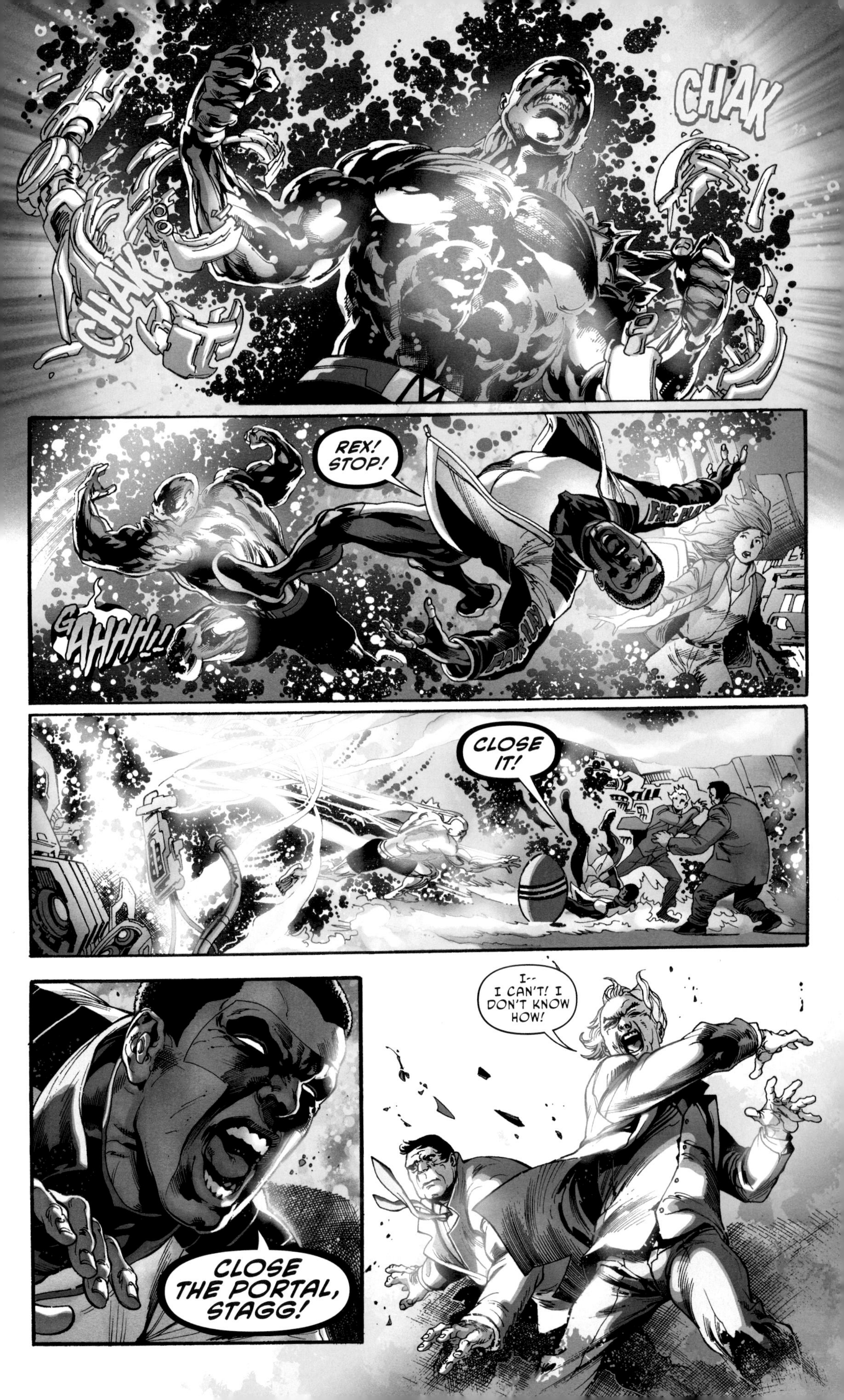
CHAK
CHAK
REX! STOP!
GAHHH!!
CLOSE IT!
CLOSE THE PORTAL, STAGG!
I-- I CAN'T! I DON'T KNOW HOW!

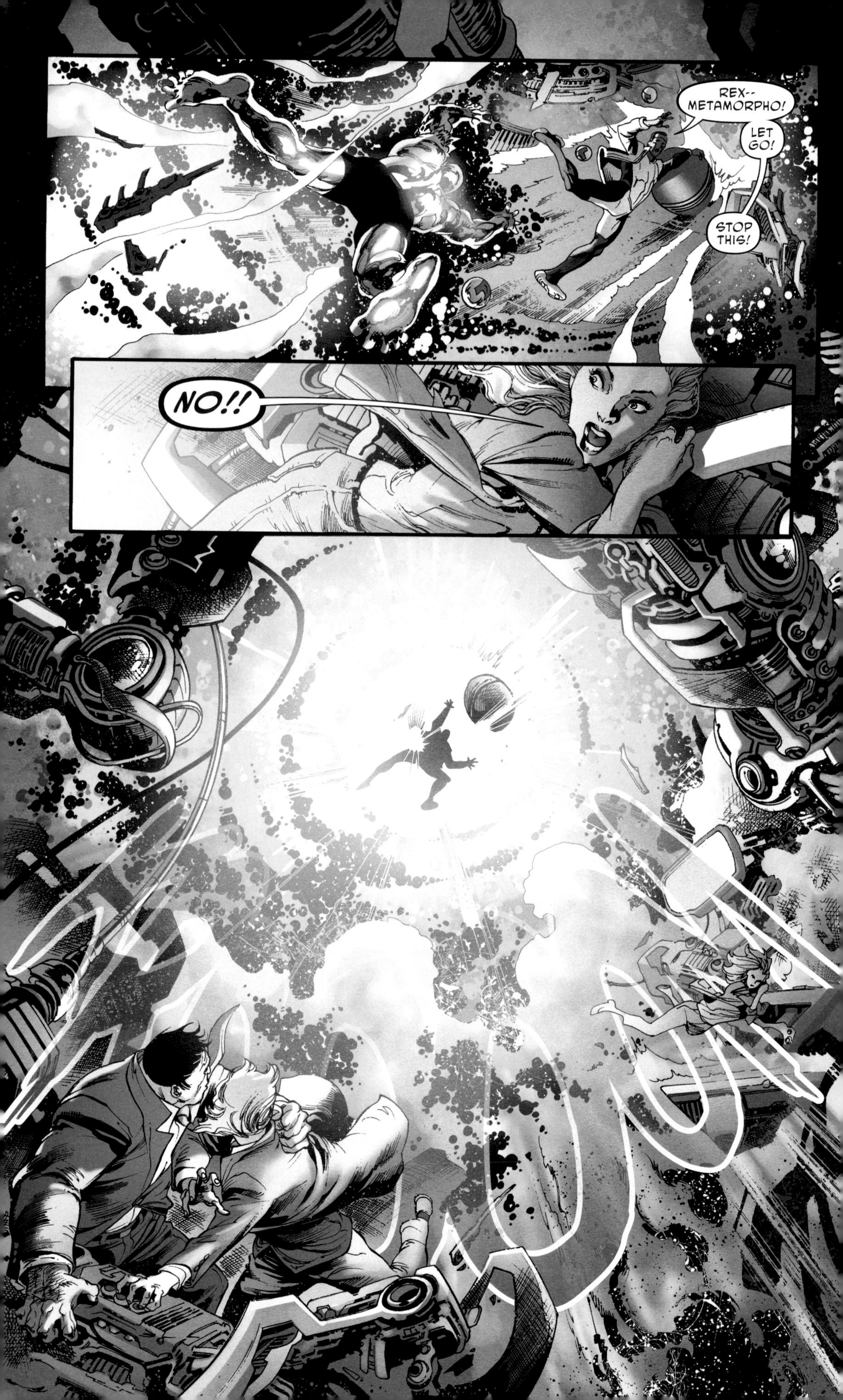
REX--
METAMORPHO!
LET GO!
STOP THIS!
NO!!

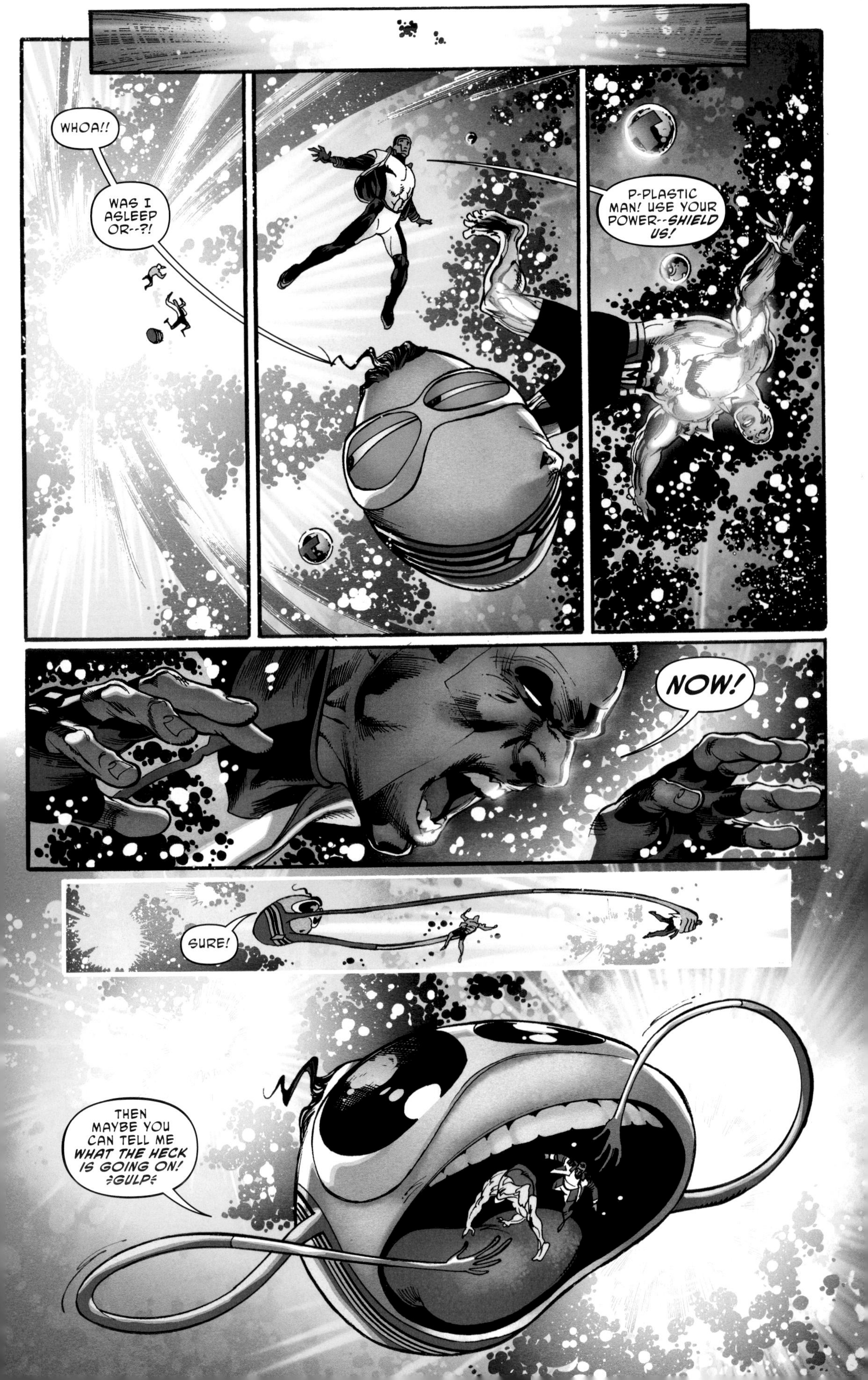
WHOA!!
WAS I ASLEEP OR--?!
P-PLASTIC MAN! USE YOUR POWER--SHIELD US!
NOW!
SURE!
THEN MAYBE YOU CAN TELL ME WHAT THE HECK IS GOING ON!
GULP

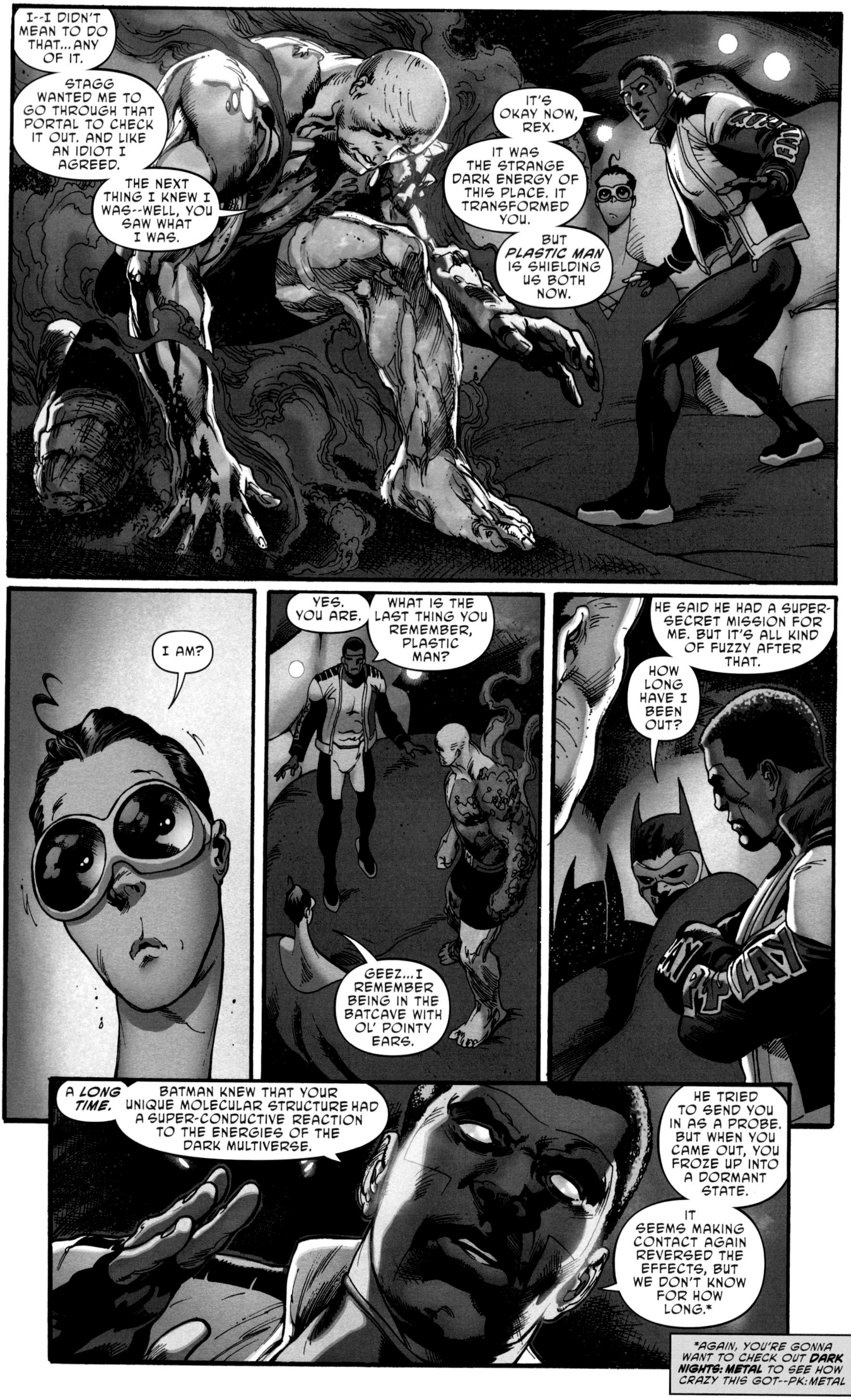
I--I DIDN'T MEAN TO DO THAT... ANY OF IT.
STAGG WANTED ME TO GO THROUGH THAT PORTAL TO CHECK IT OUT. AND LIKE AN IDIOT I AGREED.
THE NEXT THING I KNEW I WAS--WELL, YOU SAW WHAT I WAS.
IT'S OKAY NOW, REX.
IT WAS THE STRANGE DARK ENERGY OF THIS PLACE. IT TRANSFORMED YOU.
BUT *PLASTIC MAN* IS SHIELDING US BOTH NOW.
I AM?
YES. YOU ARE.
WHAT IS THE LAST THING YOU REMEMBER, PLASTIC MAN?
GEEZ...I REMEMBER BEING IN THE BATCAVE WITH OL' POINTY EARS.
HE SAID HE HAD A SUPER-SECRET MISSION FOR ME. BUT IT'S ALL KIND OF FUZZY AFTER THAT.
HOW LONG HAVE I BEEN OUT?
A *LONG TIME.*
BATMAN KNEW THAT YOUR UNIQUE MOLECULAR STRUCTURE HAD A SUPER-CONDUCTIVE REACTION TO THE ENERGIES OF THE DARK MULTIVERSE.
HE TRIED TO SEND YOU IN AS A PROBE. BUT WHEN YOU CAME OUT, YOU FROZE UP INTO A DORMANT STATE.
IT SEEMS MAKING CONTACT AGAIN REVERSED THE EFFECTS, BUT WE DON'T KNOW FOR HOW LONG.*
*AGAIN, YOU'RE GONNA WANT TO CHECK OUT **DARK NIGHTS: METAL** TO SEE HOW CRAZY THIS GOT--PK:METAL

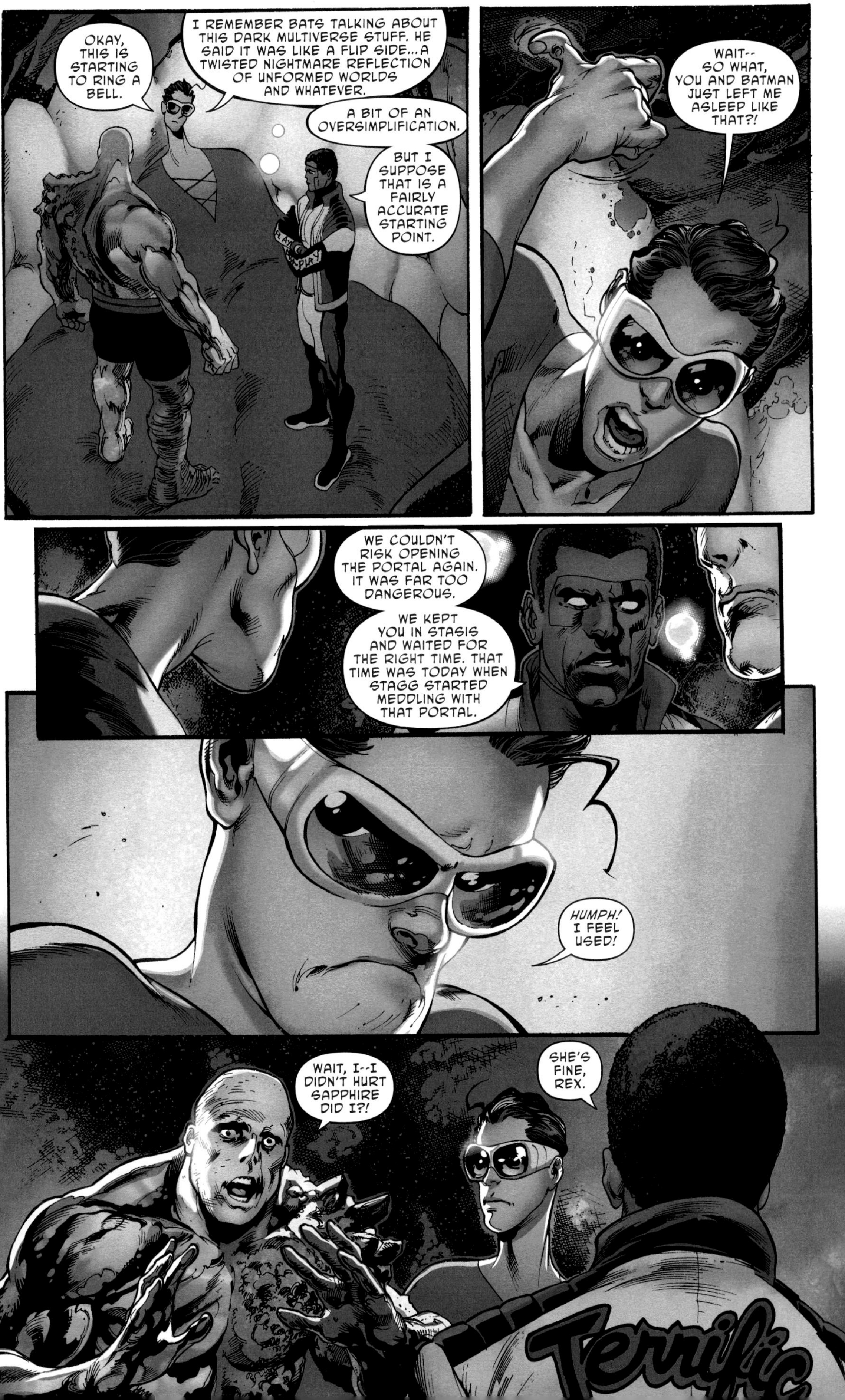
OKAY, THIS IS STARTING TO RING A BELL.
I REMEMBER BATS TALKING ABOUT THIS DARK MULTIVERSE STUFF. HE SAID IT WAS LIKE A FLIP SIDE...A TWISTED NIGHTMARE REFLECTION OF UNFORMED WORLDS AND WHATEVER.
A BIT OF AN OVERSIMPLIFICATION.
BUT I SUPPOSE THAT IS A FAIRLY ACCURATE STARTING POINT.
WAIT-- SO WHAT, YOU AND BATMAN JUST LEFT ME ASLEEP LIKE THAT?!
WE COULDN'T RISK OPENING THE PORTAL AGAIN. IT WAS FAR TOO DANGEROUS.
WE KEPT YOU IN STASIS AND WAITED FOR THE RIGHT TIME. THAT TIME WAS TODAY WHEN STAGG STARTED MEDDLING WITH THAT PORTAL.
HUMPH! I FEEL USED!
WAIT, I--I DIDN'T HURT SAPPHIRE DID I?!
SHE'S FINE, REX.
Terrific

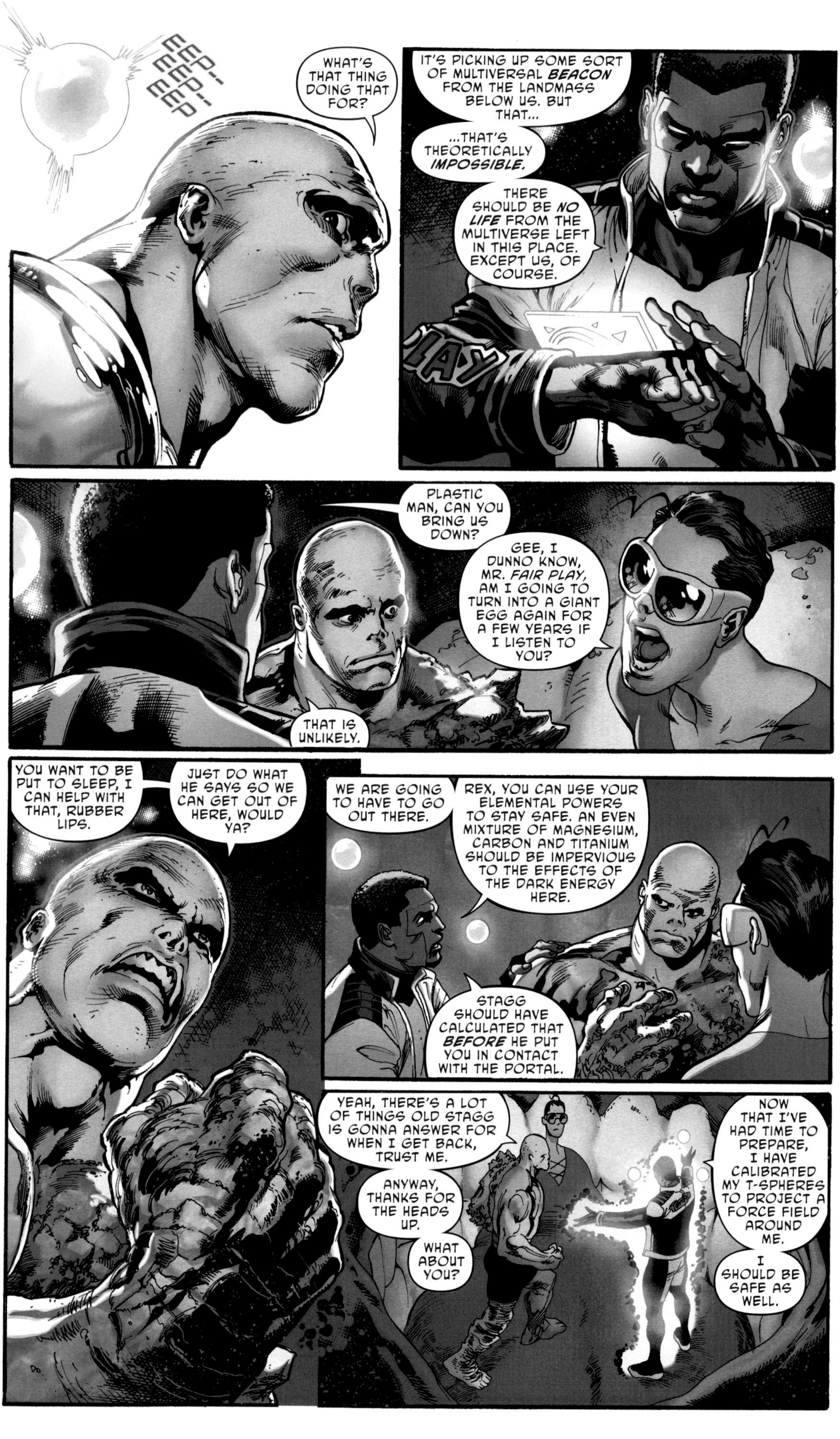
EEP! EEP! EEP
WHAT'S THAT THING DOING THAT FOR?
IT'S PICKING UP SOME SORT OF MULTIVERSAL BEACON FROM THE LANDMASS BELOW US. BUT THAT...
...THAT'S THEORETICALLY IMPOSSIBLE.
THERE SHOULD BE NO LIFE FROM THE MULTIVERSE LEFT IN THIS PLACE. EXCEPT US, OF COURSE.
PLASTIC MAN, CAN YOU BRING US DOWN?
GEE, I DUNNO KNOW, MR. FAIR PLAY, AM I GOING TO TURN INTO A GIANT EGG AGAIN FOR A FEW YEARS IF I LISTEN TO YOU?
THAT IS UNLIKELY.
YOU WANT TO BE PUT TO SLEEP, I CAN HELP WITH THAT, RUBBER LIPS.
JUST DO WHAT HE SAYS SO WE CAN GET OUT OF HERE, WOULD YA?
WE ARE GOING TO HAVE TO GO OUT THERE.
REX, YOU CAN USE YOUR ELEMENTAL POWERS TO STAY SAFE. AN EVEN MIXTURE OF MAGNESIUM, CARBON AND TITANIUM SHOULD BE IMPERVIOUS TO THE EFFECTS OF THE DARK ENERGY HERE.
STAGG SHOULD HAVE CALCULATED THAT BEFORE HE PUT YOU IN CONTACT WITH THE PORTAL.
YEAH, THERE'S A LOT OF THINGS OLD STAGG IS GONNA ANSWER FOR WHEN I GET BACK, TRUST ME.
ANYWAY, THANKS FOR THE HEADS UP.
WHAT ABOUT YOU?
NOW THAT I'VE HAD TIME TO PREPARE, I HAVE CALIBRATED MY T-SPHERES TO PROJECT A FORCE FIELD AROUND ME.
I SHOULD BE SAFE AS WELL.

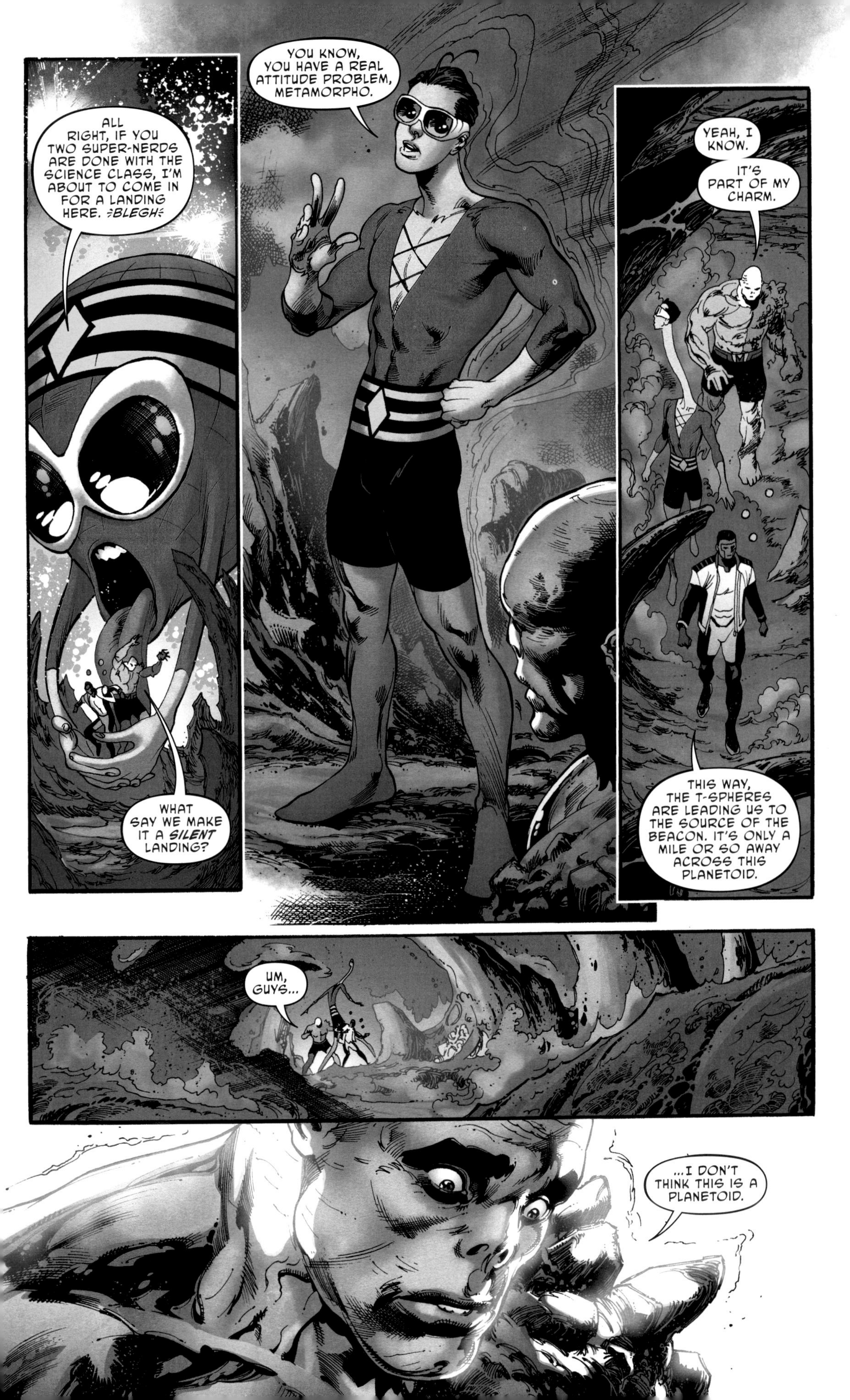
ALL RIGHT, IF YOU TWO SUPER-NERDS ARE DONE WITH THE SCIENCE CLASS, I'M ABOUT TO COME IN FOR A LANDING HERE. ⇒BLEGH⇐
WHAT SAY WE MAKE IT A SILENT LANDING?
YOU KNOW, YOU HAVE A REAL ATTITUDE PROBLEM, METAMORPHO.
YEAH, I KNOW.
IT'S PART OF MY CHARM.
THIS WAY, THE T-SPHERES ARE LEADING US TO THE SOURCE OF THE BEACON. IT'S ONLY A MILE OR SO AWAY ACROSS THIS PLANETOID.
UM, GUYS...
...I DON'T THINK THIS IS A PLANETOID.

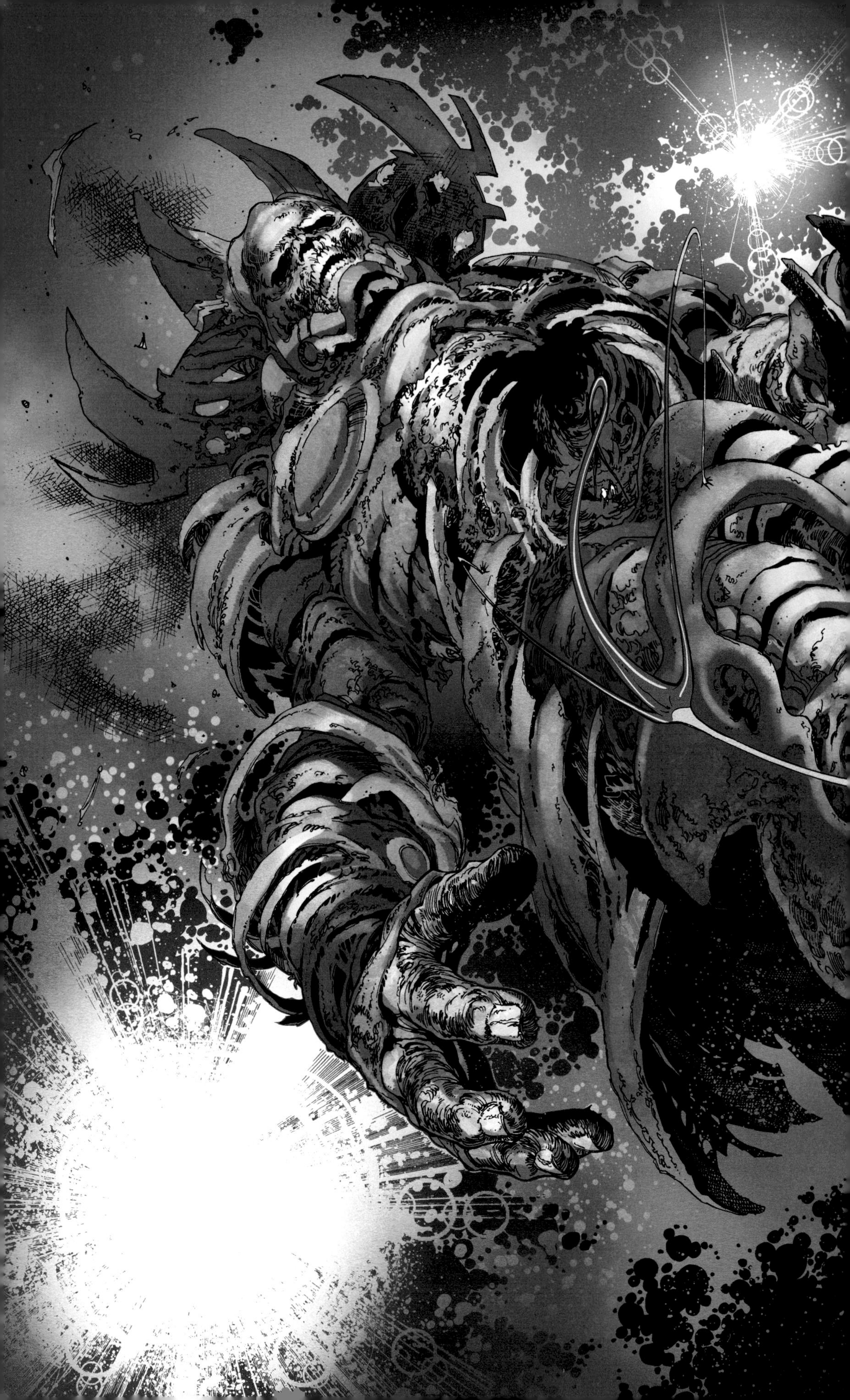

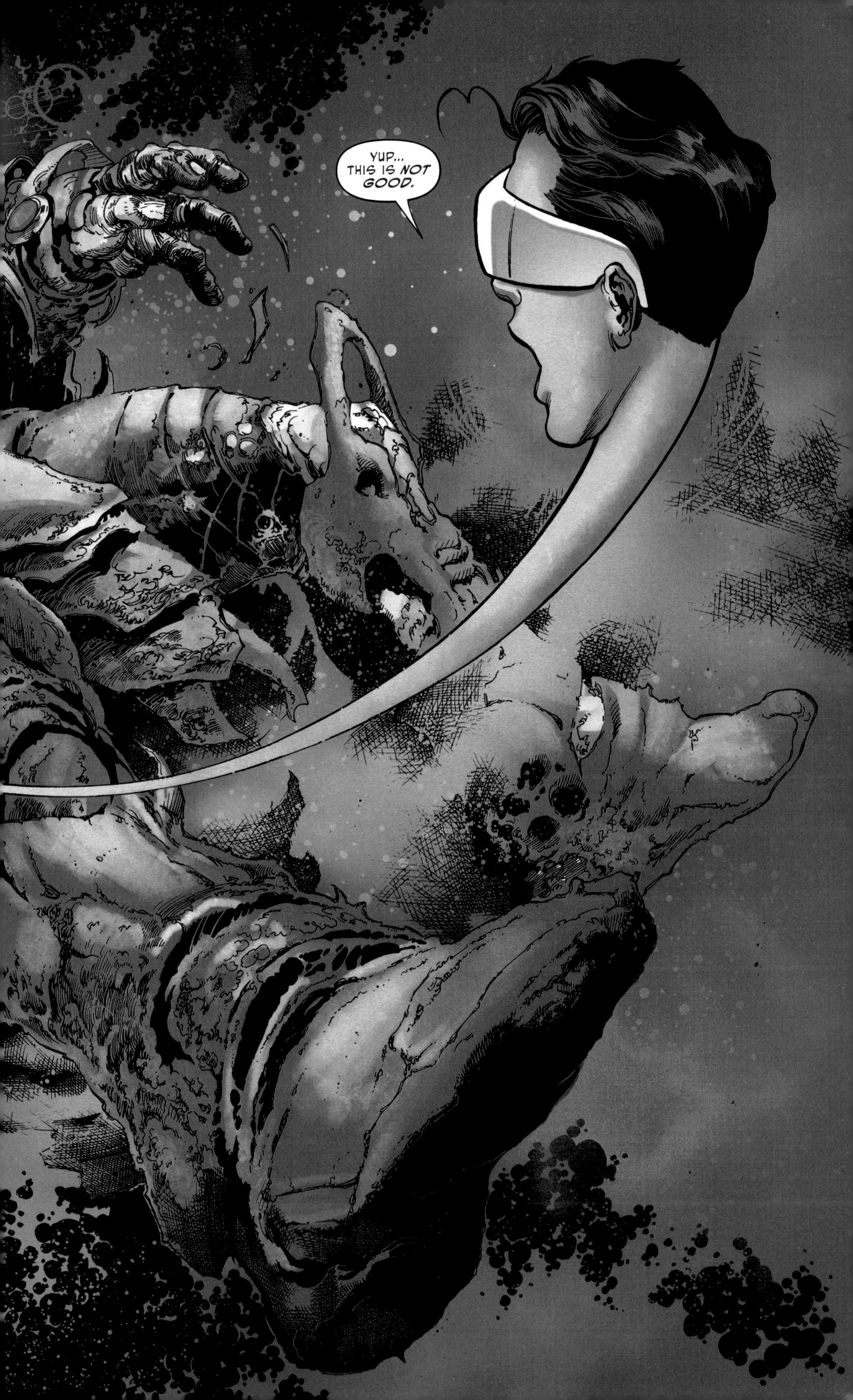
YUP... THIS IS *NOT* GOOD.

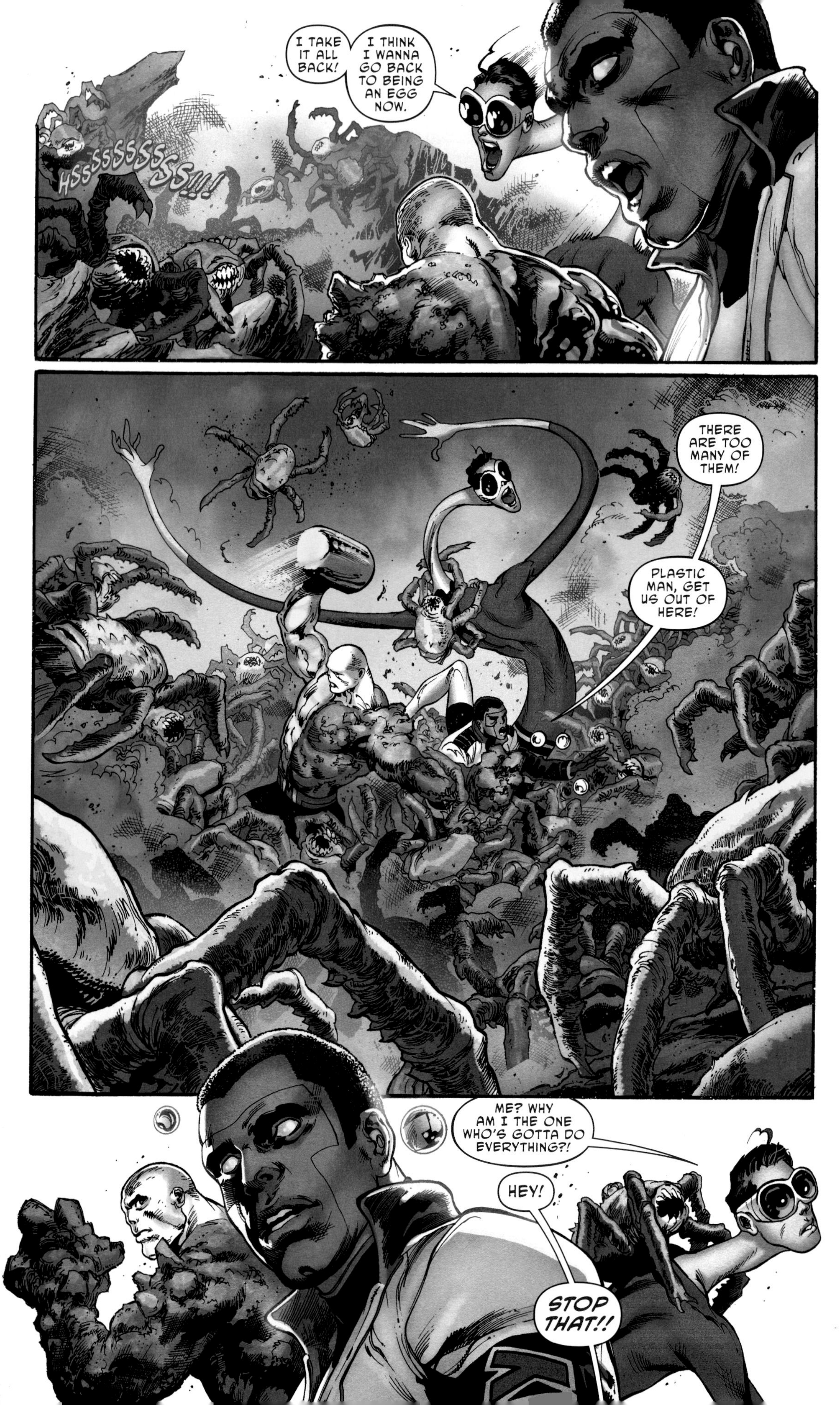
I TAKE IT ALL BACK!
I THINK I WANNA GO BACK TO BEING AN EGG NOW.
HSSSSSSSSSSSS!!!
THERE ARE TOO MANY OF THEM!
PLASTIC MAN, GET US OUT OF HERE!
ME? WHY AM I THE ONE WHO'S GOTTA DO EVERYTHING?!
HEY!
STOP THAT!!

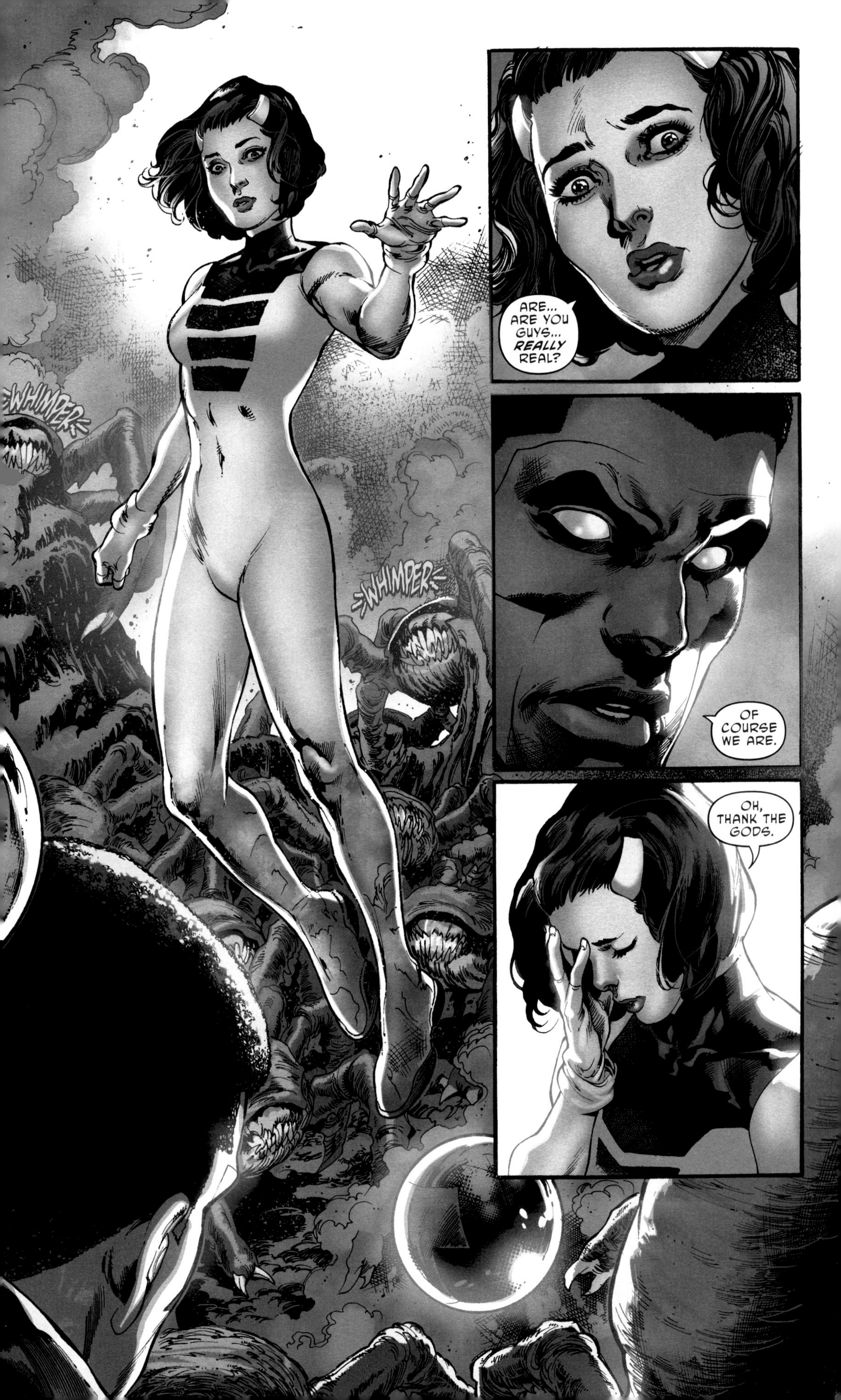
WHIMPER
WHIMPER
ARE... ARE YOU GUYS... REALLY REAL?
OF COURSE WE ARE.
OH, THANK THE GODS.

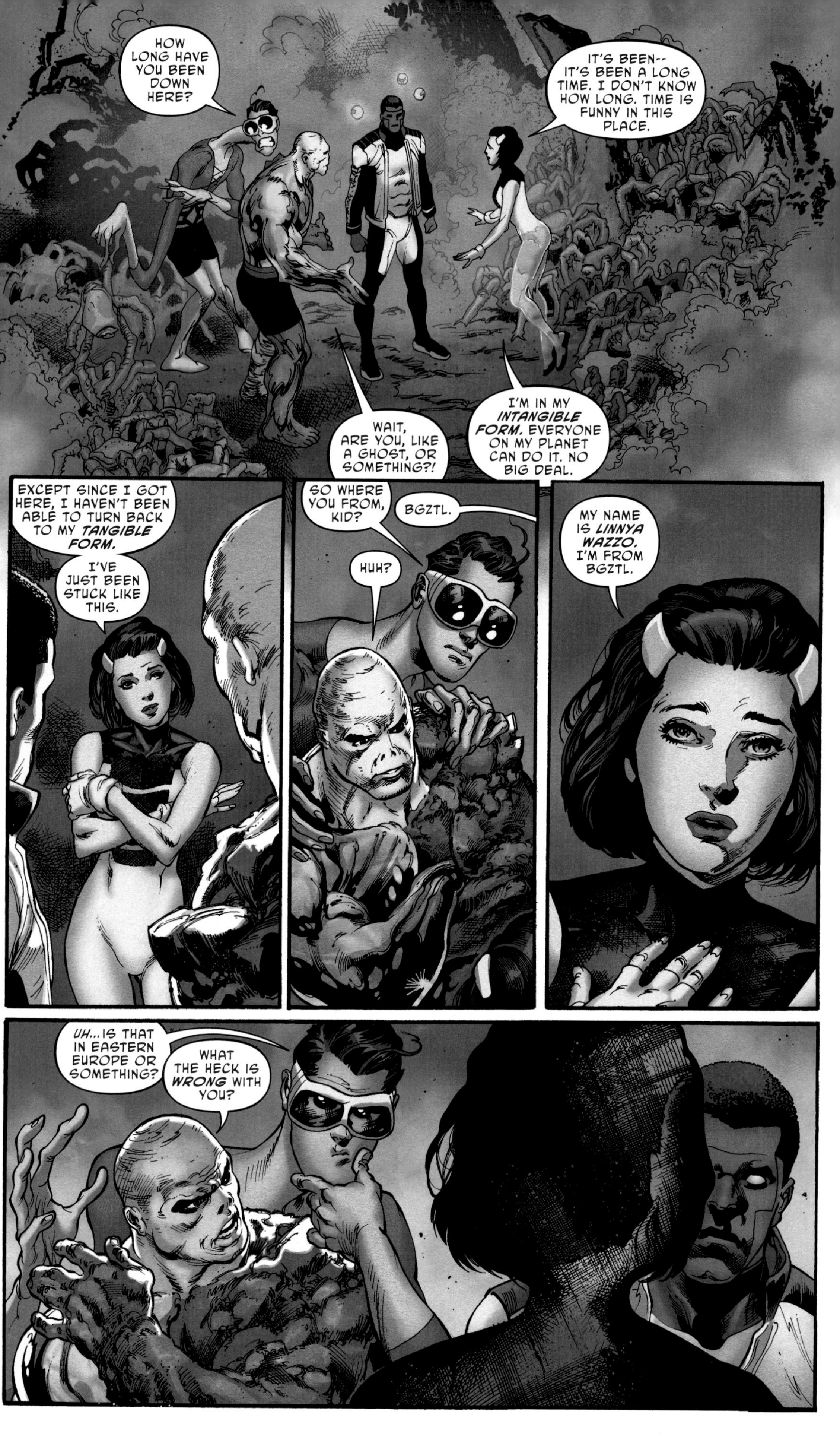

HOW LONG HAVE YOU BEEN DOWN HERE?
IT'S BEEN-- IT'S BEEN A LONG TIME. I DON'T KNOW HOW LONG. TIME IS FUNNY IN THIS PLACE.
WAIT, ARE YOU, LIKE A GHOST, OR SOMETHING?!
I'M IN MY *INTANGIBLE FORM.* EVERYONE ON MY PLANET CAN DO IT. NO BIG DEAL.
EXCEPT SINCE I GOT HERE, I HAVEN'T BEEN ABLE TO TURN BACK TO MY *TANGIBLE FORM.*
I'VE JUST BEEN STUCK LIKE THIS.
SO WHERE YOU FROM, KID?
BGZTL.
HUH?
MY NAME IS *LINNYA WAZZO.* I'M FROM BGZTL.
UH... IS THAT IN EASTERN EUROPE OR SOMETHING?
WHAT THE HECK IS *WRONG* WITH YOU?

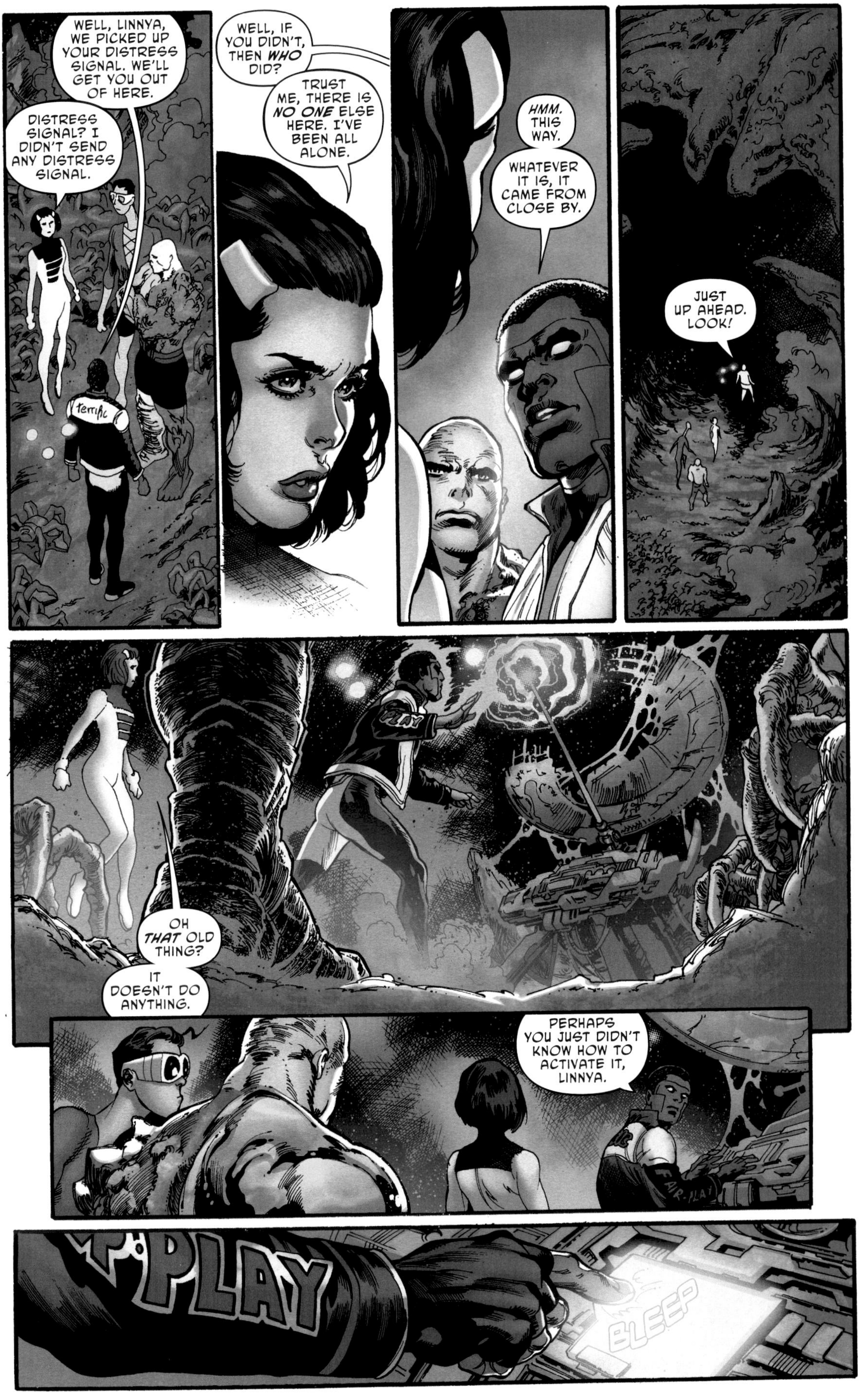
WELL, LINNYA, WE PICKED UP YOUR DISTRESS SIGNAL. WE'LL GET YOU OUT OF HERE.
DISTRESS SIGNAL? I DIDN'T SEND ANY DISTRESS SIGNAL.
terrific
WELL, IF YOU DIDN'T, THEN *WHO* DID?
TRUST ME, THERE IS *NO ONE* ELSE HERE. I'VE BEEN ALL ALONE.
HMM. THIS WAY.
WHATEVER IT IS, IT CAME FROM CLOSE BY.
JUST UP AHEAD. LOOK!
OH *THAT* OLD THING?
IT DOESN'T DO ANYTHING.
PERHAPS YOU JUST DIDN'T KNOW HOW TO ACTIVATE IT, LINNYA.
FAIR PLAY
PLAY
BLEEP

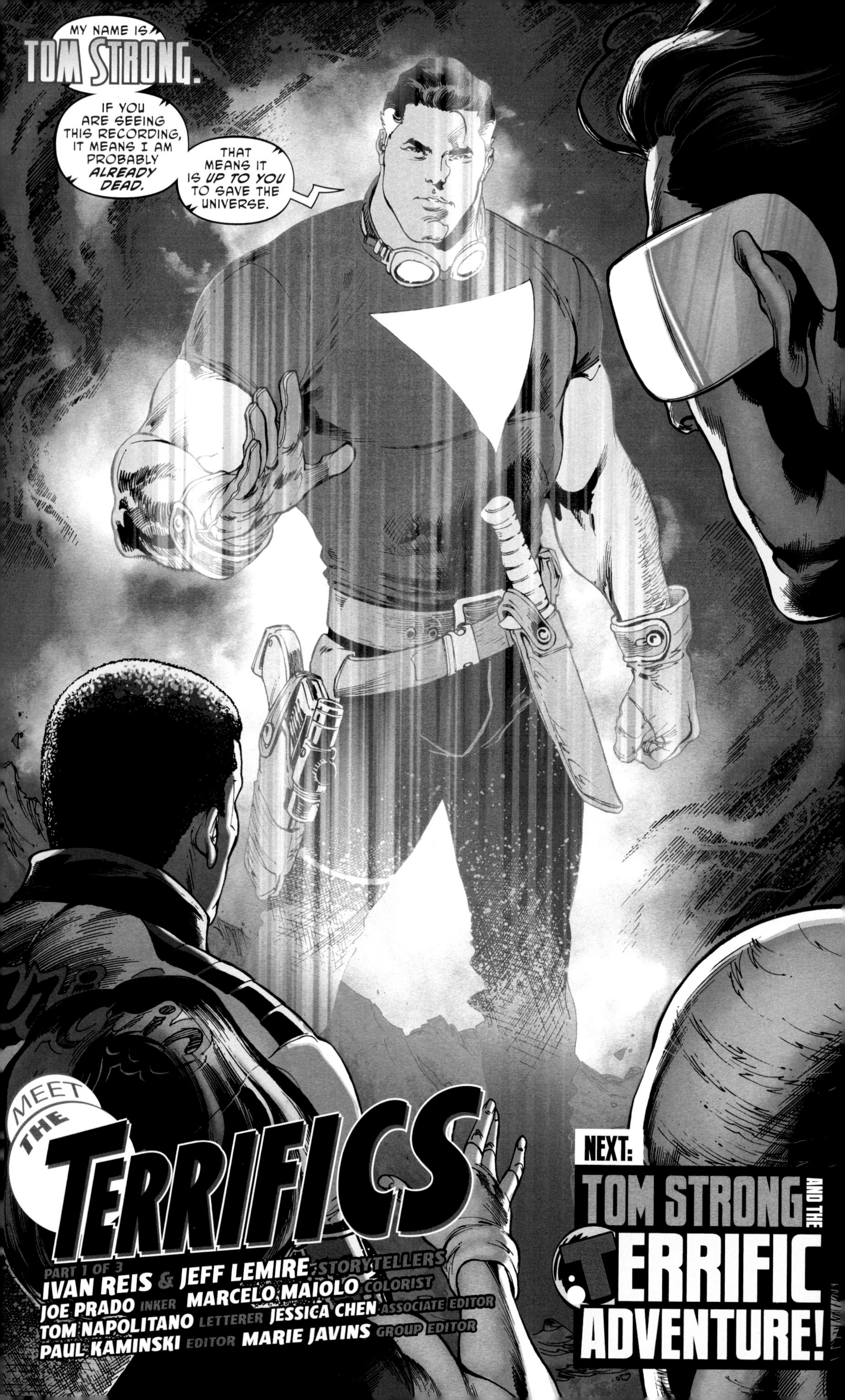

MY NAME IS TOM STRONG.
IF YOU ARE SEEING THIS RECORDING, IT MEANS I AM PROBABLY *ALREADY DEAD.*
THAT MEANS IT IS *UP TO YOU* TO SAVE THE UNIVERSE.
MEET THE TERRIFICS
PART 1 OF 3
IVAN REIS & JEFF LEMIRE STORYTELLERS
JOE PRADO INKER MARCELO MAIOLO COLORIST
TOM NAPOLITANO LETTERER JESSICA CHEN ASSOCIATE EDITOR
PAUL KAMINSKI EDITOR MARIE JAVINS GROUP EDITOR
NEXT: TOM STRONG AND THE TERRIFIC ADVENTURE!

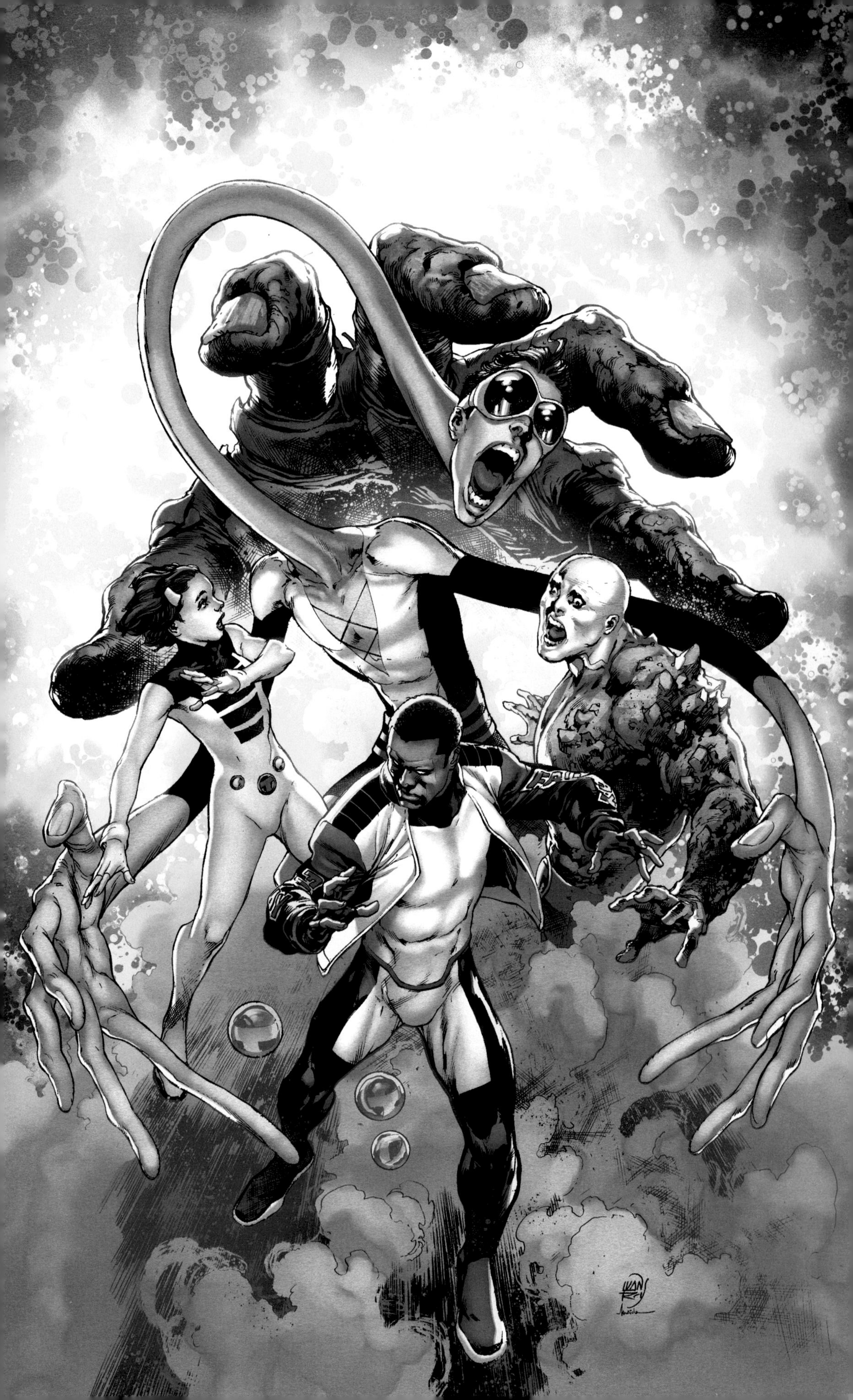

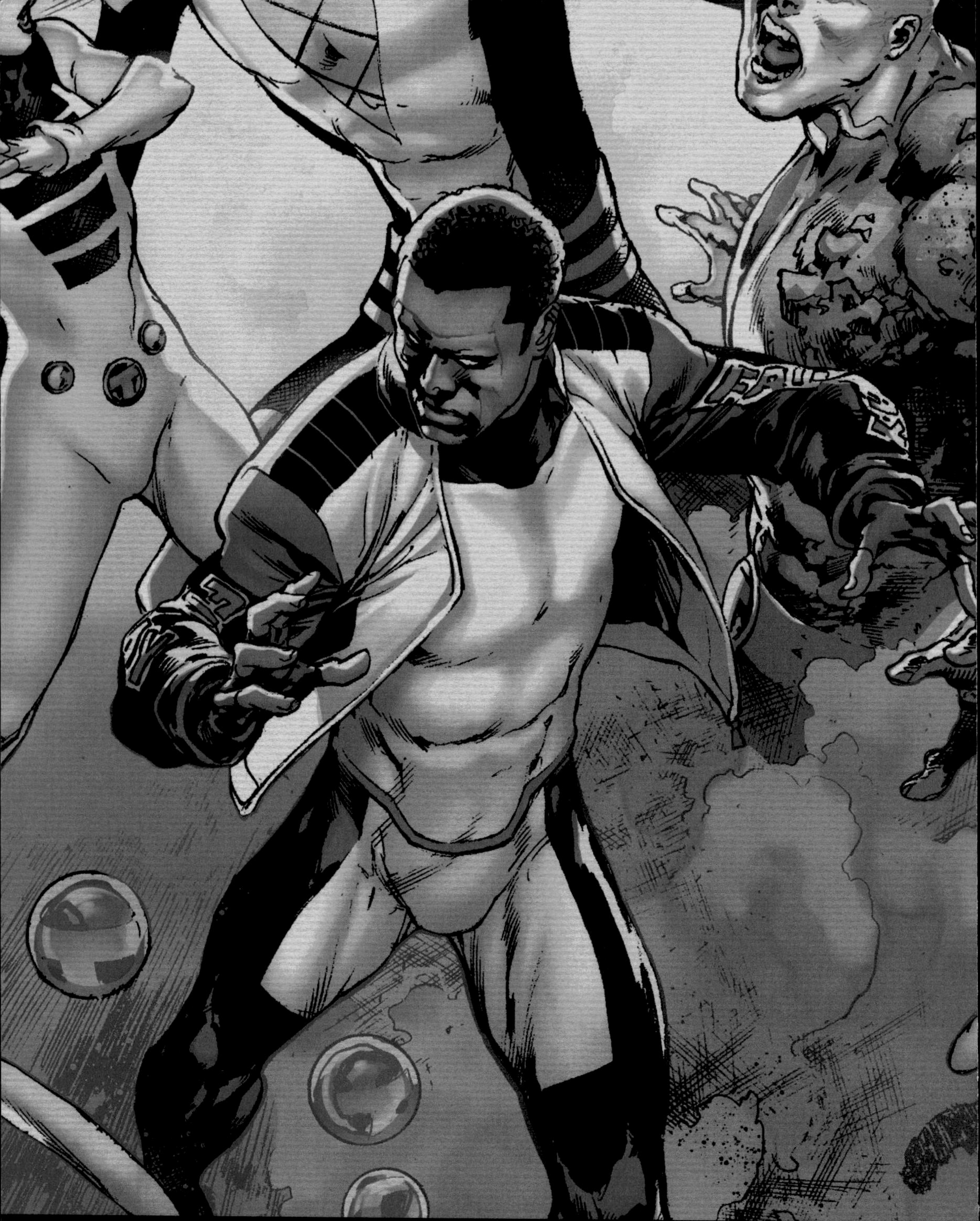

THE
TERRIFICS

#2 cover by IVAN REIS with MARCELO MAIOLO

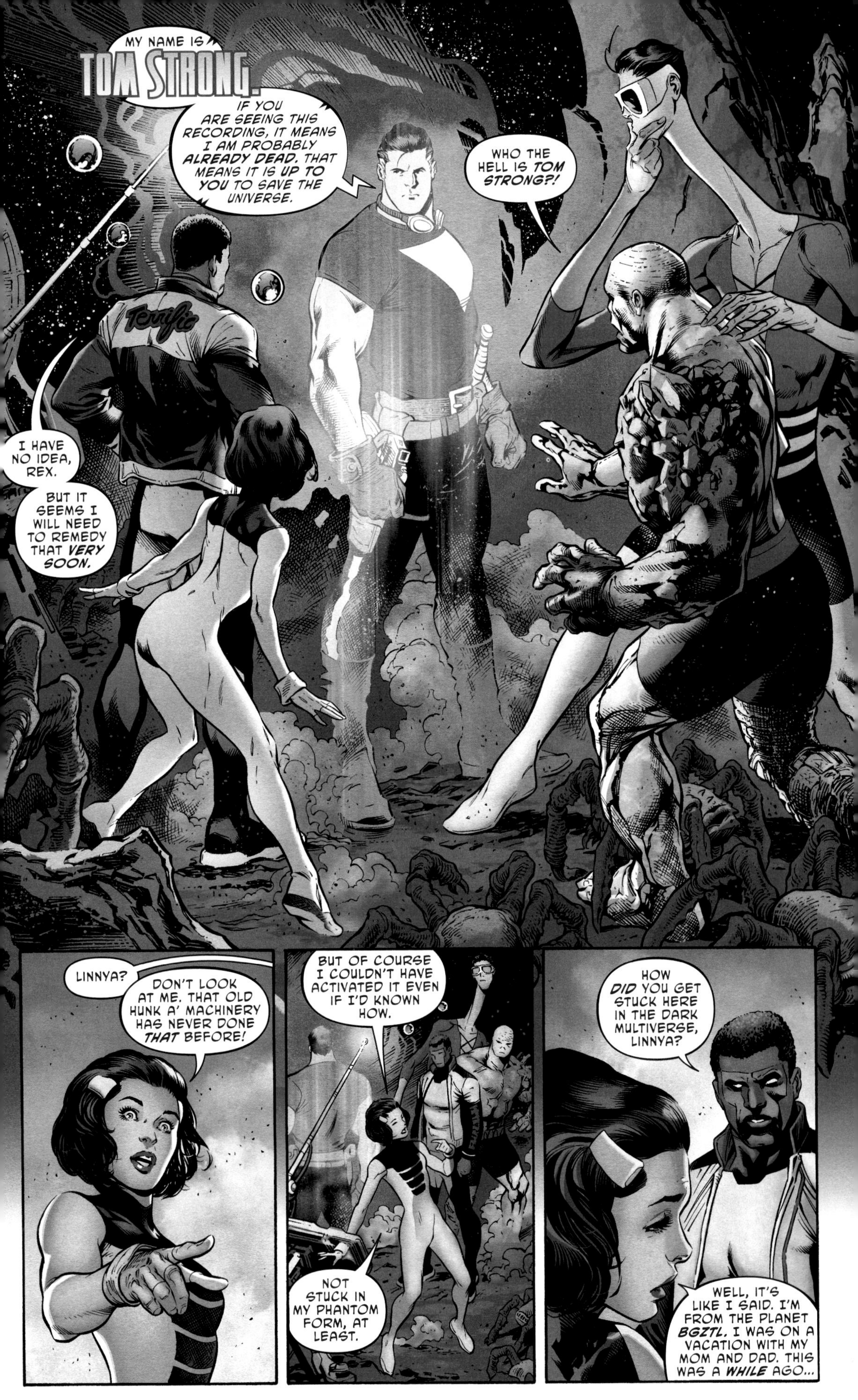
MY NAME IS TOM STRONG.
IF YOU ARE SEEING THIS RECORDING, IT MEANS I AM PROBABLY ALREADY DEAD. THAT MEANS IT IS UP TO YOU TO SAVE THE UNIVERSE.
WHO THE HELL IS TOM STRONG?!
I HAVE NO IDEA, REX.
BUT IT SEEMS I WILL NEED TO REMEDY THAT VERY SOON.
LINNYA?
DON'T LOOK AT ME. THAT OLD HUNK A' MACHINERY HAS NEVER DONE THAT BEFORE!
BUT OF COURSE I COULDN'T HAVE ACTIVATED IT EVEN IF I'D KNOWN HOW.
NOT STUCK IN MY PHANTOM FORM, AT LEAST.
HOW DID YOU GET STUCK HERE IN THE DARK MULTIVERSE, LINNYA?
WELL, IT'S LIKE I SAID. I'M FROM THE PLANET BGZTL. I WAS ON A VACATION WITH MY MOM AND DAD. THIS WAS A WHILE AGO...

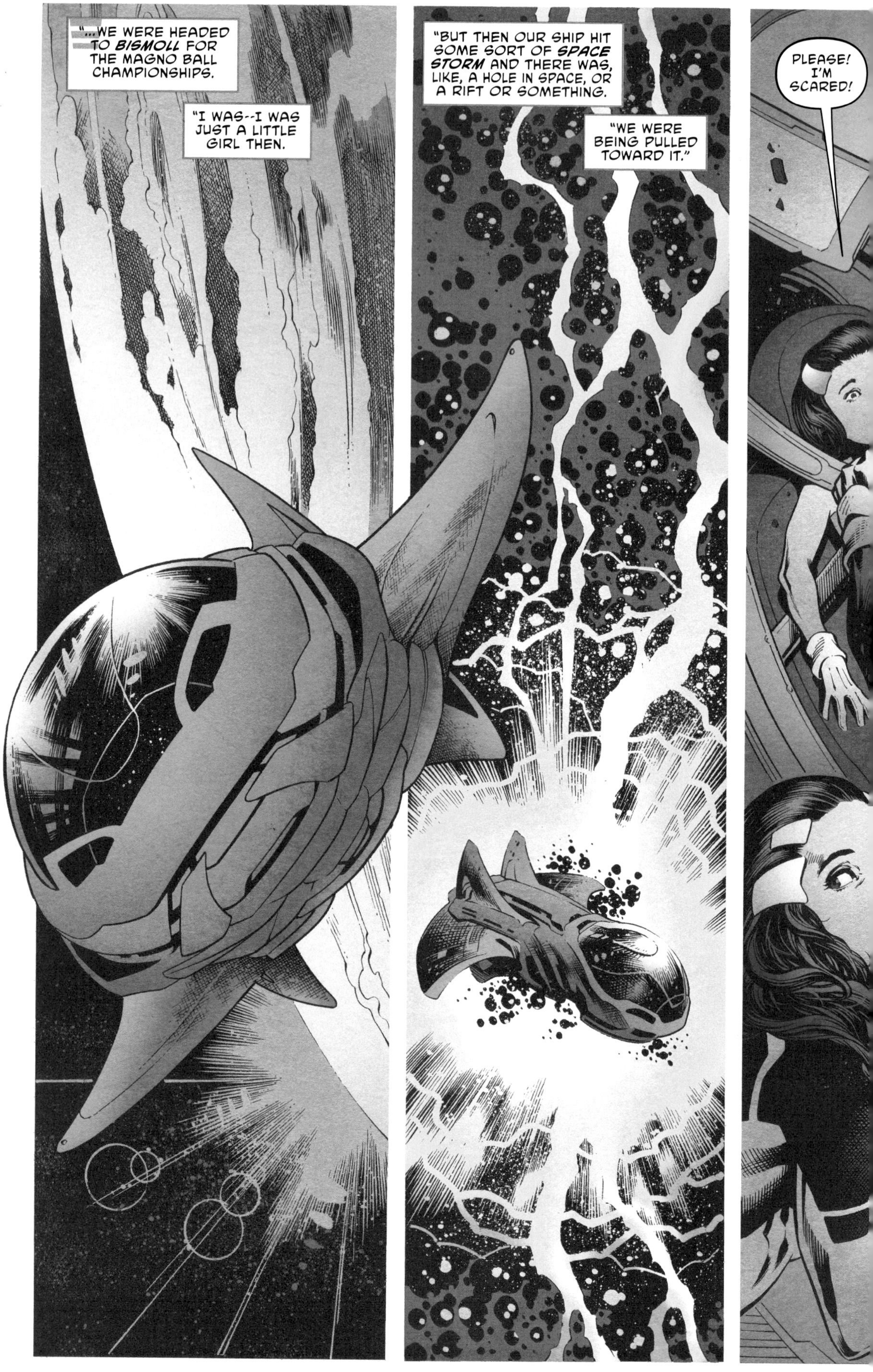
"...WE WERE HEADED TO BISMOLL FOR THE MAGNO BALL CHAMPIONSHIPS.
"I WAS--I WAS JUST A LITTLE GIRL THEN.
"BUT THEN OUR SHIP HIT SOME SORT OF SPACE STORM AND THERE WAS, LIKE, A HOLE IN SPACE, OR A RIFT OR SOMETHING.
"WE WERE BEING PULLED TOWARD IT."
PLEASE! I'M SCARED!

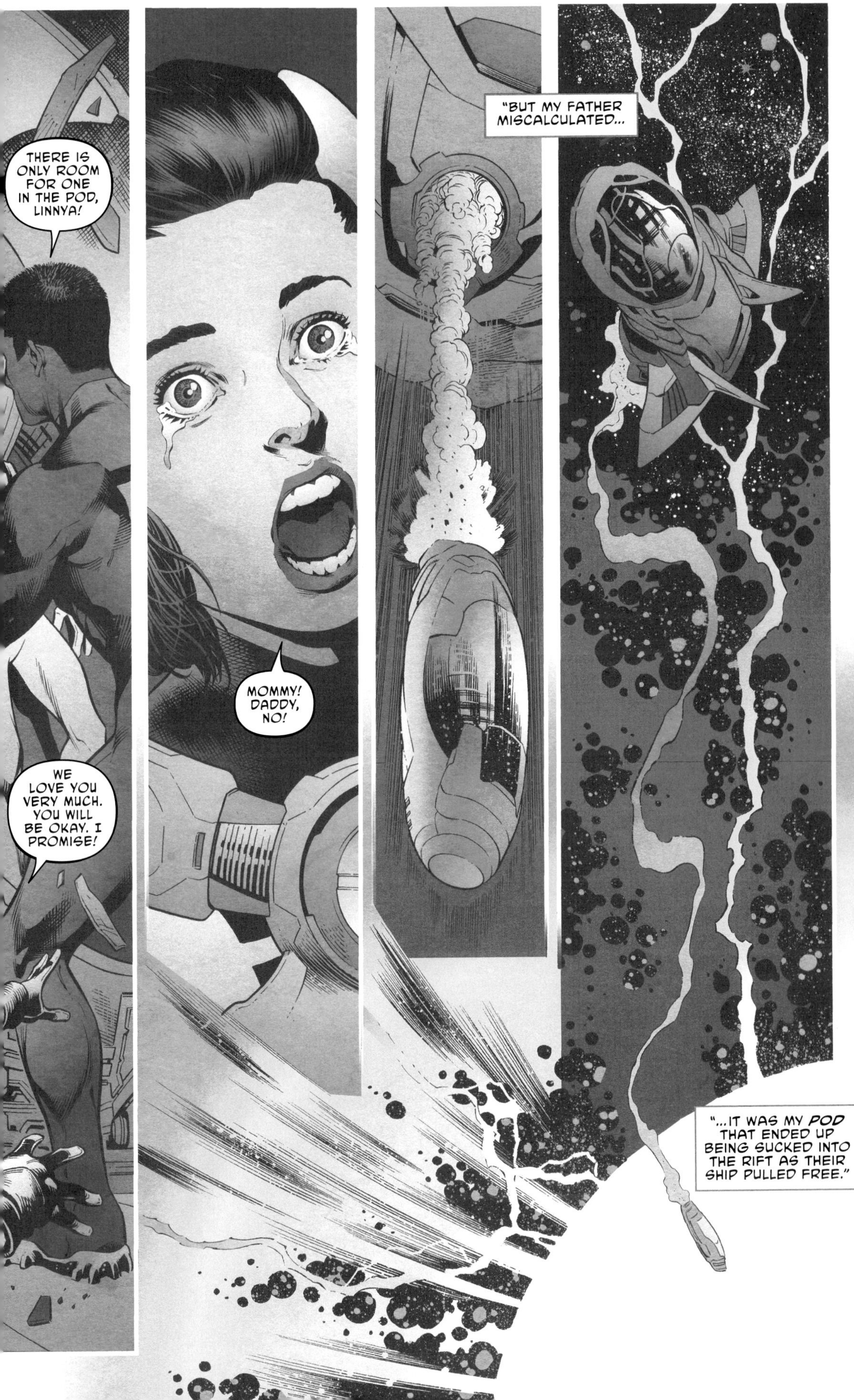
THERE IS ONLY ROOM FOR ONE IN THE POD, LINNYA!
WE LOVE YOU VERY MUCH. YOU WILL BE OKAY. I PROMISE!
MOMMY! DADDY, NO!
"BUT MY FATHER MISCALCULATED...
"...IT WAS MY *POD* THAT ENDED UP BEING SUCKED INTO THE RIFT AS THEIR SHIP PULLED FREE."

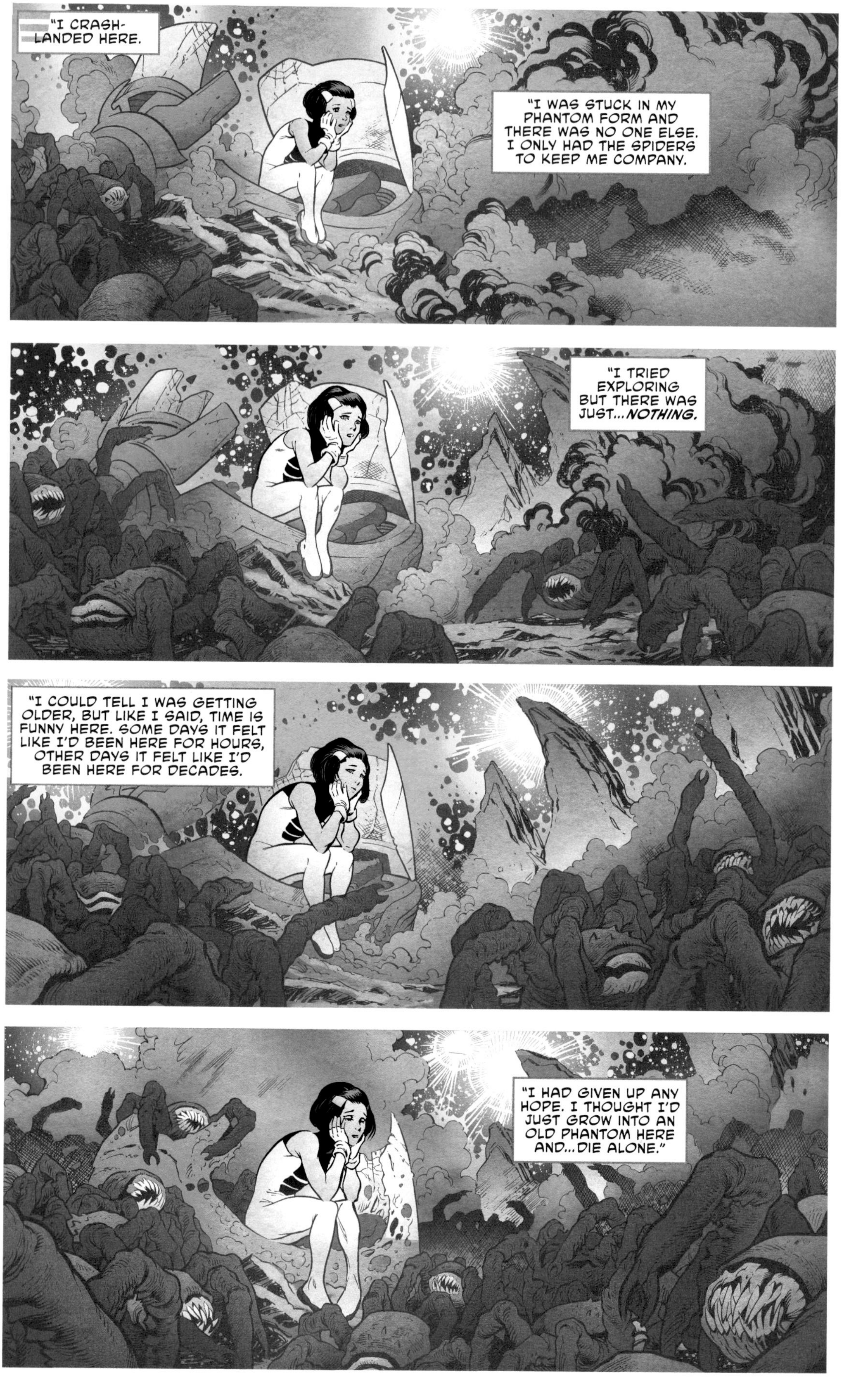
"I CRASH-LANDED HERE.
"I WAS STUCK IN MY PHANTOM FORM AND THERE WAS NO ONE ELSE. I ONLY HAD THE SPIDERS TO KEEP ME COMPANY.
"I TRIED EXPLORING BUT THERE WAS JUST... NOTHING.
"I COULD TELL I WAS GETTING OLDER, BUT LIKE I SAID, TIME IS FUNNY HERE. SOME DAYS IT FELT LIKE I'D BEEN HERE FOR HOURS, OTHER DAYS IT FELT LIKE I'D BEEN HERE FOR DECADES.
"I HAD GIVEN UP ANY HOPE. I THOUGHT I'D JUST GROW INTO AN OLD PHANTOM HERE AND...DIE ALONE."

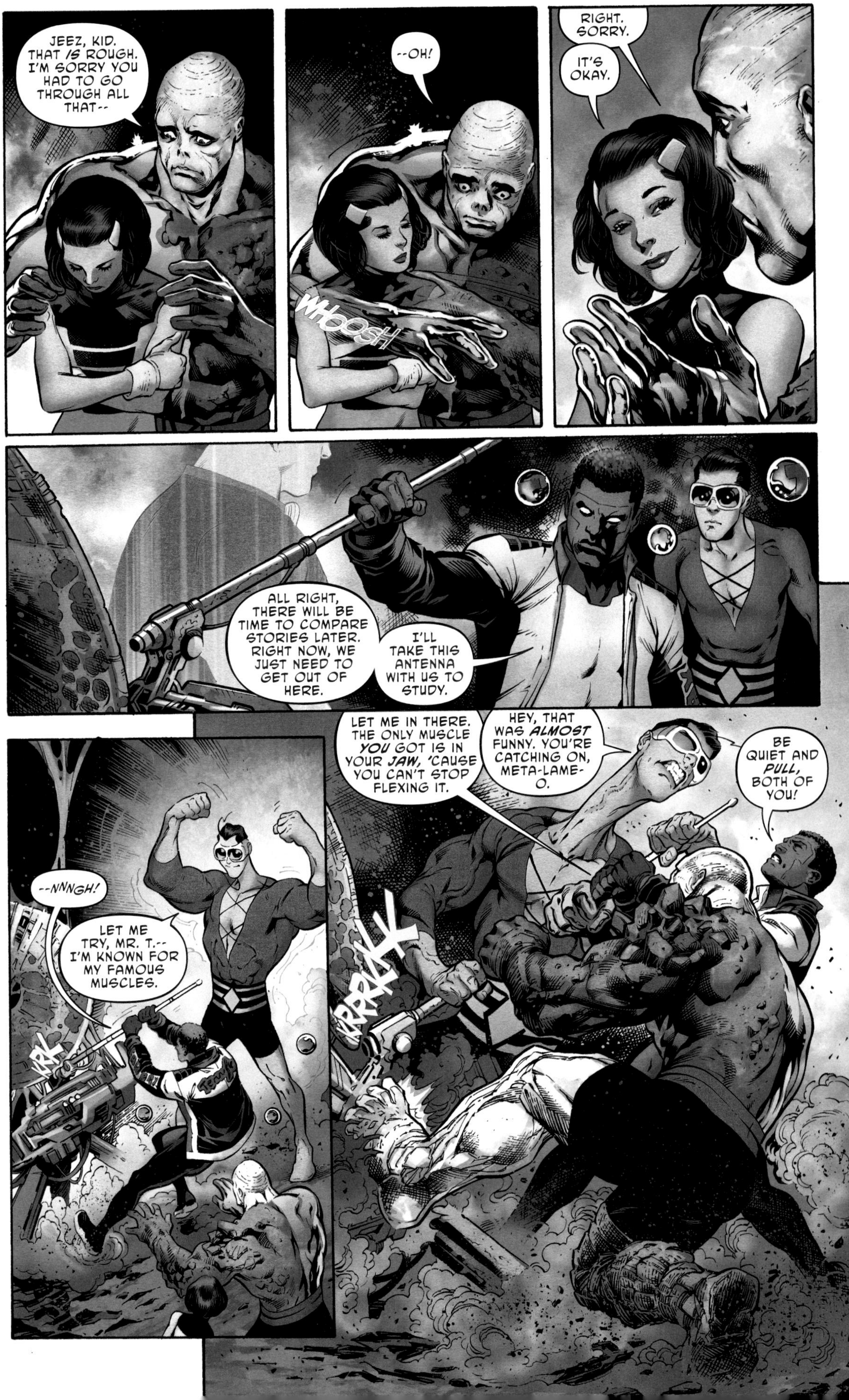
JEEZ, KID. THAT *IS* ROUGH. I'M SORRY YOU HAD TO GO THROUGH ALL THAT--
--OH!
WHOOSH
RIGHT. SORRY.
IT'S OKAY.
ALL RIGHT, THERE WILL BE TIME TO COMPARE STORIES LATER. RIGHT NOW, WE JUST NEED TO GET OUT OF HERE.
I'LL TAKE THIS ANTENNA WITH US TO STUDY.
--NNNGH!
LET ME TRY, MR. T.-- I'M KNOWN FOR MY FAMOUS MUSCLES.
KRK
LET ME IN THERE. THE ONLY MUSCLE *YOU* GOT IS IN YOUR *JAW*, 'CAUSE YOU CAN'T STOP FLEXING IT.
HEY, THAT WAS *ALMOST* FUNNY. YOU'RE CATCHING ON, META-LAME-O.
BE QUIET AND *PULL*, BOTH OF YOU!
KRRRAKK

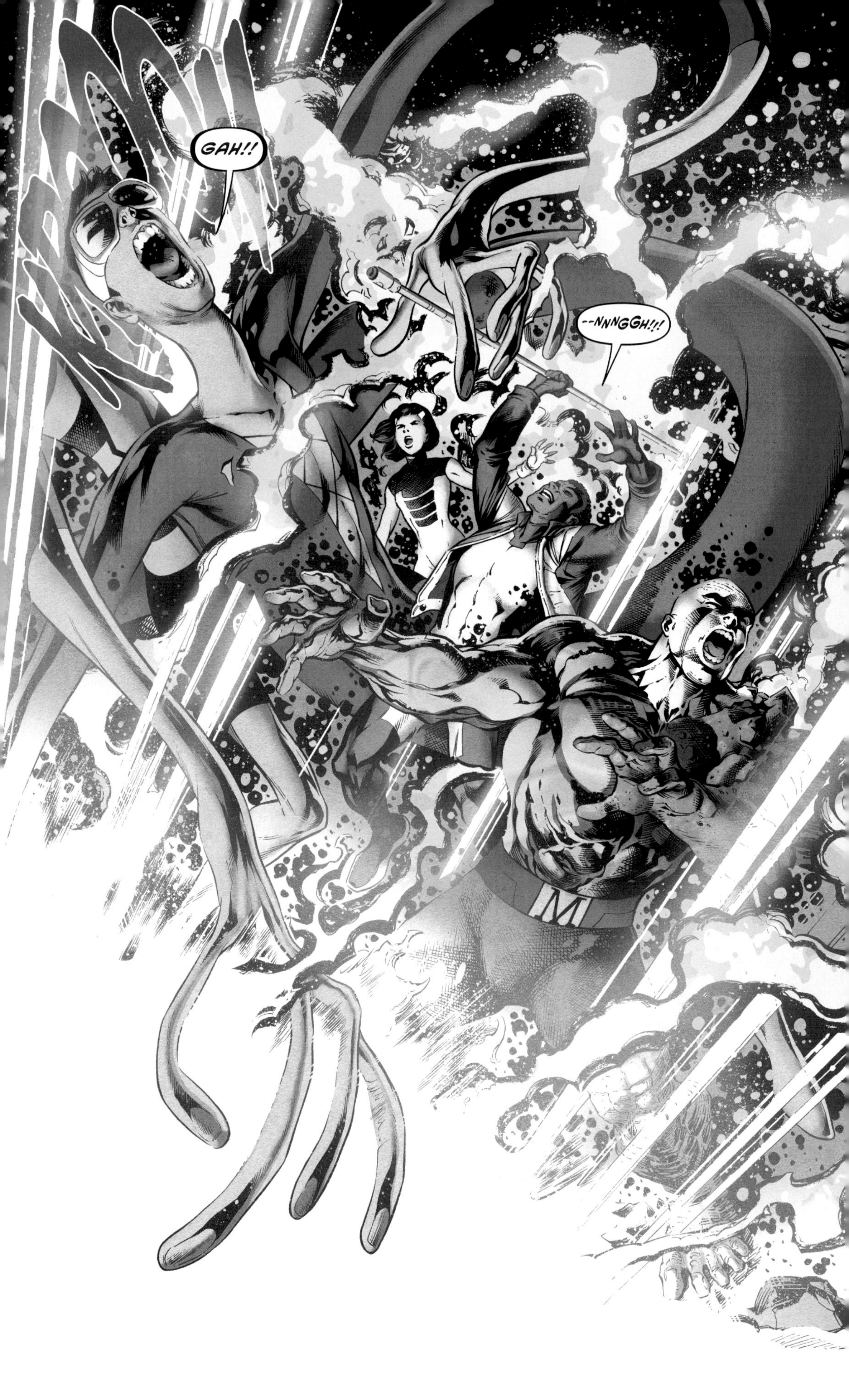
GAH!!
--NNNGGH!!!

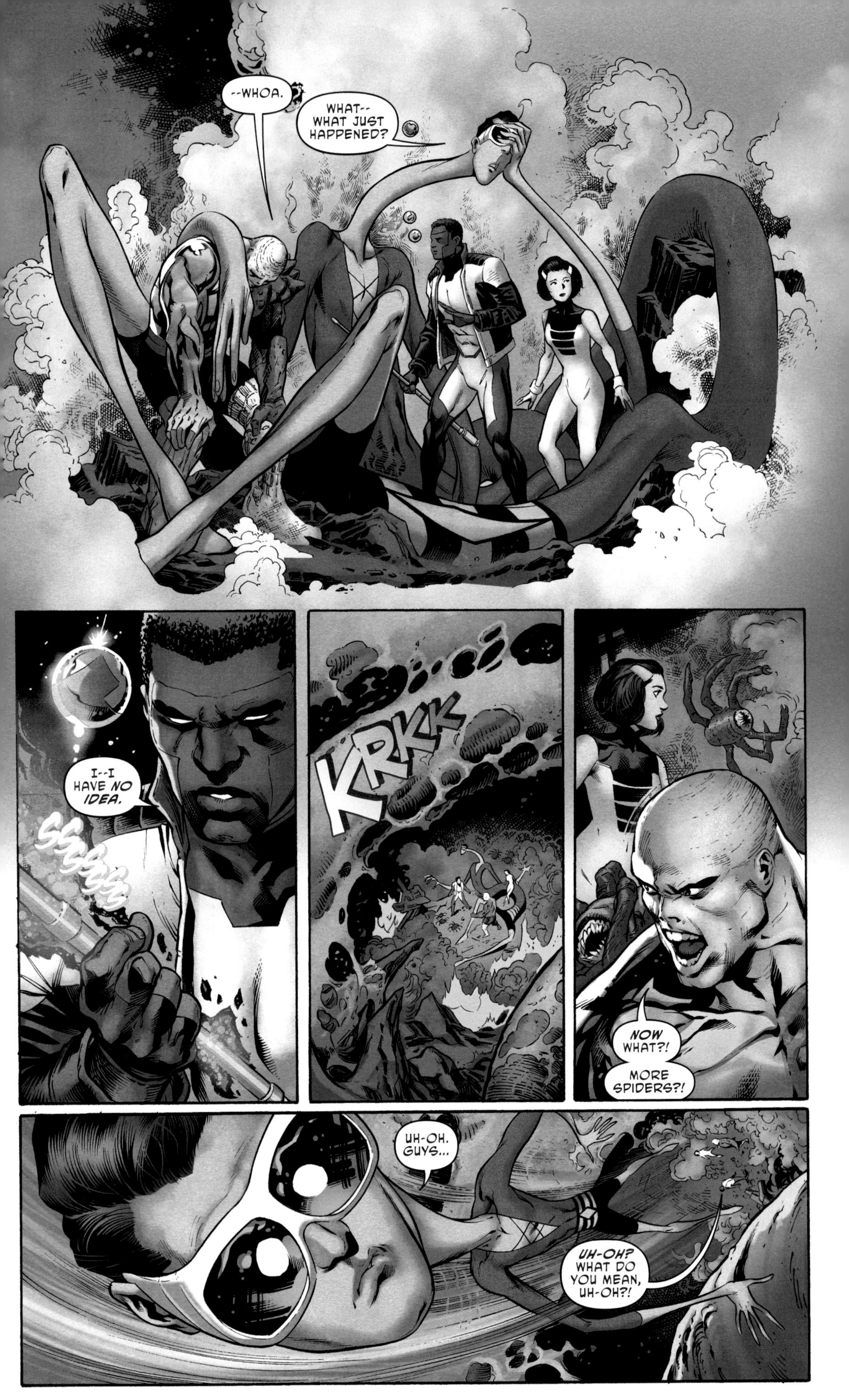
--WHOA.
WHAT-- WHAT JUST HAPPENED?
I--I HAVE *NO IDEA.*
SSSSSSS
KRKK
NOW WHAT?!
MORE SPIDERS?!
UH-OH. GUYS...
UH-OH? WHAT DO YOU MEAN, UH-OH?!

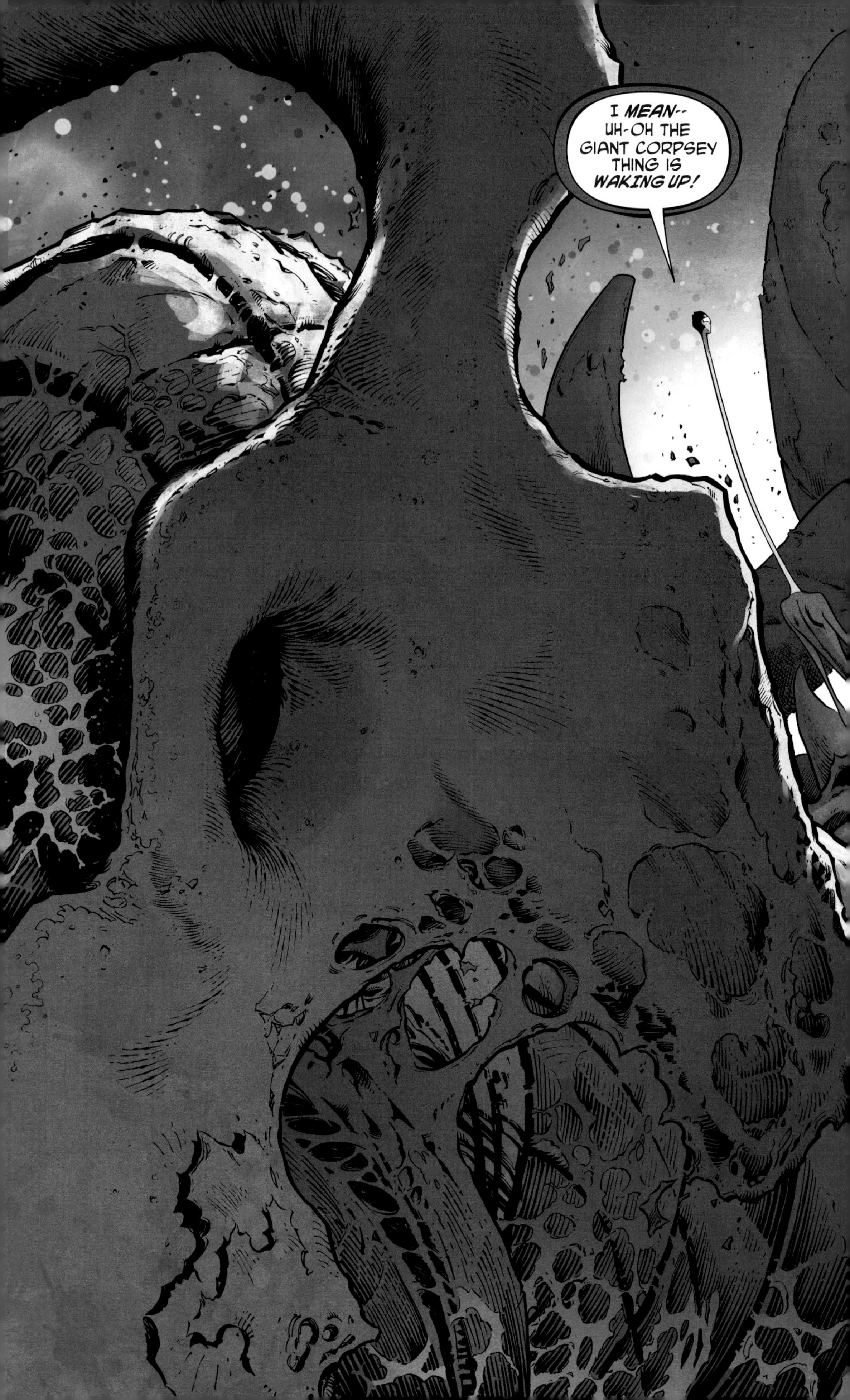
I *MEAN*--
UH-OH THE GIANT CORPSEY THING IS *WAKING UP!*

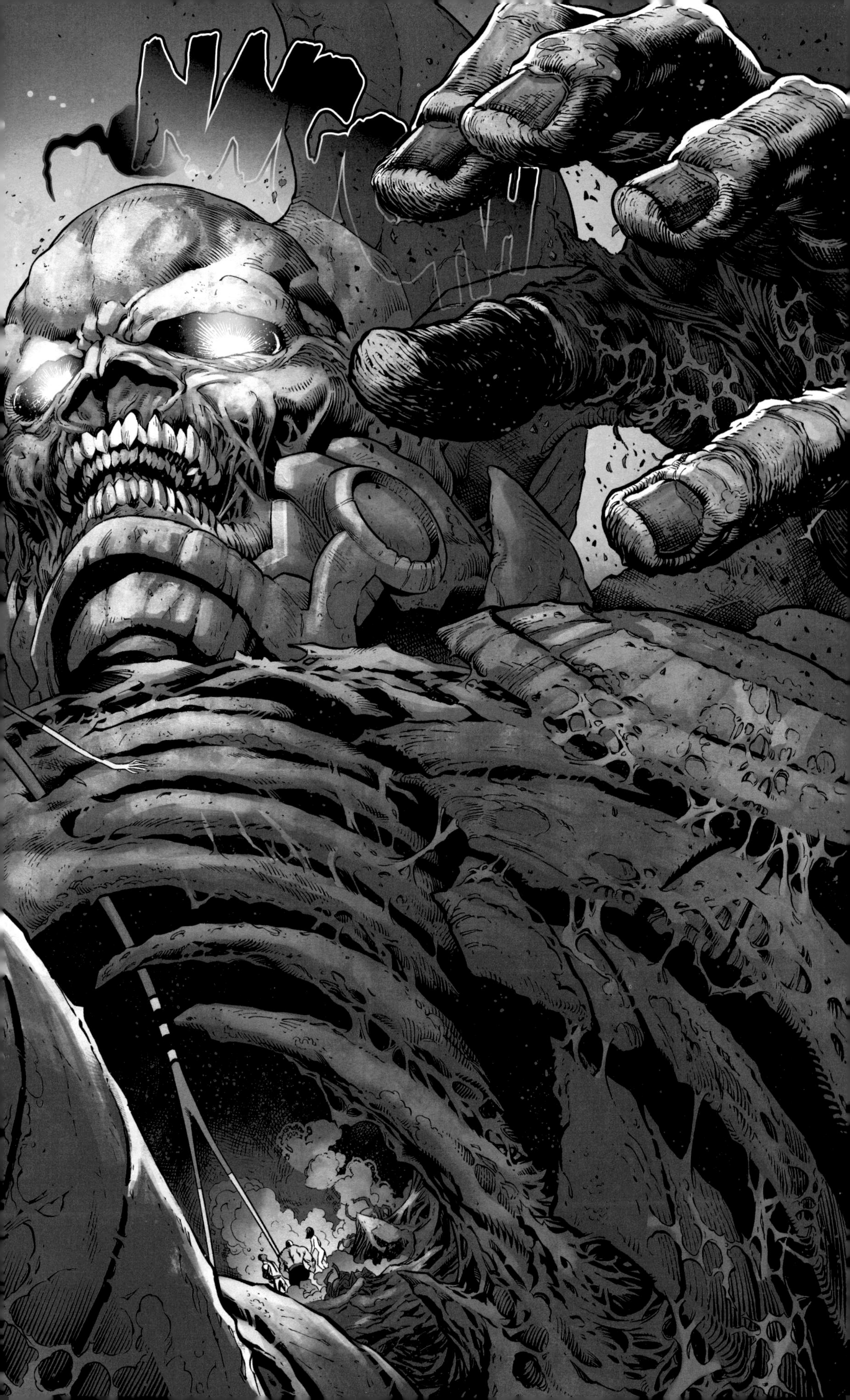

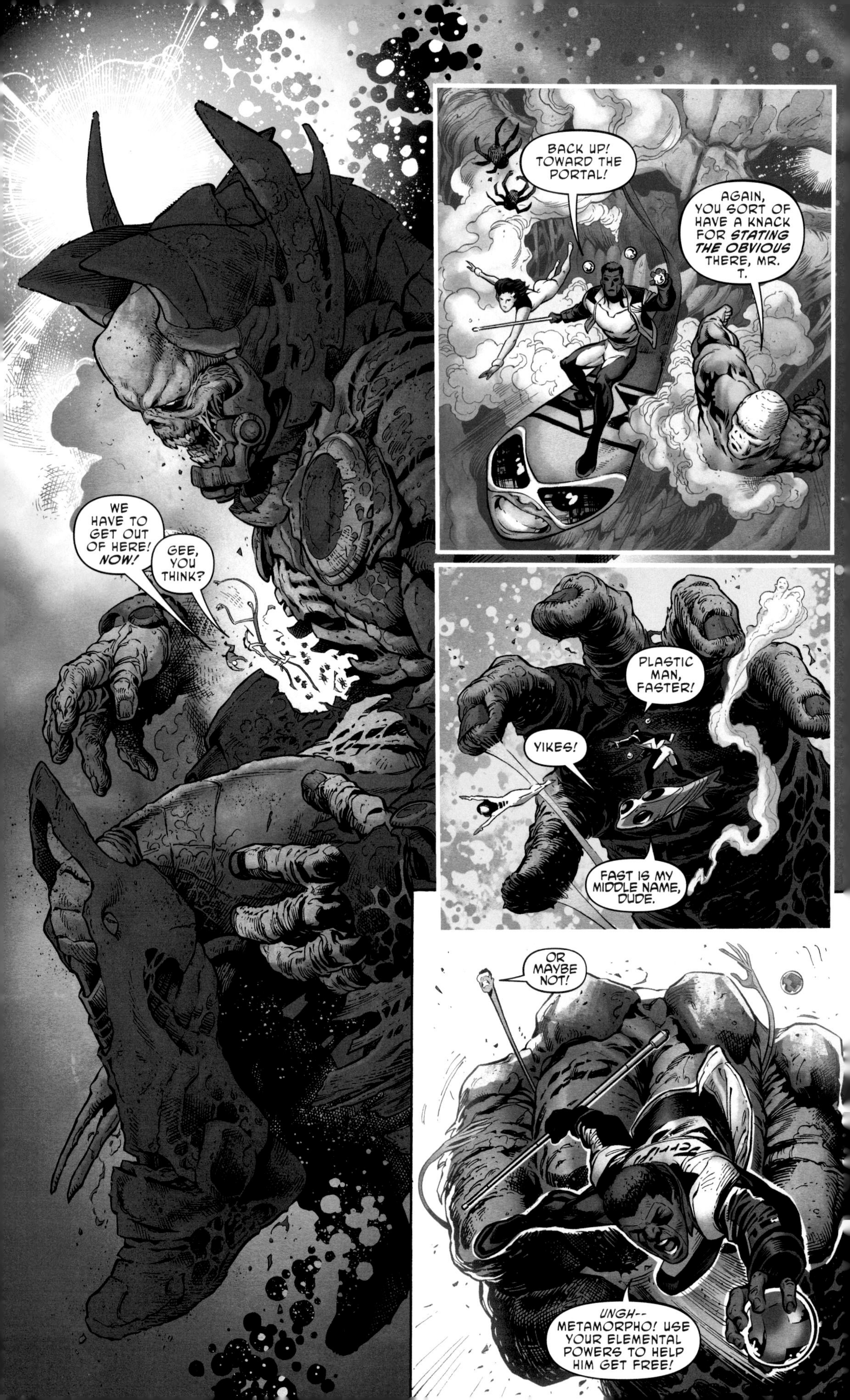
BACK UP! TOWARD THE PORTAL!
AGAIN, YOU SORT OF HAVE A KNACK FOR *STATING THE OBVIOUS* THERE, MR. T.
WE HAVE TO GET OUT OF HERE! *NOW!*
GEE, YOU THINK?
PLASTIC MAN, FASTER!
YIKES!
FAST IS MY MIDDLE NAME, DUDE.
OR MAYBE NOT!
UNGH-- METAMORPHO! USE YOUR ELEMENTAL POWERS TO HELP HIM GET FREE!

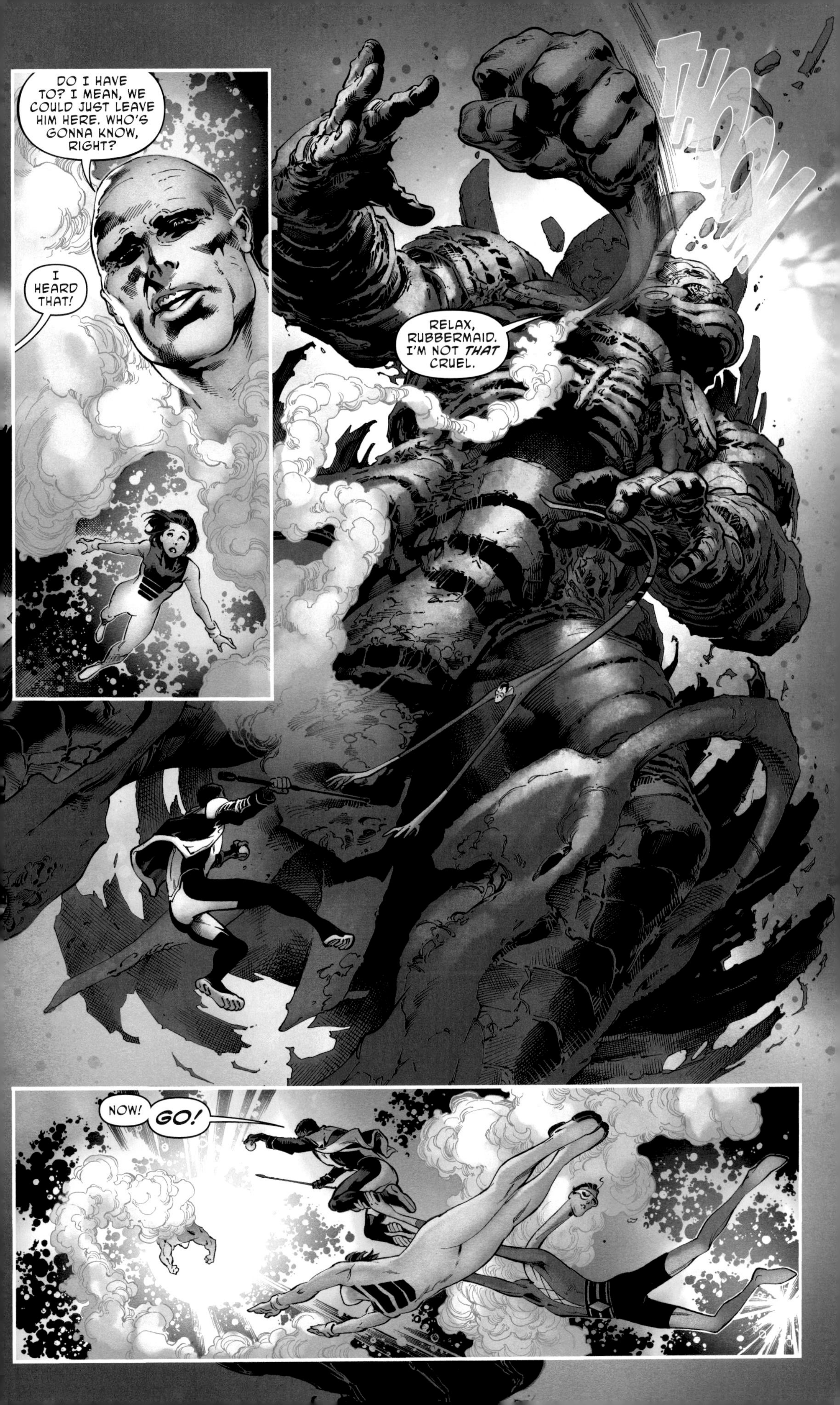
THOOOM
DO I HAVE TO? I MEAN, WE COULD JUST LEAVE HIM HERE. WHO'S GONNA KNOW, RIGHT?
I HEARD THAT!
RELAX, RUBBERMAID. I'M NOT *THAT* CRUEL.
NOW!
GO!

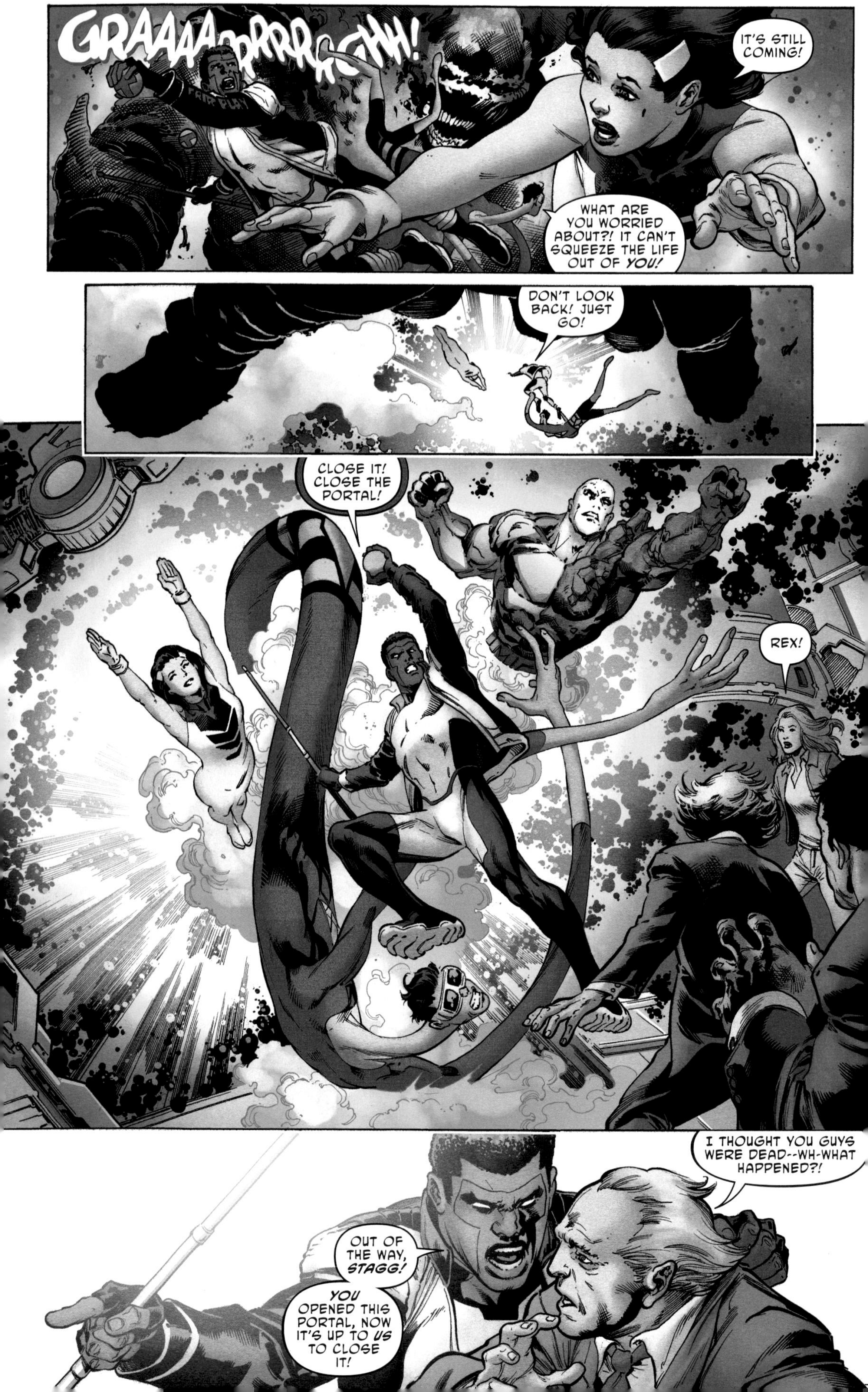
GRAAAARRRRAGHH!
IT'S STILL COMING!
WHAT ARE YOU WORRIED ABOUT?! IT CAN'T SQUEEZE THE LIFE OUT OF YOU!
DON'T LOOK BACK! JUST GO!
CLOSE IT! CLOSE THE PORTAL!
REX!
I THOUGHT YOU GUYS WERE DEAD--WH-WHAT HAPPENED?!
OUT OF THE WAY, STAGG!
YOU OPENED THIS PORTAL, NOW IT'S UP TO US TO CLOSE IT!

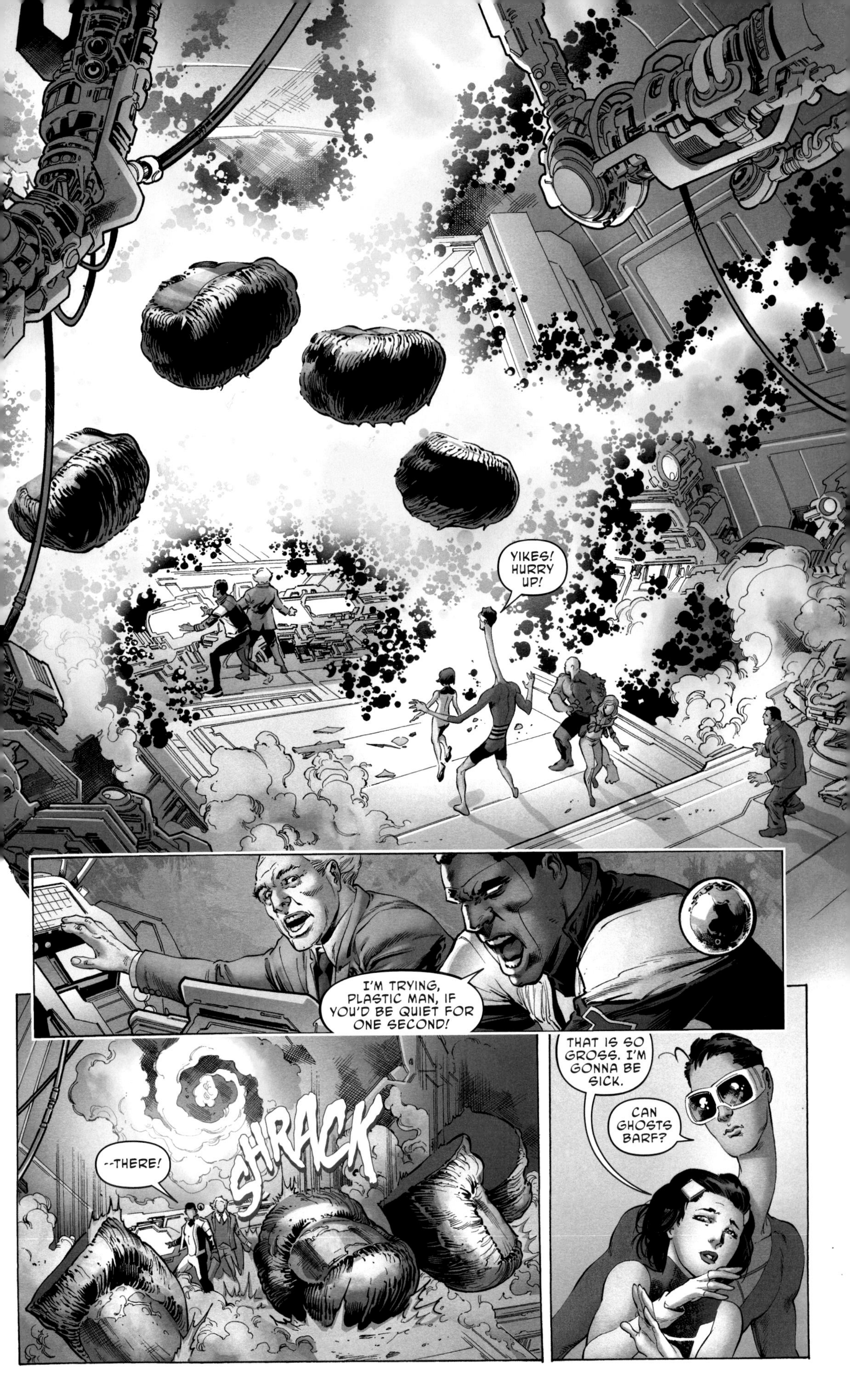
YIKES! HURRY UP!
I'M TRYING, PLASTIC MAN, IF YOU'D BE QUIET FOR ONE SECOND!
--THERE!
SHRACK
THAT IS SO GROSS. I'M GONNA BE SICK.
CAN GHOSTS BARF?

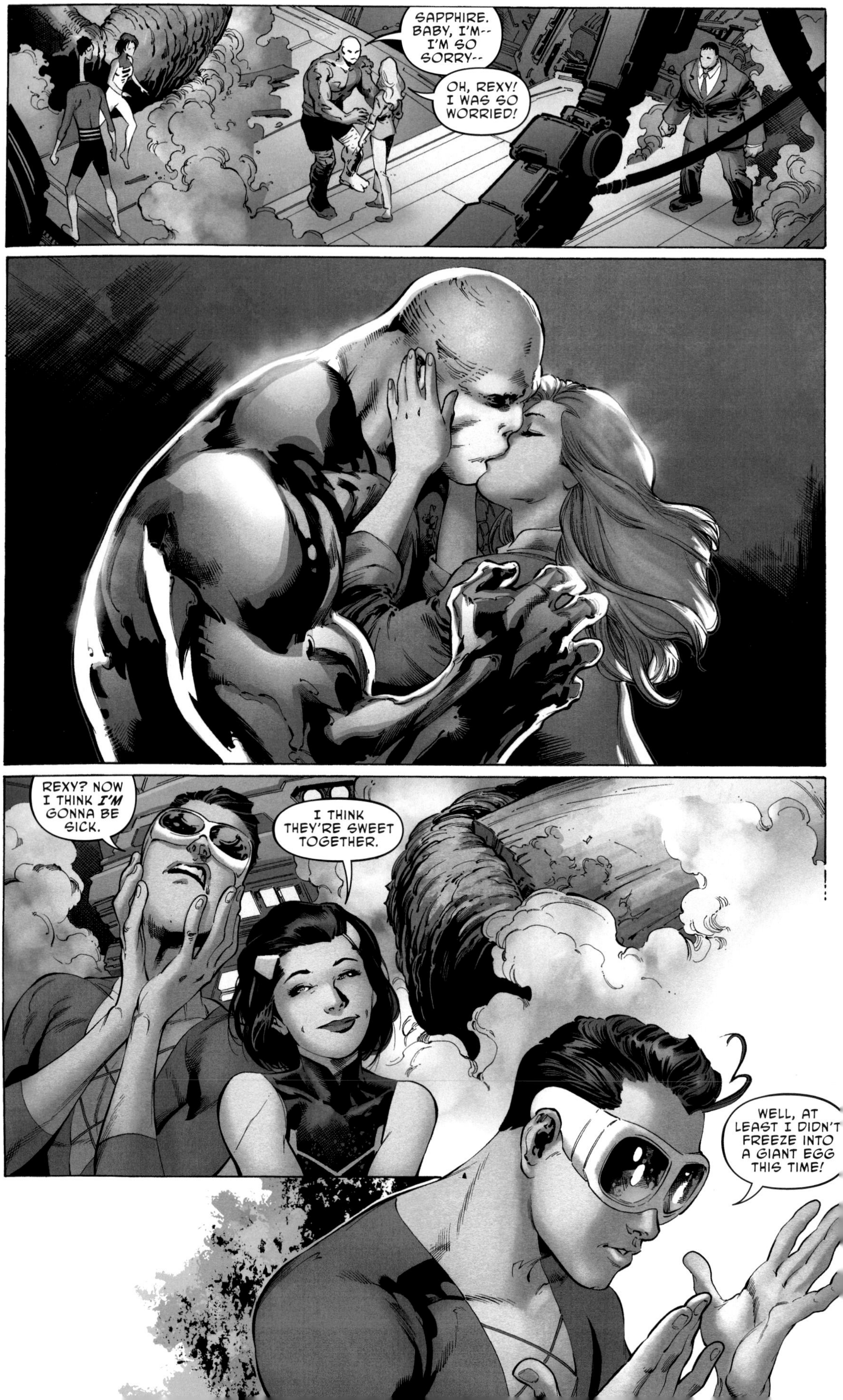
SAPPHIRE. BABY, I'M-- I'M SO SORRY--
OH, REXY! I WAS SO WORRIED!
REXY? NOW I THINK *I'M* GONNA BE SICK.
I THINK THEY'RE SWEET TOGETHER.
WELL, AT LEAST I DIDN'T FREEZE INTO A GIANT EGG THIS TIME!

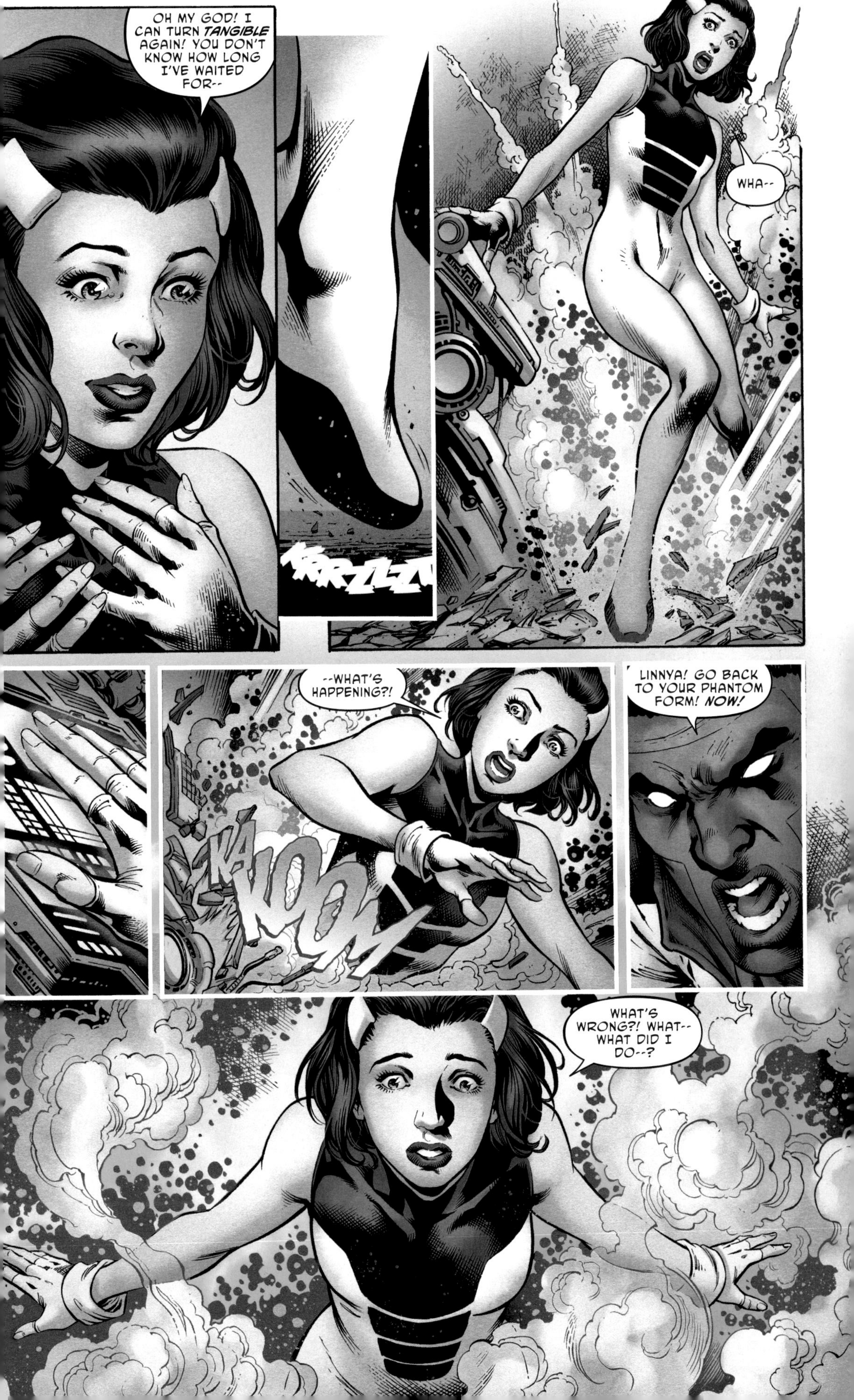
OH MY GOD! I CAN TURN TANGIBLE AGAIN! YOU DON'T KNOW HOW LONG I'VE WAITED FOR--
KRRZZZZ
WHA--
--WHAT'S HAPPENING?!
KA-BOOM
LINNYA! GO BACK TO YOUR PHANTOM FORM! NOW!
WHAT'S WRONG?! WHAT-- WHAT DID I DO--?

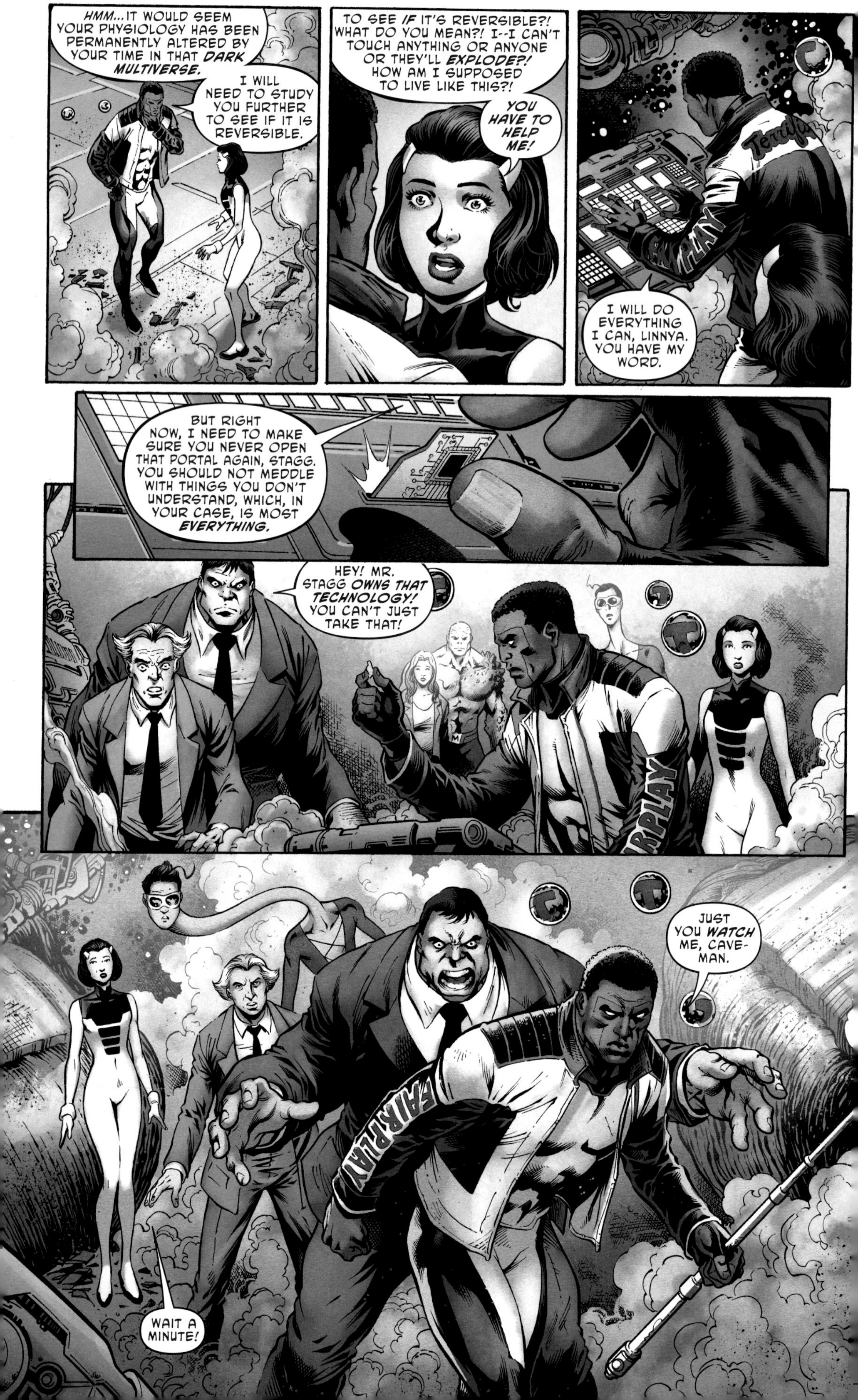
HMM...IT WOULD SEEM YOUR PHYSIOLOGY HAS BEEN PERMANENTLY ALTERED BY YOUR TIME IN THAT DARK MULTIVERSE.
I WILL NEED TO STUDY YOU FURTHER TO SEE IF IT IS REVERSIBLE.
TO SEE IF IT'S REVERSIBLE?! WHAT DO YOU MEAN?! I--I CAN'T TOUCH ANYTHING OR ANYONE OR THEY'LL EXPLODE?! HOW AM I SUPPOSED TO LIVE LIKE THIS?!
YOU HAVE TO HELP ME!
I WILL DO EVERYTHING I CAN, LINNYA. YOU HAVE MY WORD.
BUT RIGHT NOW, I NEED TO MAKE SURE YOU NEVER OPEN THAT PORTAL AGAIN, STAGG. YOU SHOULD NOT MEDDLE WITH THINGS YOU DON'T UNDERSTAND, WHICH, IN YOUR CASE, IS MOST EVERYTHING.
HEY! MR. STAGG OWNS THAT TECHNOLOGY! YOU CAN'T JUST TAKE THAT!
JUST YOU WATCH ME, CAVE-MAN.
WAIT A MINUTE!

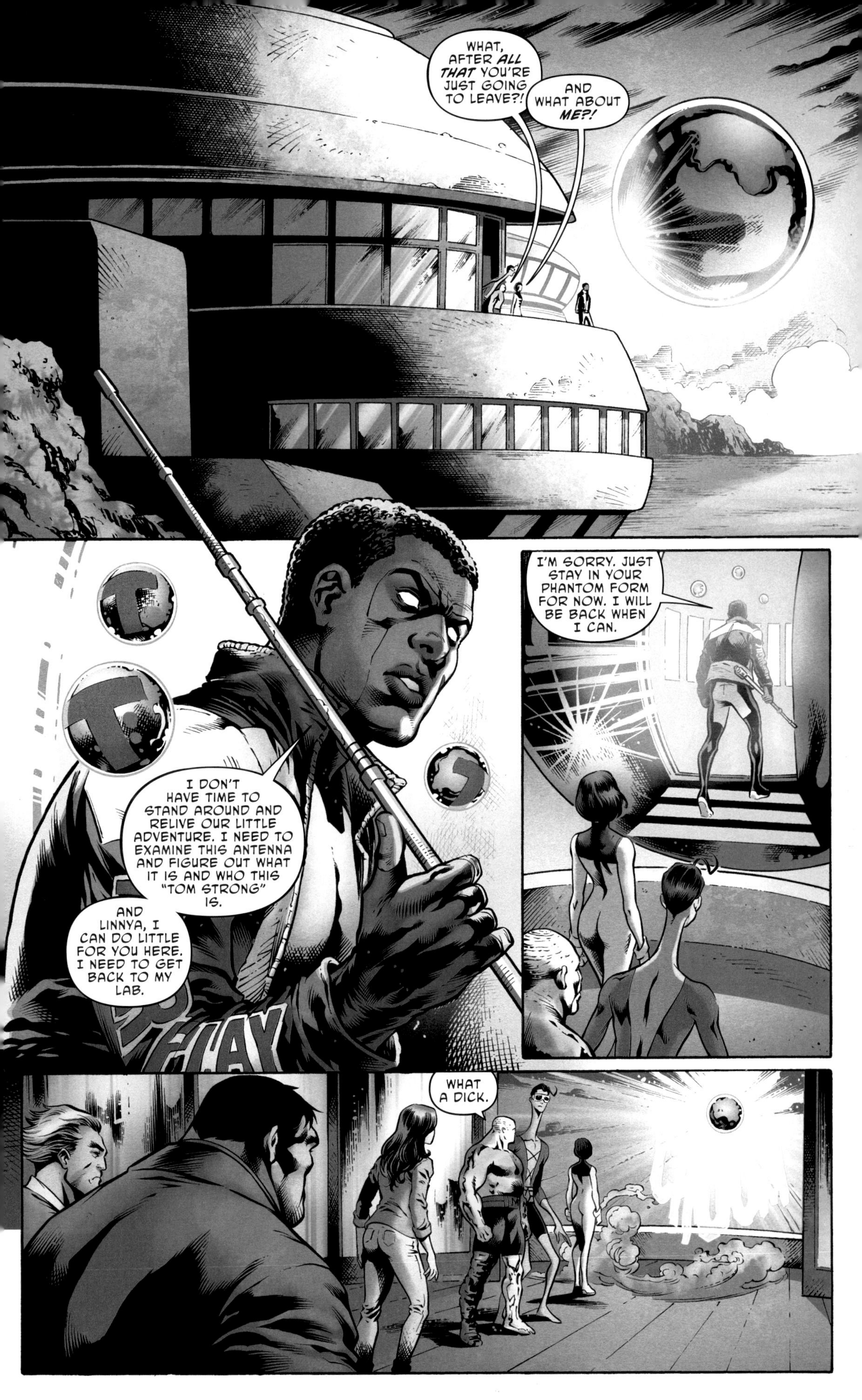
WHAT, AFTER ALL THAT YOU'RE JUST GOING TO LEAVE?!
AND WHAT ABOUT ME?!
I DON'T HAVE TIME TO STAND AROUND AND RELIVE OUR LITTLE ADVENTURE. I NEED TO EXAMINE THIS ANTENNA AND FIGURE OUT WHAT IT IS AND WHO THIS "TOM STRONG" IS.
AND LINNYA, I CAN DO LITTLE FOR YOU HERE. I NEED TO GET BACK TO MY LAB.
I'M SORRY. JUST STAY IN YOUR PHANTOM FORM FOR NOW. I WILL BE BACK WHEN I CAN.
WHAT A DICK.

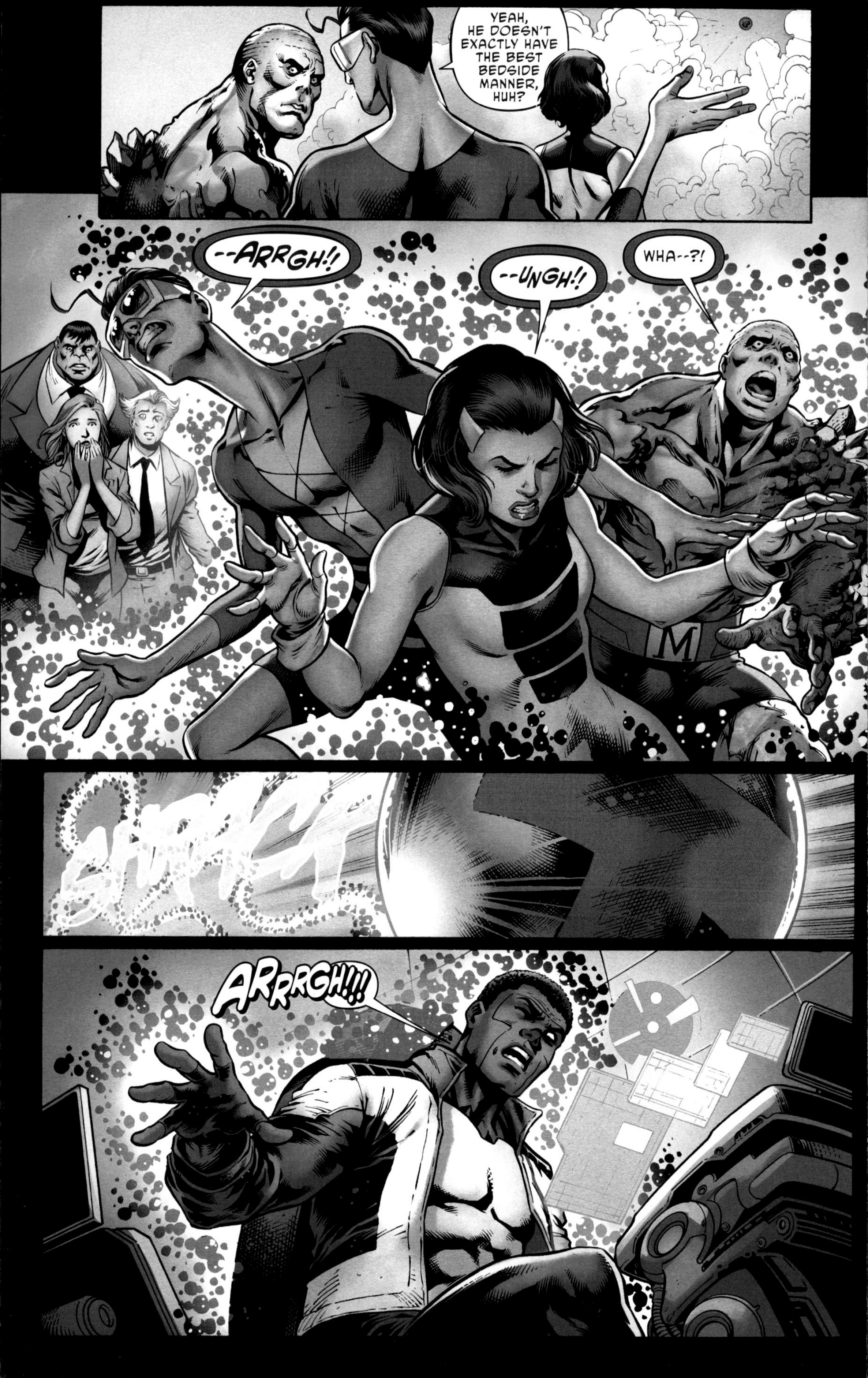
YEAH, HE DOESN'T EXACTLY HAVE THE BEST BEDSIDE MANNER, HUH?
--ARRGH!!
--UNGH!!
WHA--?!
ARRRGH!!!

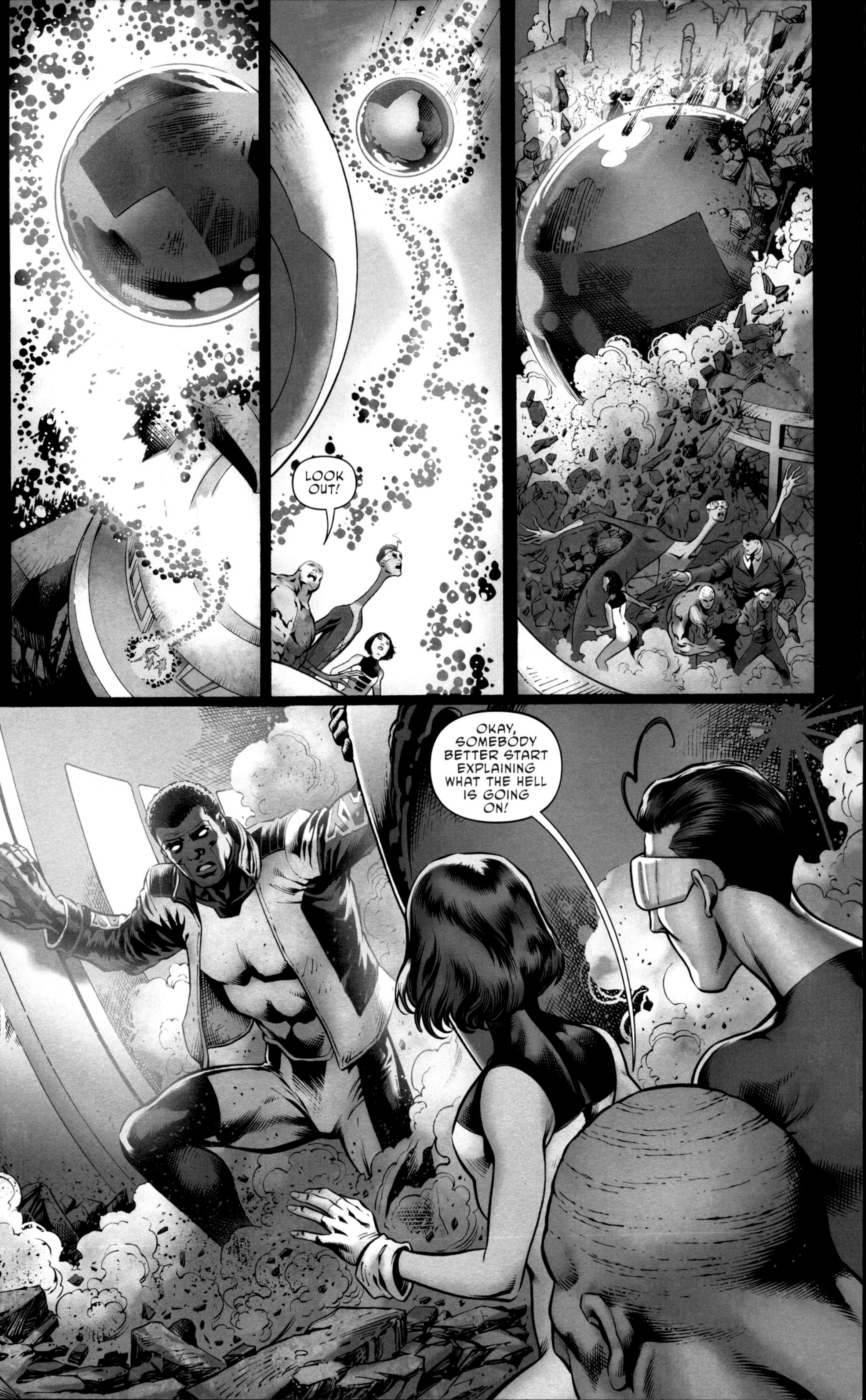
LOOK OUT!
OKAY, SOMEBODY BETTER START EXPLAINING WHAT THE HELL IS GOING ON!

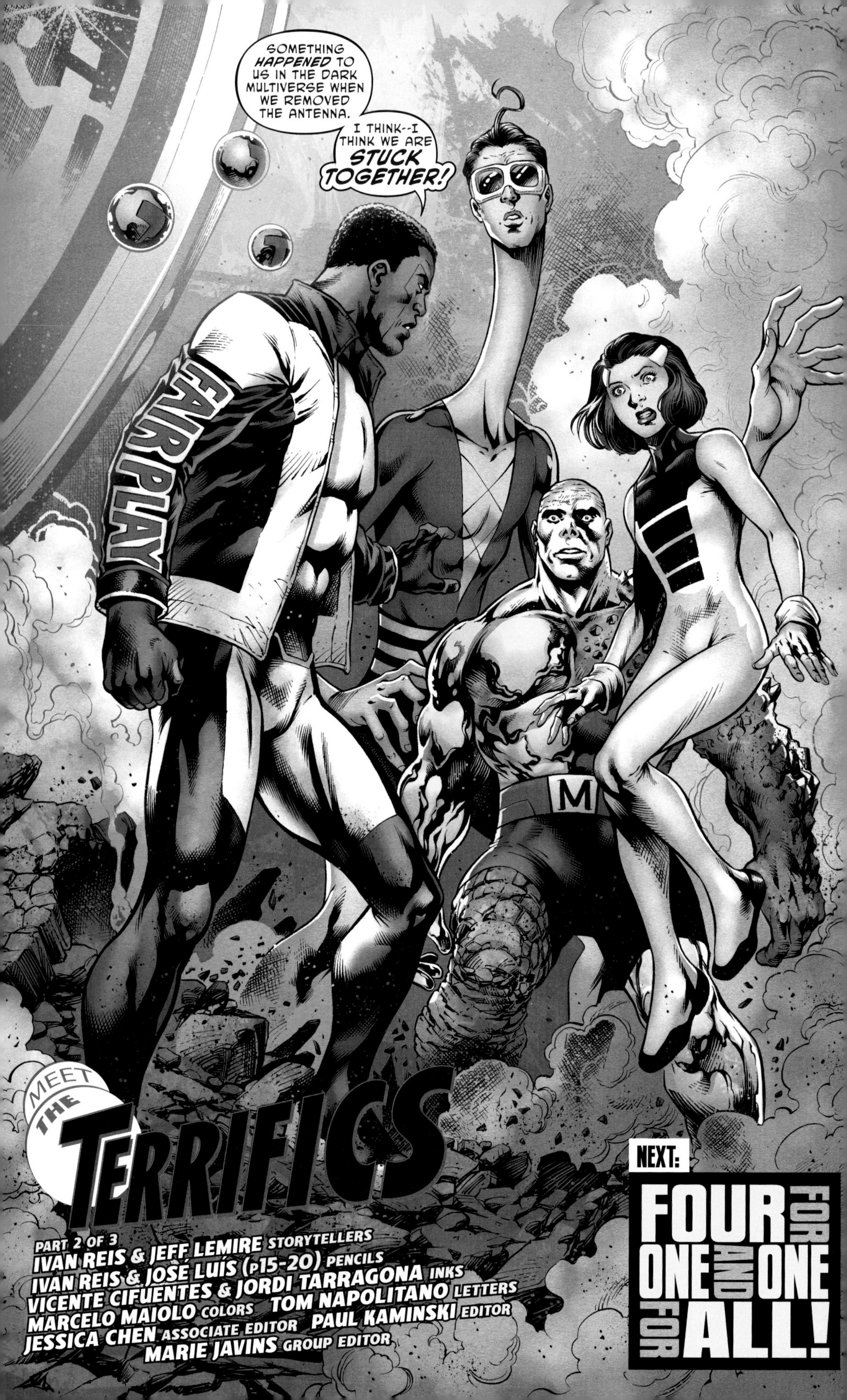
SOMETHING HAPPENED TO US IN THE DARK MULTIVERSE WHEN WE REMOVED THE ANTENNA.
I THINK--I THINK WE ARE STUCK TOGETHER!
FAIR PLAY
M
MEET THE TERRIFICS
PART 2 OF 3
IVAN REIS & JEFF LEMIRE STORYTELLERS
IVAN REIS & JOSÉ LUÍS (p15-20) PENCILS
VICENTE CIFUENTES & JORDI TARRAGONA INKS
MARCELO MAIOLO COLORS TOM NAPOLITANO LETTERS
JESSICA CHEN ASSOCIATE EDITOR PAUL KAMINSKI EDITOR
MARIE JAVINS GROUP EDITOR
NEXT:
FOUR FOR ONE AND ONE FOR ALL!

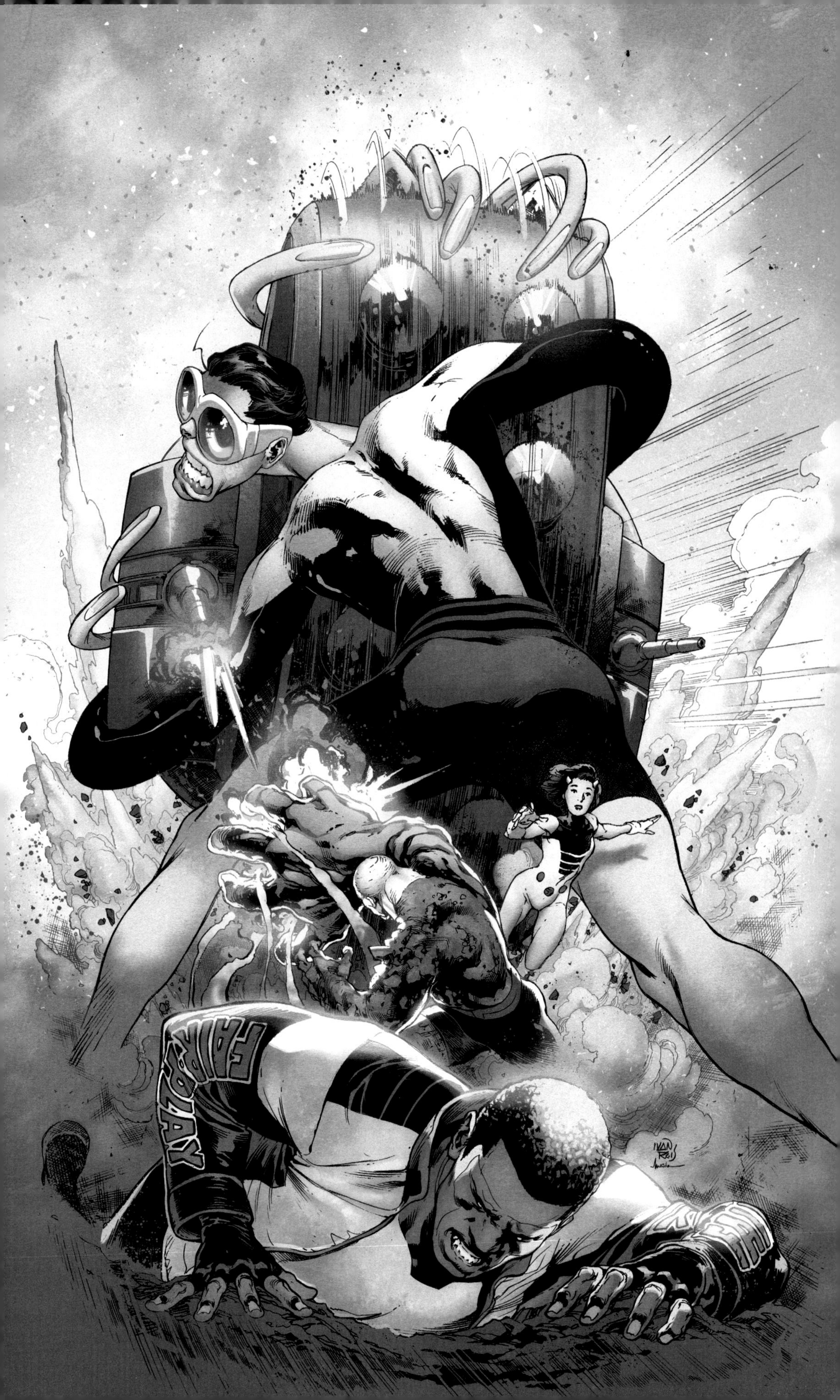
FAIR PLAY

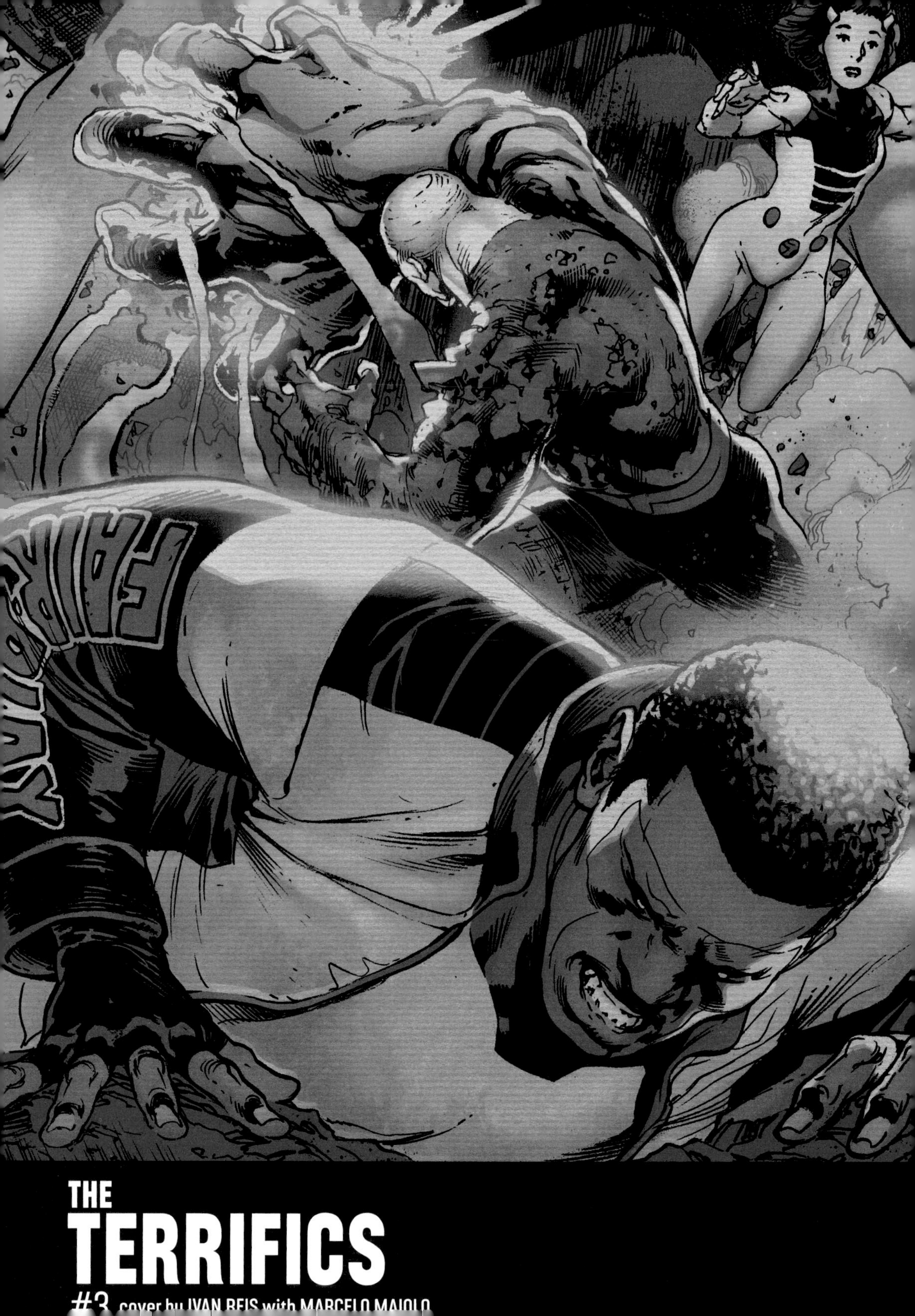

THE
TERRIFICS
#3 cover by IVAN REIS with MARCELO MAIOLO

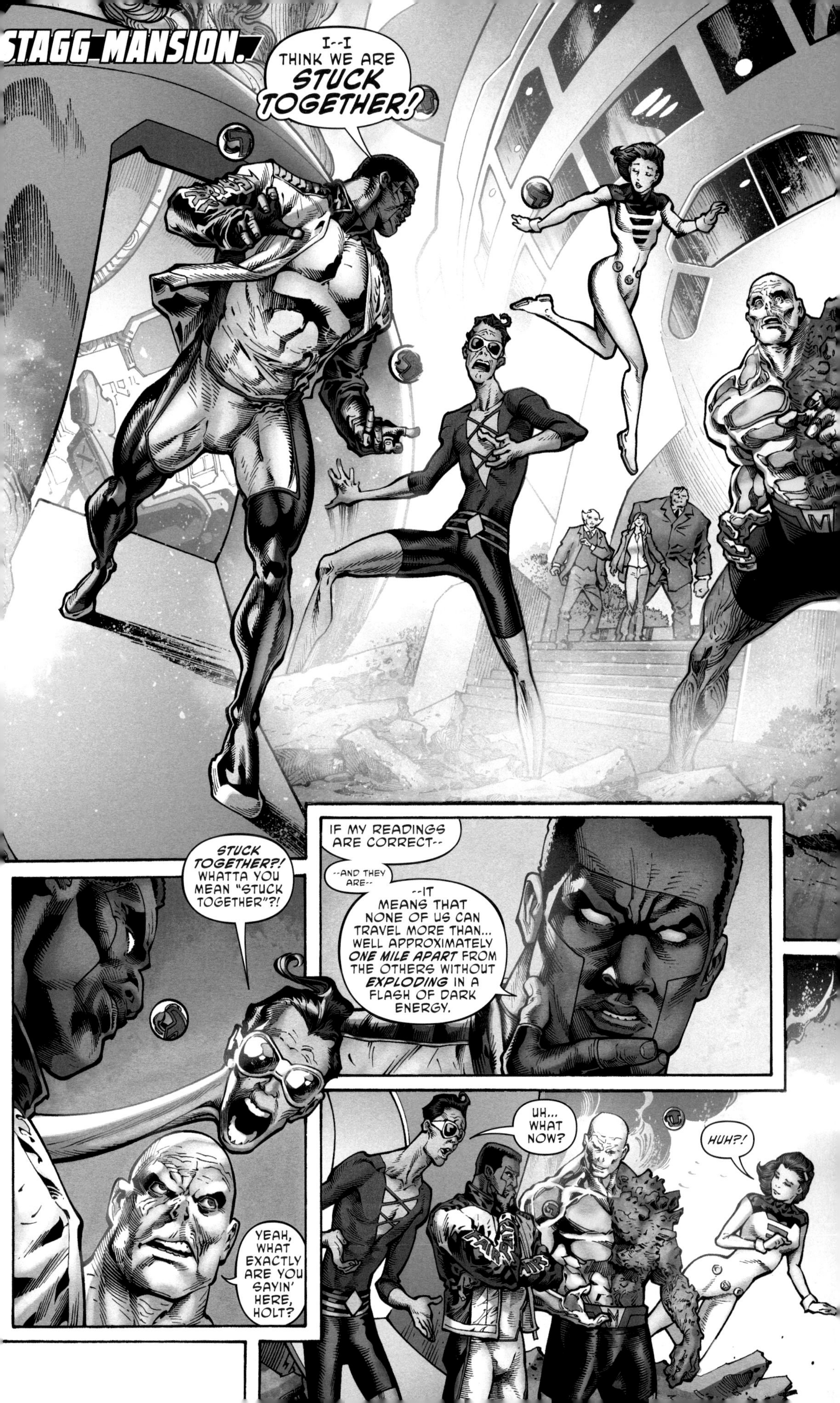
STAGG MANSION.
I--I THINK WE ARE STUCK TOGETHER?!
STUCK TOGETHER?! WHATTA YOU MEAN "STUCK TOGETHER"?!
IF MY READINGS ARE CORRECT--
--AND THEY ARE--
--IT MEANS THAT NONE OF US CAN TRAVEL MORE THAN... WELL APPROXIMATELY ONE MILE APART FROM THE OTHERS WITHOUT EXPLODING IN A FLASH OF DARK ENERGY.
YEAH, WHAT EXACTLY ARE YOU SAYIN' HERE, HOLT?
UH... WHAT NOW?
HUH?!

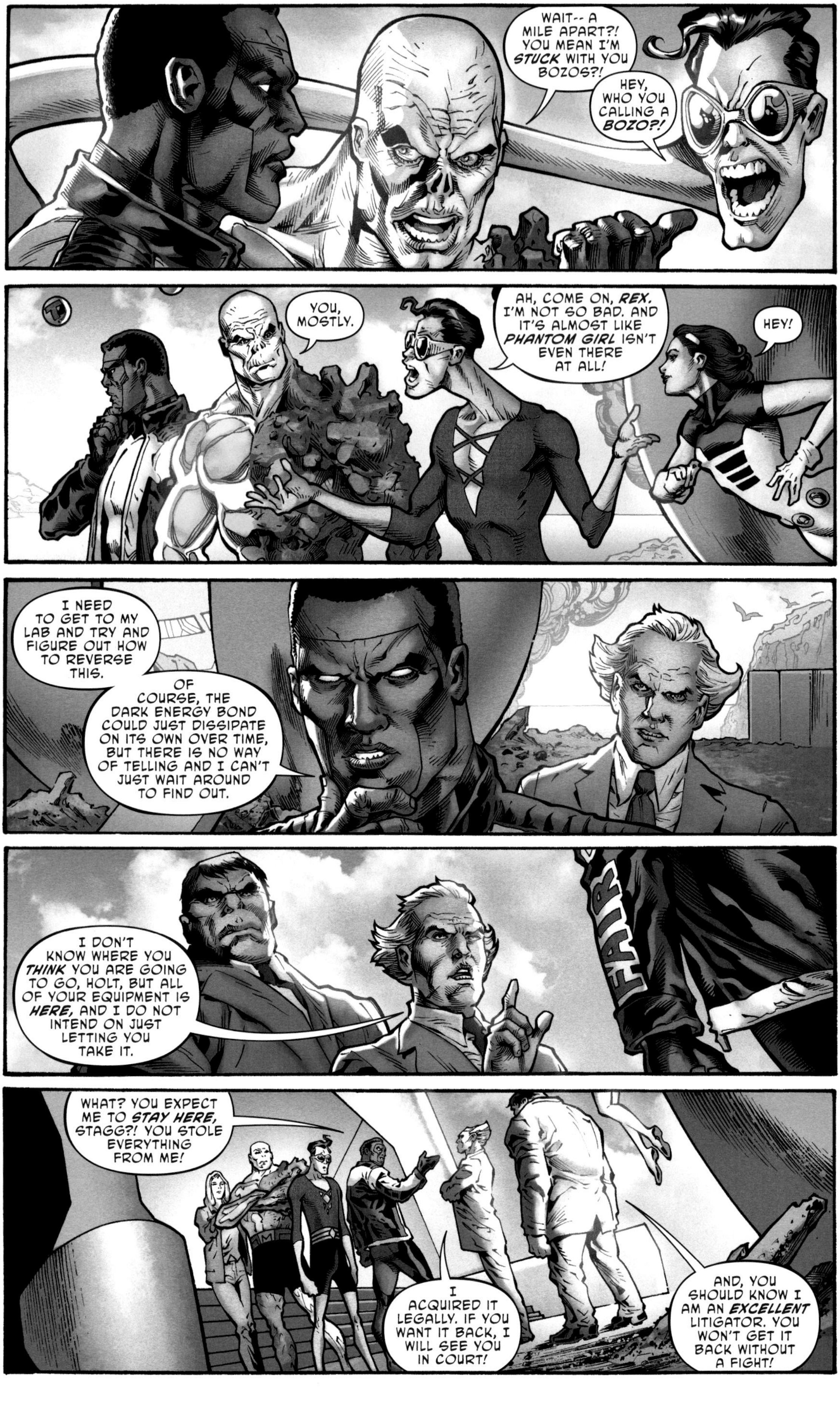
WAIT-- A MILE APART?! YOU MEAN I'M STUCK WITH YOU BOZOS?!
HEY, WHO YOU CALLING A BOZO?!
YOU, MOSTLY.
AH, COME ON, REX. I'M NOT SO BAD. AND IT'S ALMOST LIKE PHANTOM GIRL ISN'T EVEN THERE AT ALL!
HEY!
I NEED TO GET TO MY LAB AND TRY AND FIGURE OUT HOW TO REVERSE THIS.
OF COURSE, THE DARK ENERGY BOND COULD JUST DISSIPATE ON ITS OWN OVER TIME, BUT THERE IS NO WAY OF TELLING AND I CAN'T JUST WAIT AROUND TO FIND OUT.
I DON'T KNOW WHERE YOU THINK YOU ARE GOING TO GO, HOLT, BUT ALL OF YOUR EQUIPMENT IS HERE, AND I DO NOT INTEND ON JUST LETTING YOU TAKE IT.
WHAT? YOU EXPECT ME TO STAY HERE, STAGG?! YOU STOLE EVERYTHING FROM ME!
I ACQUIRED IT LEGALLY. IF YOU WANT IT BACK, I WILL SEE YOU IN COURT!
AND, YOU SHOULD KNOW I AM AN EXCELLENT LITIGATOR. YOU WON'T GET IT BACK WITHOUT A FIGHT!

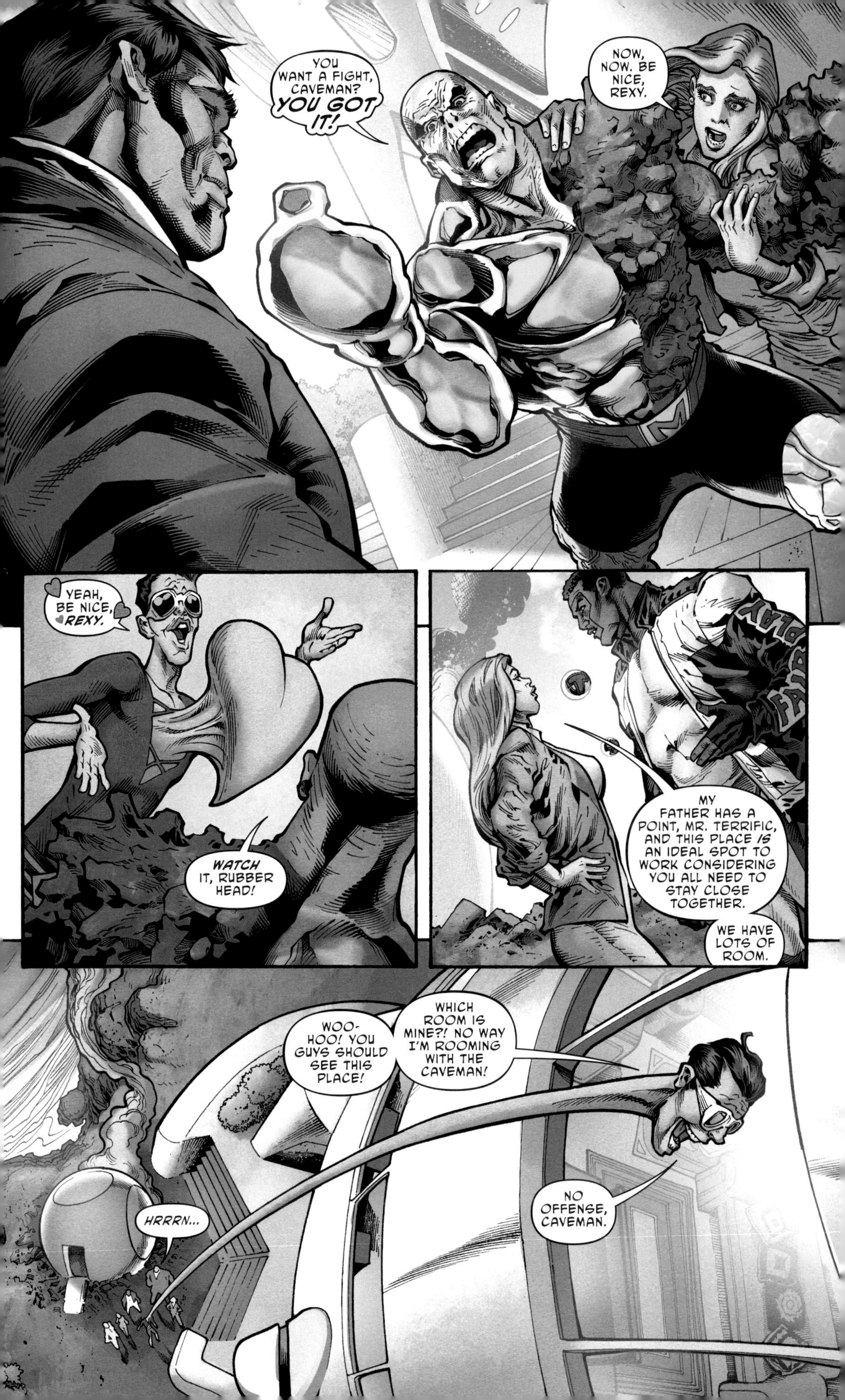

YOU WANT A FIGHT, CAVEMAN? YOU GOT IT!
NOW, NOW. BE NICE, REXY.
YEAH, BE NICE, REXY.
WATCH IT, RUBBER HEAD!
MY FATHER HAS A POINT, MR. TERRIFIC, AND THIS PLACE IS AN IDEAL SPOT TO WORK CONSIDERING YOU ALL NEED TO STAY CLOSE TOGETHER.
WE HAVE LOTS OF ROOM.
WOO-HOO! YOU GUYS SHOULD SEE THIS PLACE!
WHICH ROOM IS MINE?! NO WAY I'M ROOMING WITH THE CAVEMAN!
NO OFFENSE, CAVEMAN.
HRRRN...

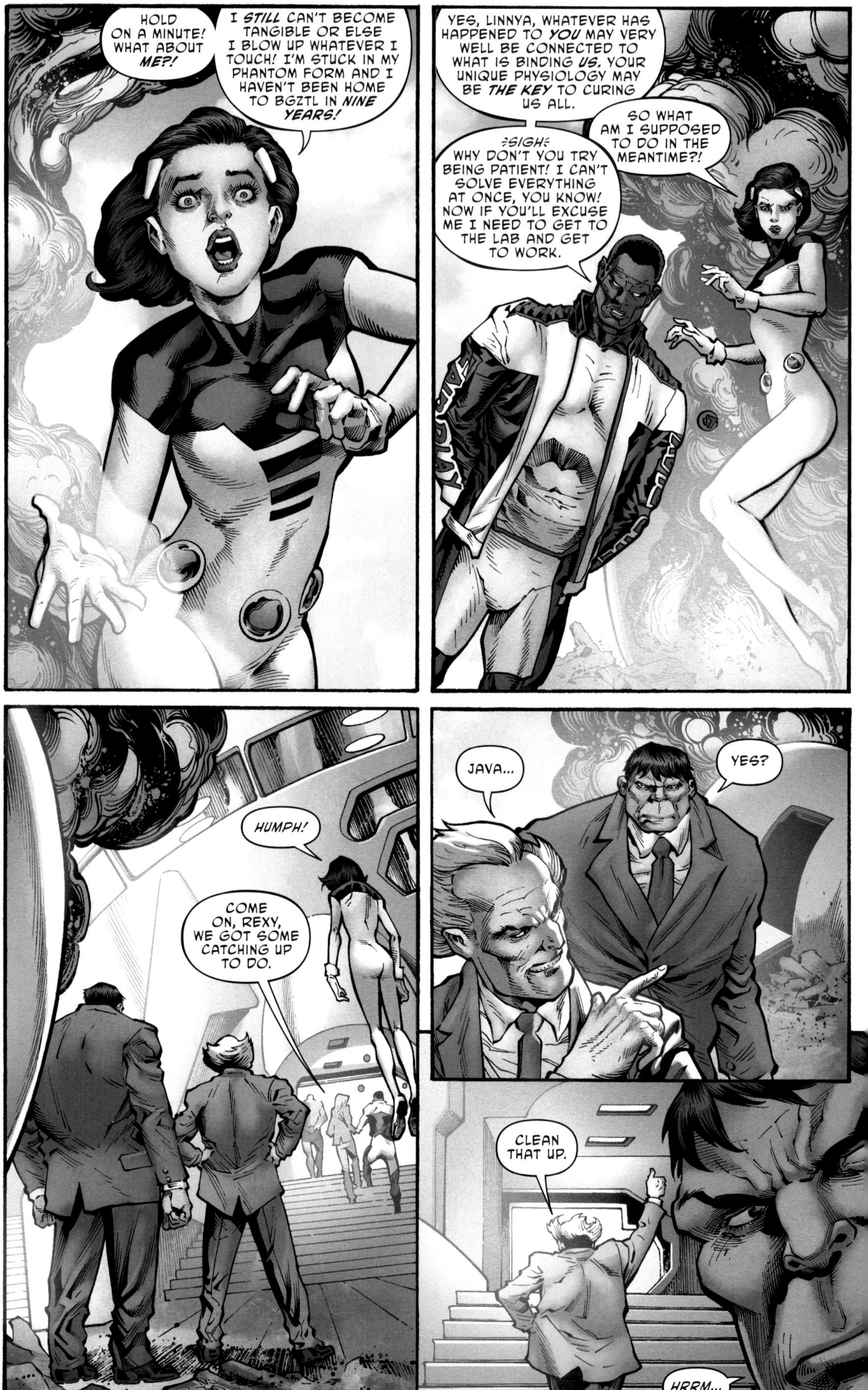
HOLD ON A MINUTE! WHAT ABOUT *ME?!*
I *STILL* CAN'T BECOME TANGIBLE OR ELSE I BLOW UP WHATEVER I TOUCH! I'M STUCK IN MY PHANTOM FORM AND I HAVEN'T BEEN HOME TO BGZTL IN *NINE YEARS!*
YES, LINNYA, WHATEVER HAS HAPPENED TO *YOU* MAY VERY WELL BE CONNECTED TO WHAT IS BINDING *US*. YOUR UNIQUE PHYSIOLOGY MAY BE *THE KEY* TO CURING US ALL.
SO WHAT AM I SUPPOSED TO DO IN THE MEANTIME?!
SIGH WHY DON'T YOU TRY BEING PATIENT! I CAN'T SOLVE EVERYTHING AT ONCE, YOU KNOW! NOW IF YOU'LL EXCUSE ME I NEED TO GET TO THE LAB AND GET TO WORK.
HUMPH!
COME ON, REXY, WE GOT SOME CATCHING UP TO DO.
JAVA...
YES?
CLEAN THAT UP.
HRRM...

MEANWHILE, IN NORTHERN MICHIGAN...

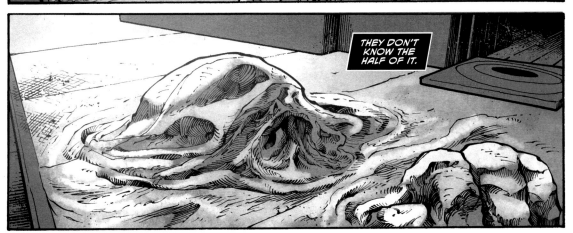

MARGE BETTMAN AND TRICIA KEELER ARE BUSY GOSSIPING, AS USUAL.

--YOU SEE THAT HAIRCUT SHE GOT?! WHO DOES SHE THINK SHE IS?!

I KNOW! I SWEAR THIS WHOLE DAMN TOWN IS GOING CRAZY.

THEY DON'T KNOW THE HALF OF IT.

BUT THEY ARE ABOUT TO.

GRRRNNN

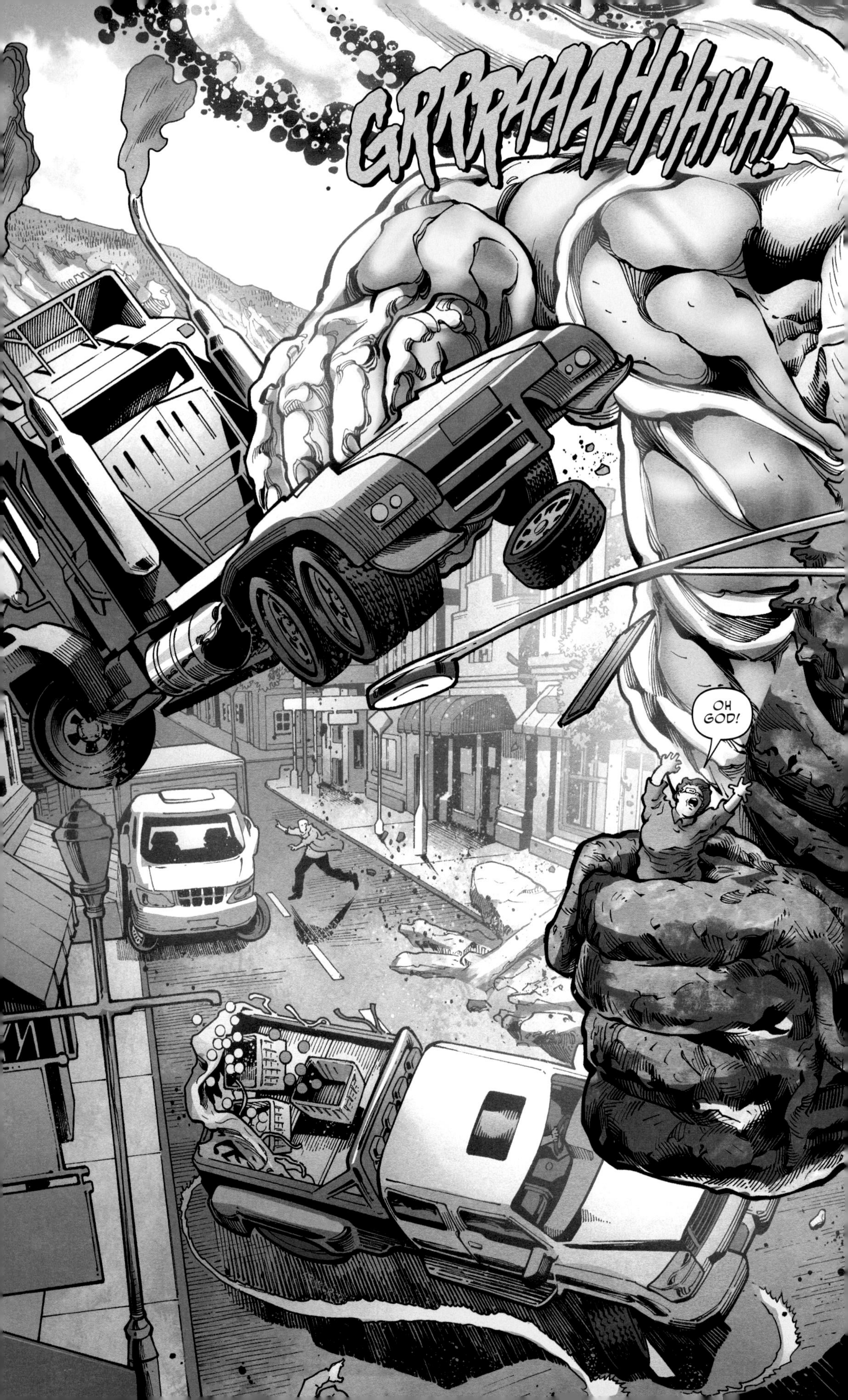
GRRRAAAAHHHHH!!
OH GOD!

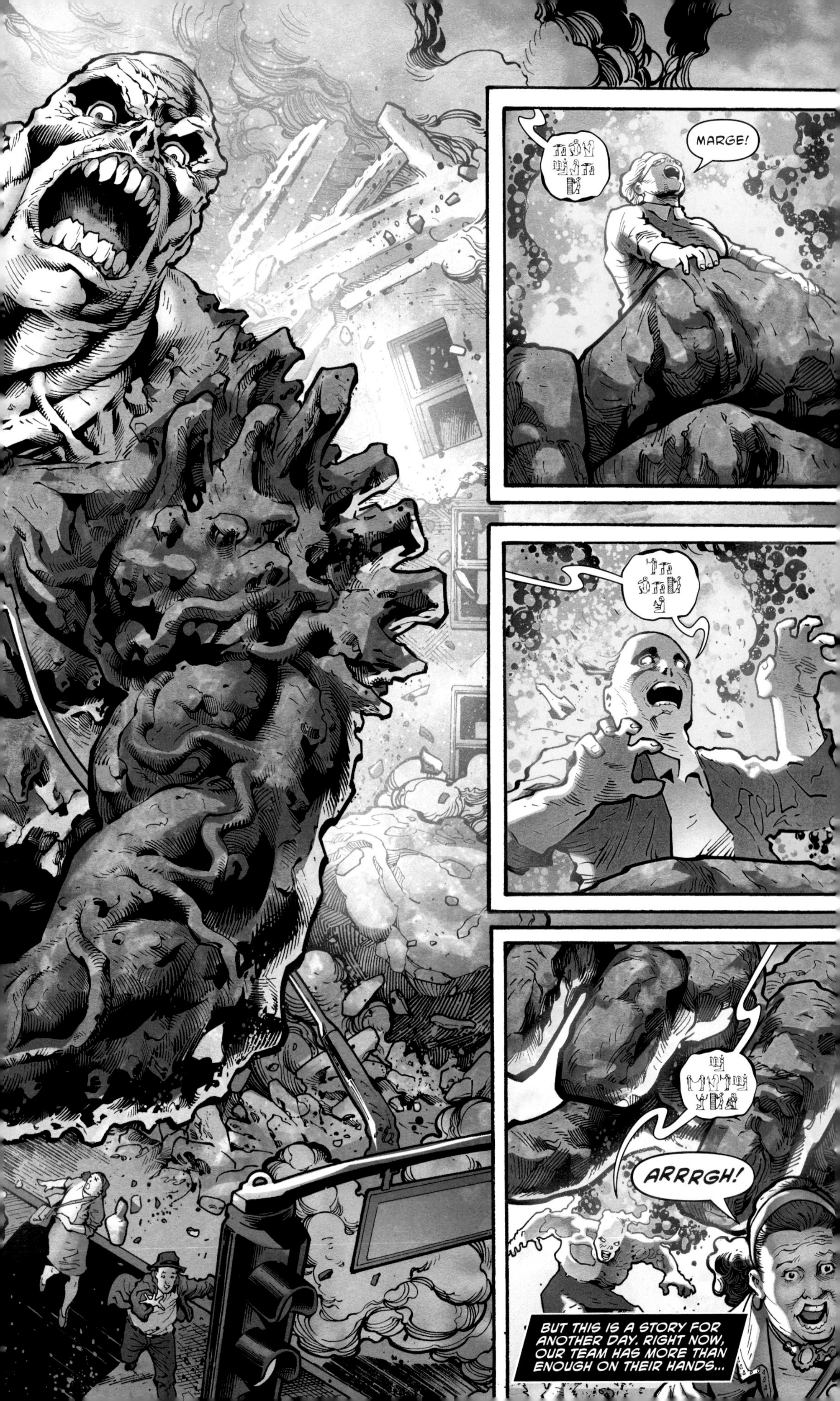
MARGE!
ARRRGH!
BUT THIS IS A STORY FOR ANOTHER DAY. RIGHT NOW, OUR TEAM HAS MORE THAN ENOUGH ON THEIR HANDS...

CASE IN POINT. BACK AT STAGG MANSION...

--I DON'T UNDERSTAND WHY YOU'RE SORE WITH ME, REX.

I AIN'T SORE WITH YOU, SAPPH. I'M JUST--

YOU'RE JUST *WHAT*, BABY?

WELL, I'M MAD AT MYSELF. I MEAN--I CAN'T BELIEVE I KEEP LETTING YOUR DAD GET ME MIXED UP IN ALL THIS CRAZY STUFF.

I JUST WISH I COULD STAND UP FOR MYSELF.

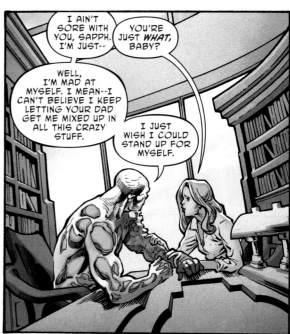

I DON'T LIKE THAT *OLD RAT,* HE'S NO GOOD AND I JUST KEEP LETTING HIM BOSS ME AROUND. AND NOW LOOK AT THE MESS I'M IN!

HE'S *MY FATHER,* REX. YOU HAVE HIM ALL WRONG. I KNOW HE'S... ECCENTRIC, BUT HE MEANS WELL.

OH COME ON, SAPPH! YOU CAN'T REALLY BELIEVE THAT! HE'S A MADMAN! AND THAT--THAT *CAVEMAN* OF HIS IS UP TO NO GOOD, TOO, I JUST KNOW IT!

WELL, IF IT'S ALL SO AWFUL, WHY DON'T YOU JUST LEAVE THEN?!

BECAUSE I CAN'T! I'M STUCK TO PLASTIC MAN, PHANTOM GIRL AND MR. PERSONALITY!

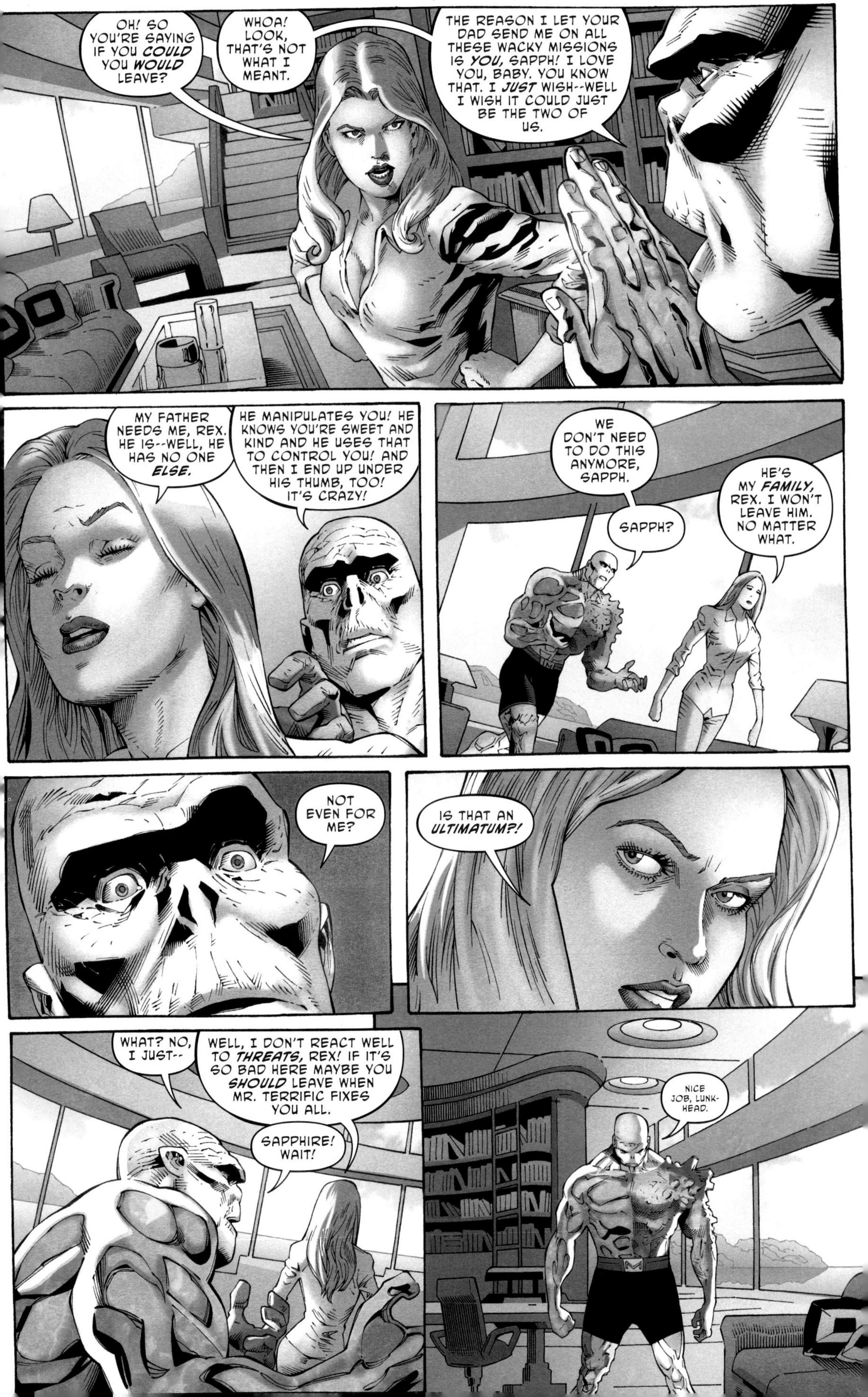
OH! SO YOU'RE SAYING IF YOU COULD YOU WOULD LEAVE?
WHOA! LOOK, THAT'S NOT WHAT I MEANT.
THE REASON I LET YOUR DAD SEND ME ON ALL THESE WACKY MISSIONS IS YOU, SAPPH! I LOVE YOU, BABY. YOU KNOW THAT. I JUST WISH--WELL I WISH IT COULD JUST BE THE TWO OF US.
MY FATHER NEEDS ME, REX. HE IS--WELL, HE HAS NO ONE ELSE.
HE MANIPULATES YOU! HE KNOWS YOU'RE SWEET AND KIND AND HE USES THAT TO CONTROL YOU! AND THEN I END UP UNDER HIS THUMB, TOO! IT'S CRAZY!
WE DON'T NEED TO DO THIS ANYMORE, SAPPH.
SAPPH?
HE'S MY FAMILY, REX. I WON'T LEAVE HIM. NO MATTER WHAT.
NOT EVEN FOR ME?
IS THAT AN ULTIMATUM?!
WHAT? NO, I JUST--
WELL, I DON'T REACT WELL TO THREATS, REX! IF IT'S SO BAD HERE MAYBE YOU SHOULD LEAVE WHEN MR. TERRIFIC FIXES YOU ALL.
SAPPHIRE! WAIT!
NICE JOB, LUNK-HEAD.

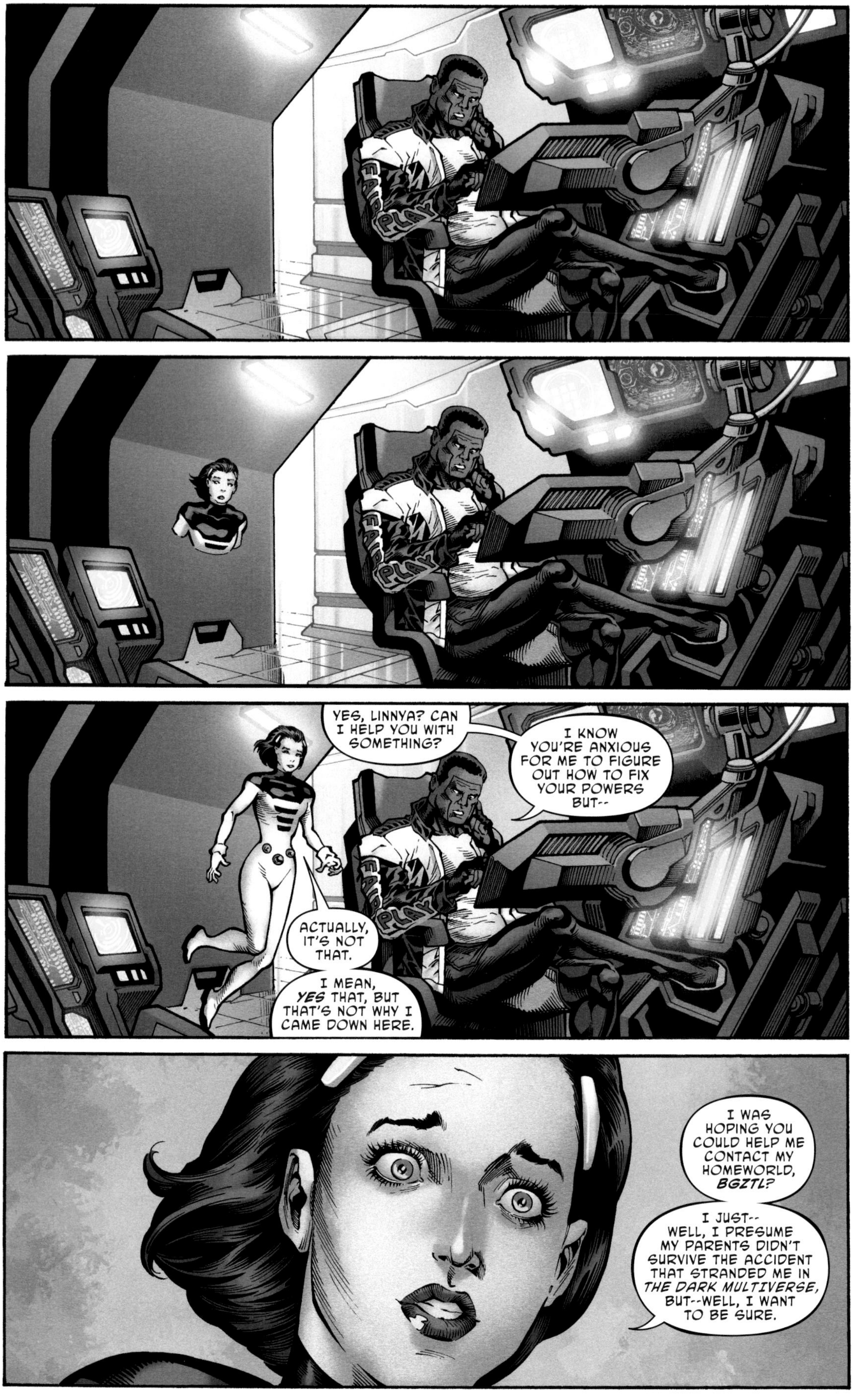
FAIR PLAY
YES, LINNYA? CAN I HELP YOU WITH SOMETHING?
I KNOW YOU'RE ANXIOUS FOR ME TO FIGURE OUT HOW TO FIX YOUR POWERS BUT--
ACTUALLY, IT'S NOT THAT.
I MEAN, *YES* THAT, BUT THAT'S NOT WHY I CAME DOWN HERE.
I WAS HOPING YOU COULD HELP ME CONTACT MY HOMEWORLD, *BGZTL?*
I JUST-- WELL, I PRESUME MY PARENTS DIDN'T SURVIVE THE ACCIDENT THAT STRANDED ME IN *THE DARK MULTIVERSE,* BUT--WELL, I WANT TO BE SURE.

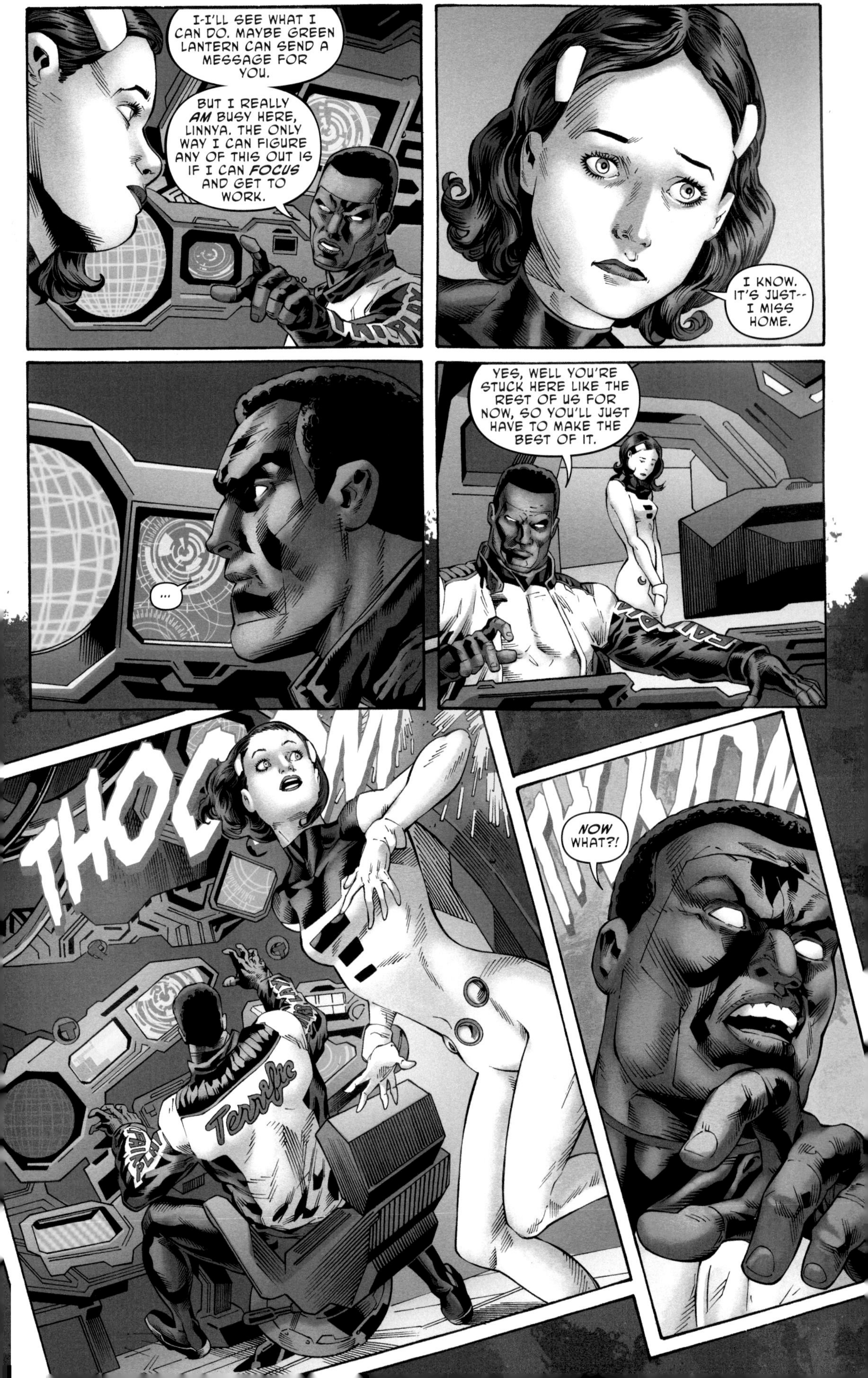
I-I'LL SEE WHAT I CAN DO. MAYBE GREEN LANTERN CAN SEND A MESSAGE FOR YOU.
BUT I REALLY AM BUSY HERE, LINNYA. THE ONLY WAY I CAN FIGURE ANY OF THIS OUT IS IF I CAN FOCUS AND GET TO WORK.
I KNOW. IT'S JUST-- I MISS HOME.
...
YES, WELL YOU'RE STUCK HERE LIKE THE REST OF US FOR NOW, SO YOU'LL JUST HAVE TO MAKE THE BEST OF IT.
THOOOM
NOW WHAT?!

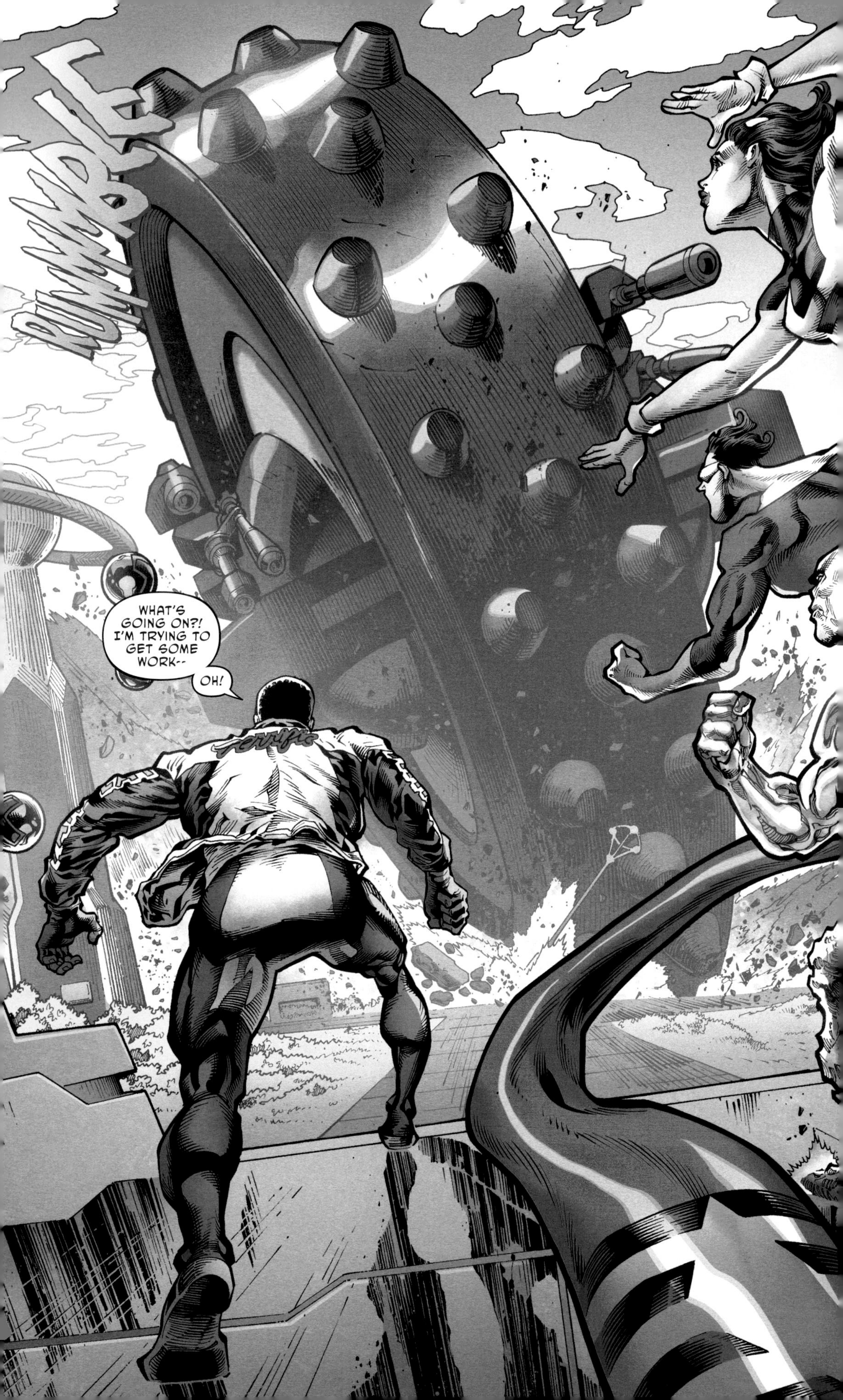

RUMMBLE
WHAT'S GOING ON?! I'M TRYING TO GET SOME WORK--
OH!

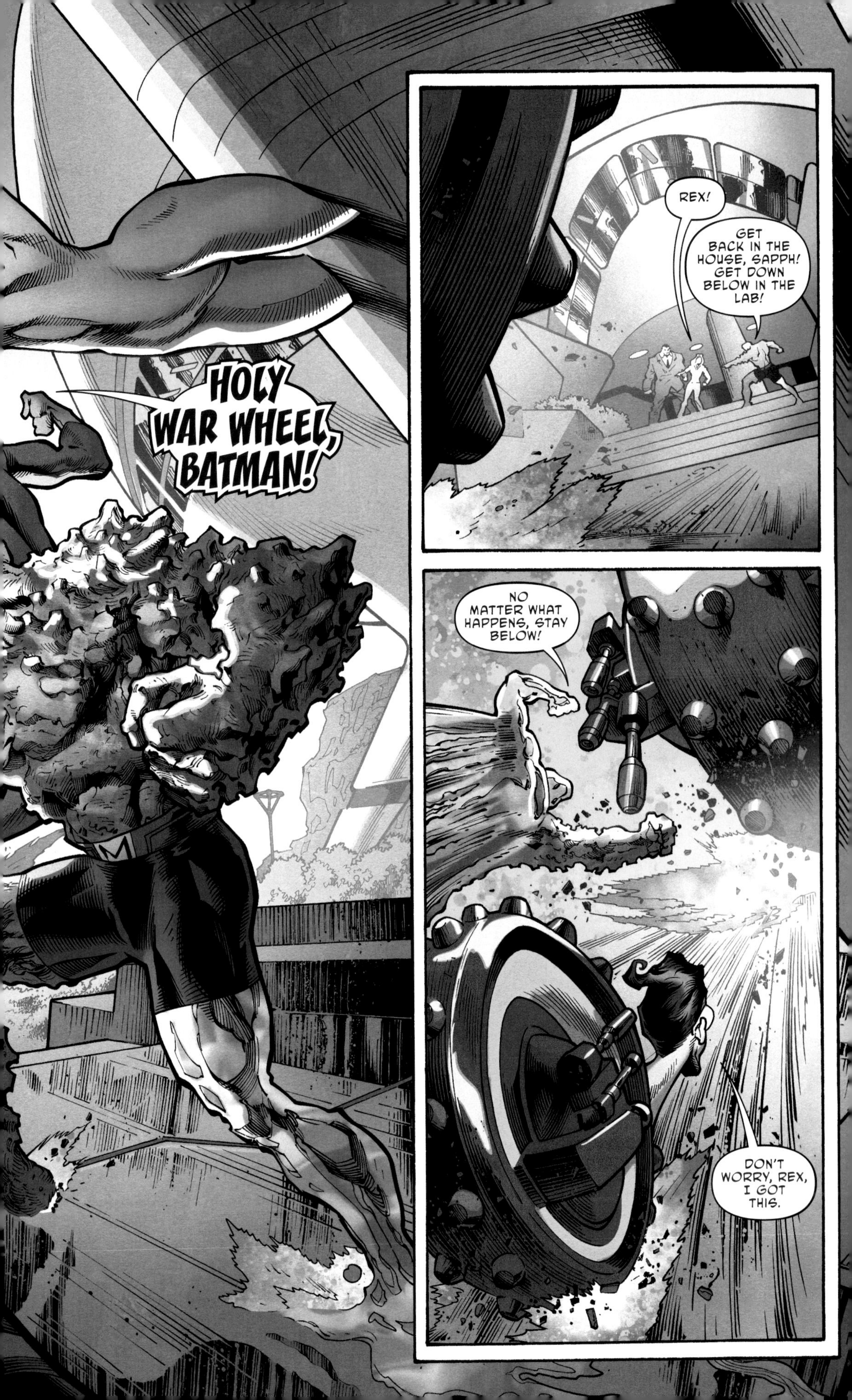
HOLY WAR WHEEL, BATMAN!
REX!
GET BACK IN THE HOUSE, SAPPH! GET DOWN BELOW IN THE LAB!
NO MATTER WHAT HAPPENS, STAY BELOW!
DON'T WORRY, REX, I GOT THIS.

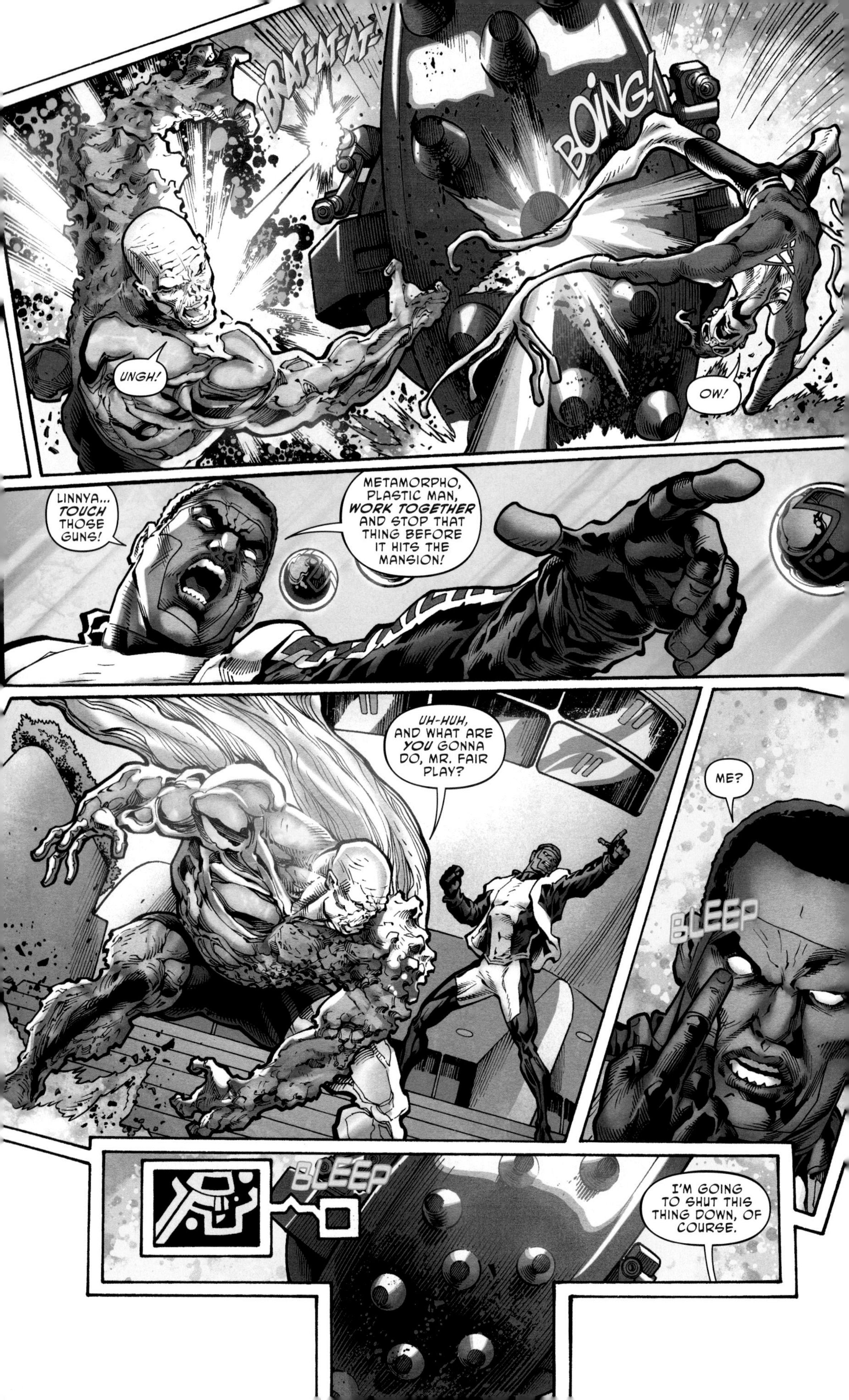
BRAT-AT-AT-
BOING!
UNGH!
OW!
LINNYA... TOUCH THOSE GUNS!
METAMORPHO, PLASTIC MAN, WORK TOGETHER AND STOP THAT THING BEFORE IT HITS THE MANSION!
UH-HUH, AND WHAT ARE YOU GONNA DO, MR. FAIR PLAY?
ME?
BLEEP
BLEEP
I'M GOING TO SHUT THIS THING DOWN, OF COURSE.

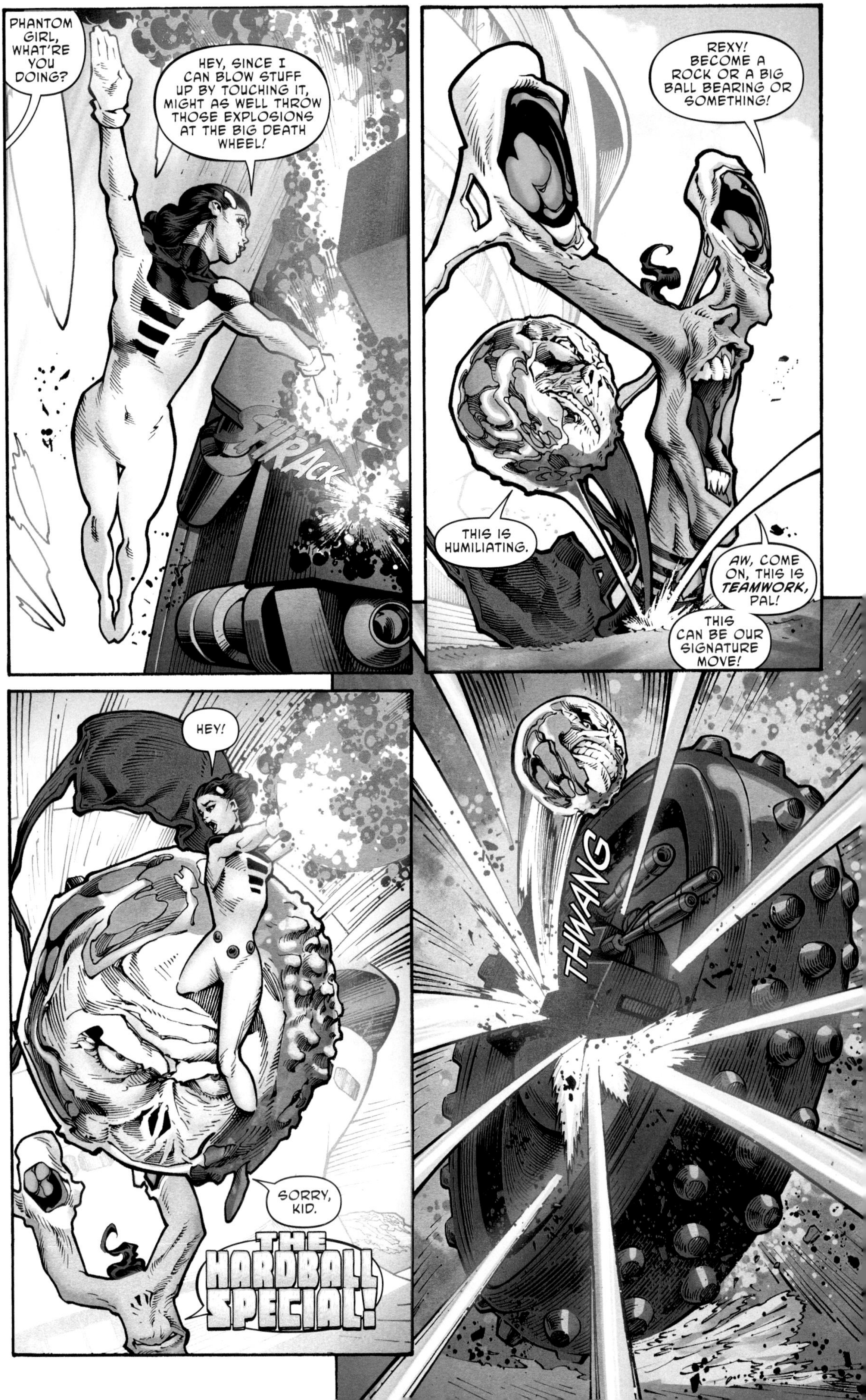
PHANTOM GIRL, WHAT'RE YOU DOING?
HEY, SINCE I CAN BLOW STUFF UP BY TOUCHING IT, MIGHT AS WELL THROW THOSE EXPLOSIONS AT THE BIG DEATH WHEEL!
SHRACK
REXY! BECOME A ROCK OR A BIG BALL BEARING OR SOMETHING!
THIS IS HUMILIATING.
AW, COME ON, THIS IS TEAMWORK, PAL!
THIS CAN BE OUR SIGNATURE MOVE!
HEY!
SORRY, KID.
THE HARDBALL SPECIAL!
THWANG

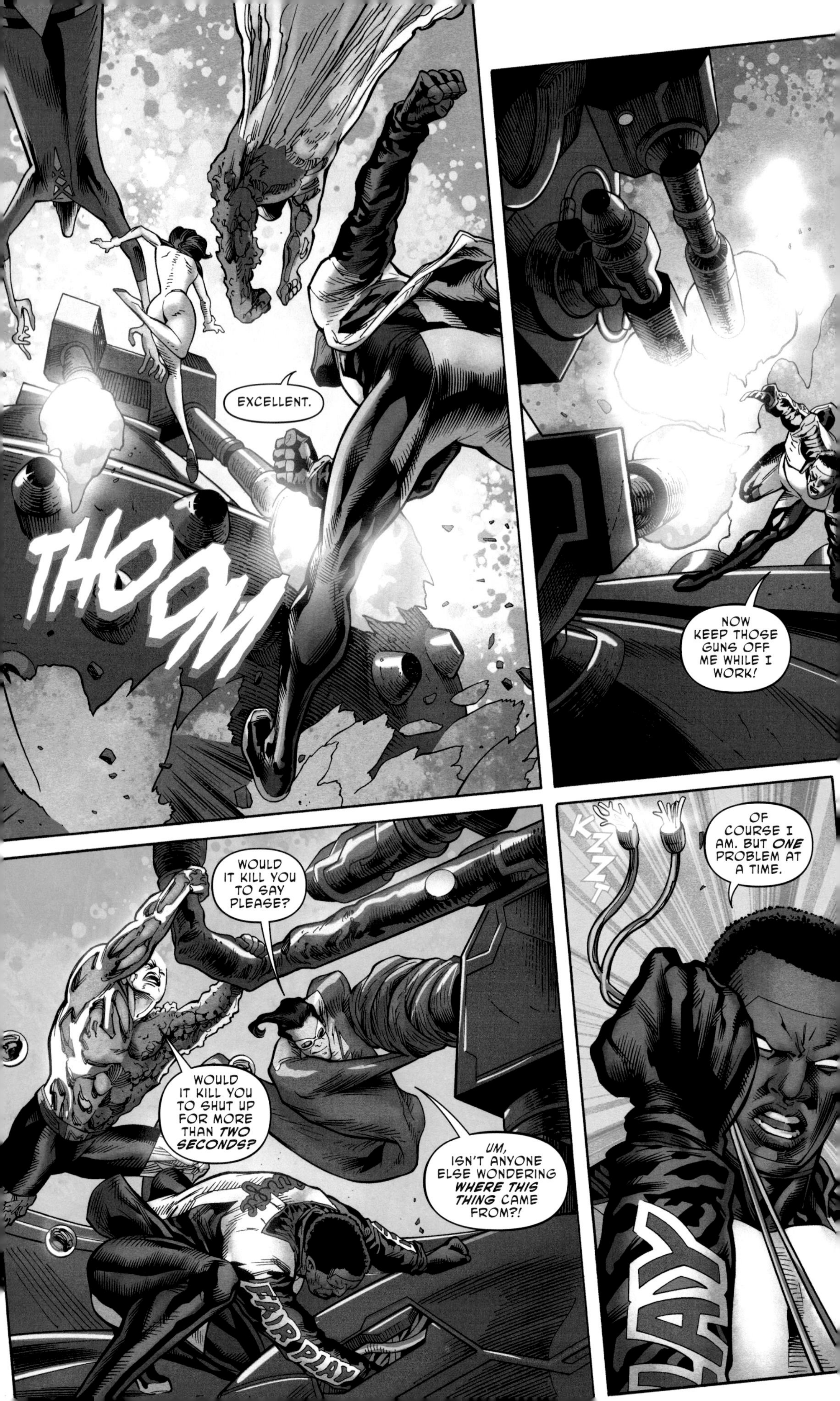

EXCELLENT.
THOOM
NOW KEEP THOSE GUNS OFF ME WHILE I WORK!
WOULD IT KILL YOU TO SAY PLEASE?
WOULD IT KILL YOU TO SHUT UP FOR MORE THAN TWO SECONDS?
UM, ISN'T ANYONE ELSE WONDERING WHERE THIS THING CAME FROM?!
FAIR PLAY
KZZZT
OF COURSE I AM. BUT ONE PROBLEM AT A TIME.

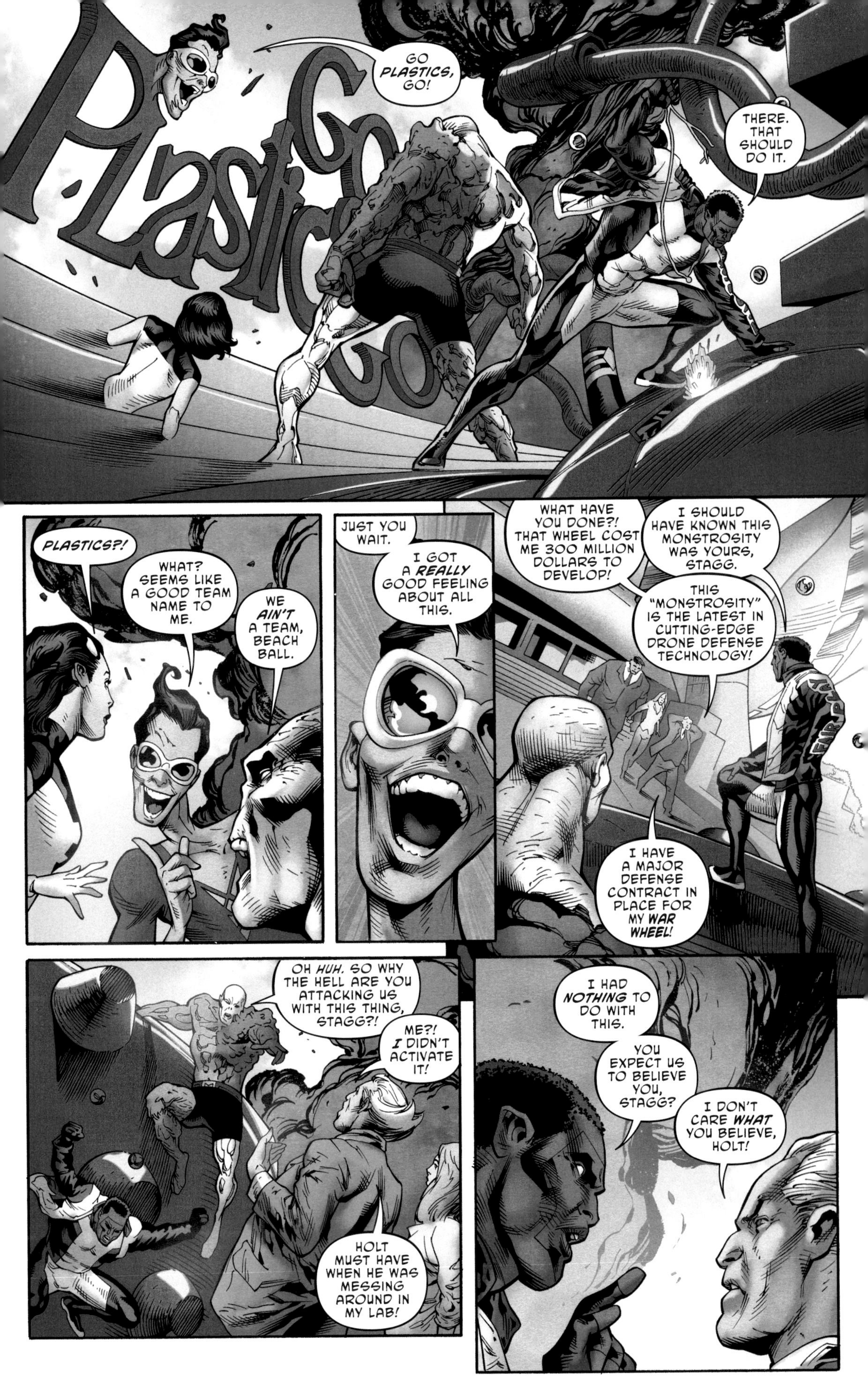

Plastic Go Go
GO PLASTICS, GO!
THERE. THAT SHOULD DO IT.
PLASTICS?!
WHAT? SEEMS LIKE A GOOD TEAM NAME TO ME.
WE AIN'T A TEAM, BEACH BALL.
JUST YOU WAIT.
I GOT A REALLY GOOD FEELING ABOUT ALL THIS.
WHAT HAVE YOU DONE?! THAT WHEEL COST ME 300 MILLION DOLLARS TO DEVELOP!
I SHOULD HAVE KNOWN THIS MONSTROSITY WAS YOURS, STAGG.
THIS "MONSTROSITY" IS THE LATEST IN CUTTING-EDGE DRONE DEFENSE TECHNOLOGY!
I HAVE A MAJOR DEFENSE CONTRACT IN PLACE FOR MY WAR WHEEL!
OH HUH. SO WHY THE HELL ARE YOU ATTACKING US WITH THIS THING, STAGG?!
ME?! I DIDN'T ACTIVATE IT!
HOLT MUST HAVE WHEN HE WAS MESSING AROUND IN MY LAB!
I HAD NOTHING TO DO WITH THIS.
YOU EXPECT US TO BELIEVE YOU, STAGG?
I DON'T CARE WHAT YOU BELIEVE, HOLT!

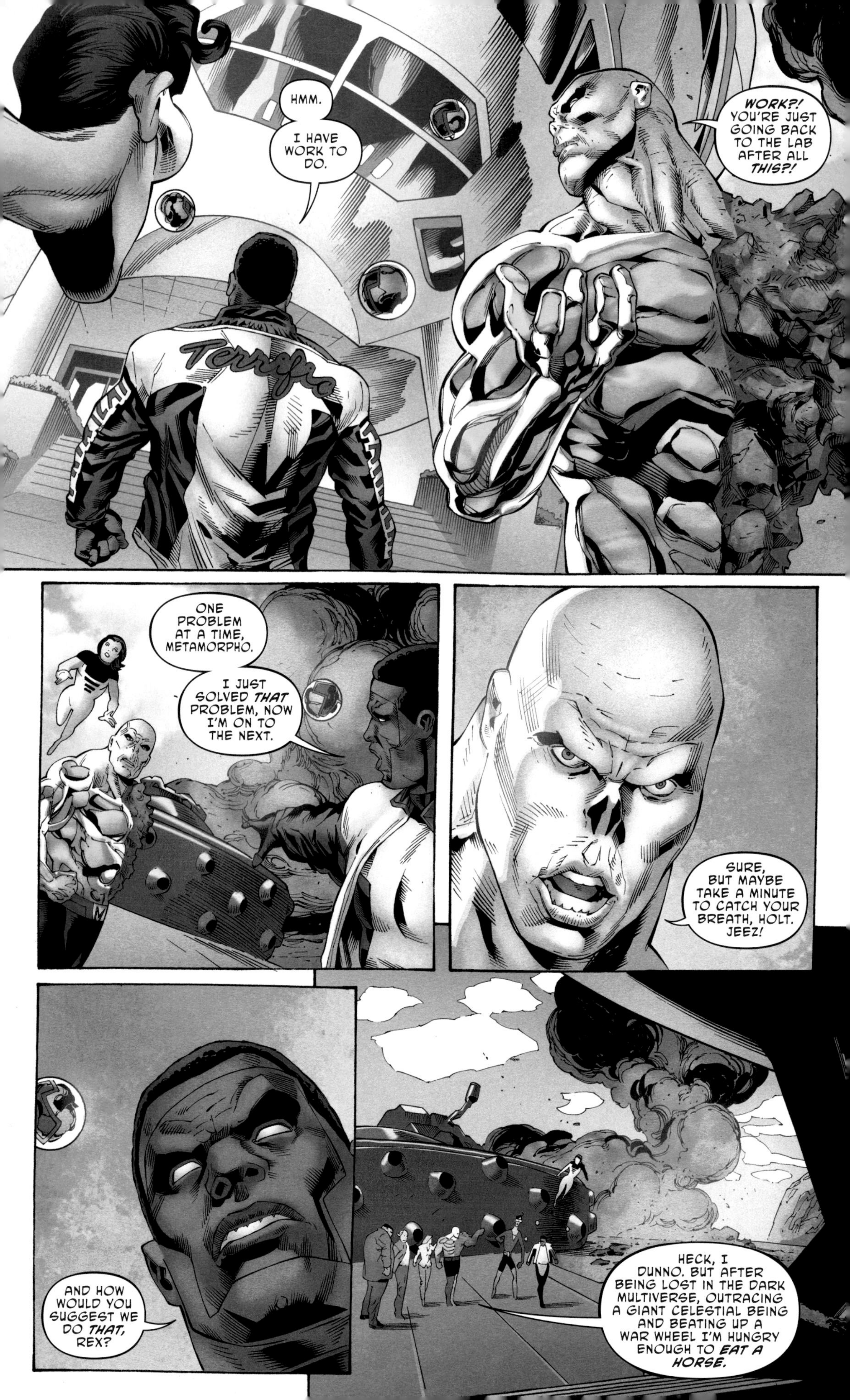

HMM.
I HAVE WORK TO DO.
WORK?! YOU'RE JUST GOING BACK TO THE LAB AFTER ALL THIS?!
Terrific
ONE PROBLEM AT A TIME, METAMORPHO.
I JUST SOLVED THAT PROBLEM, NOW I'M ON TO THE NEXT.
SURE, BUT MAYBE TAKE A MINUTE TO CATCH YOUR BREATH, HOLT. JEEZ!
AND HOW WOULD YOU SUGGEST WE DO THAT, REX?
HECK, I DUNNO. BUT AFTER BEING LOST IN THE DARK MULTIVERSE, OUTRACING A GIANT CELESTIAL BEING AND BEATING UP A WAR WHEEL I'M HUNGRY ENOUGH TO EAT A HORSE.

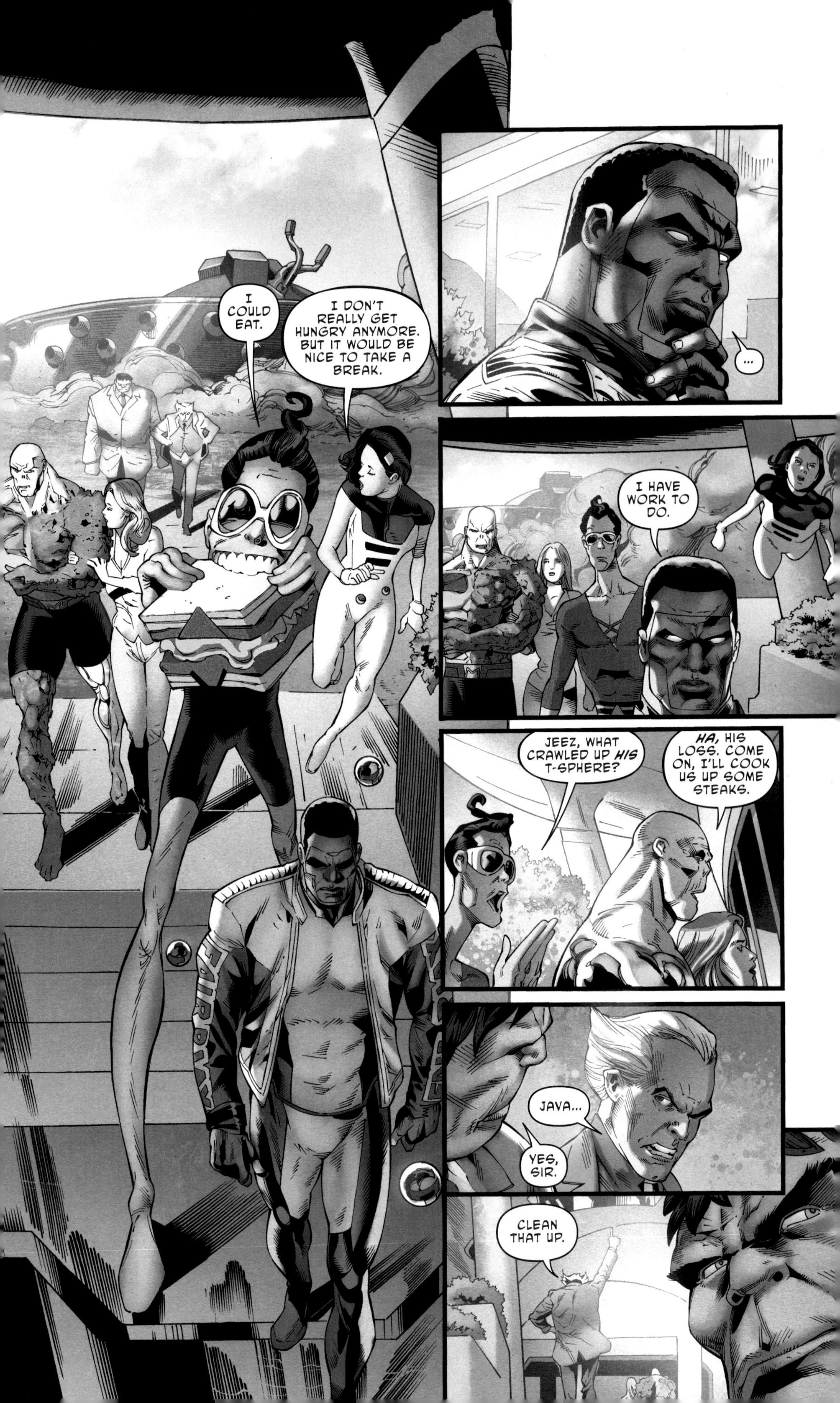
I COULD EAT.
I DON'T REALLY GET HUNGRY ANYMORE. BUT IT WOULD BE NICE TO TAKE A BREAK.
...
I HAVE WORK TO DO.
JEEZ, WHAT CRAWLED UP HIS T-SPHERE?
HA, HIS LOSS. COME ON, I'LL COOK US UP SOME STEAKS.
JAVA...
YES, SIR.
CLEAN THAT UP.

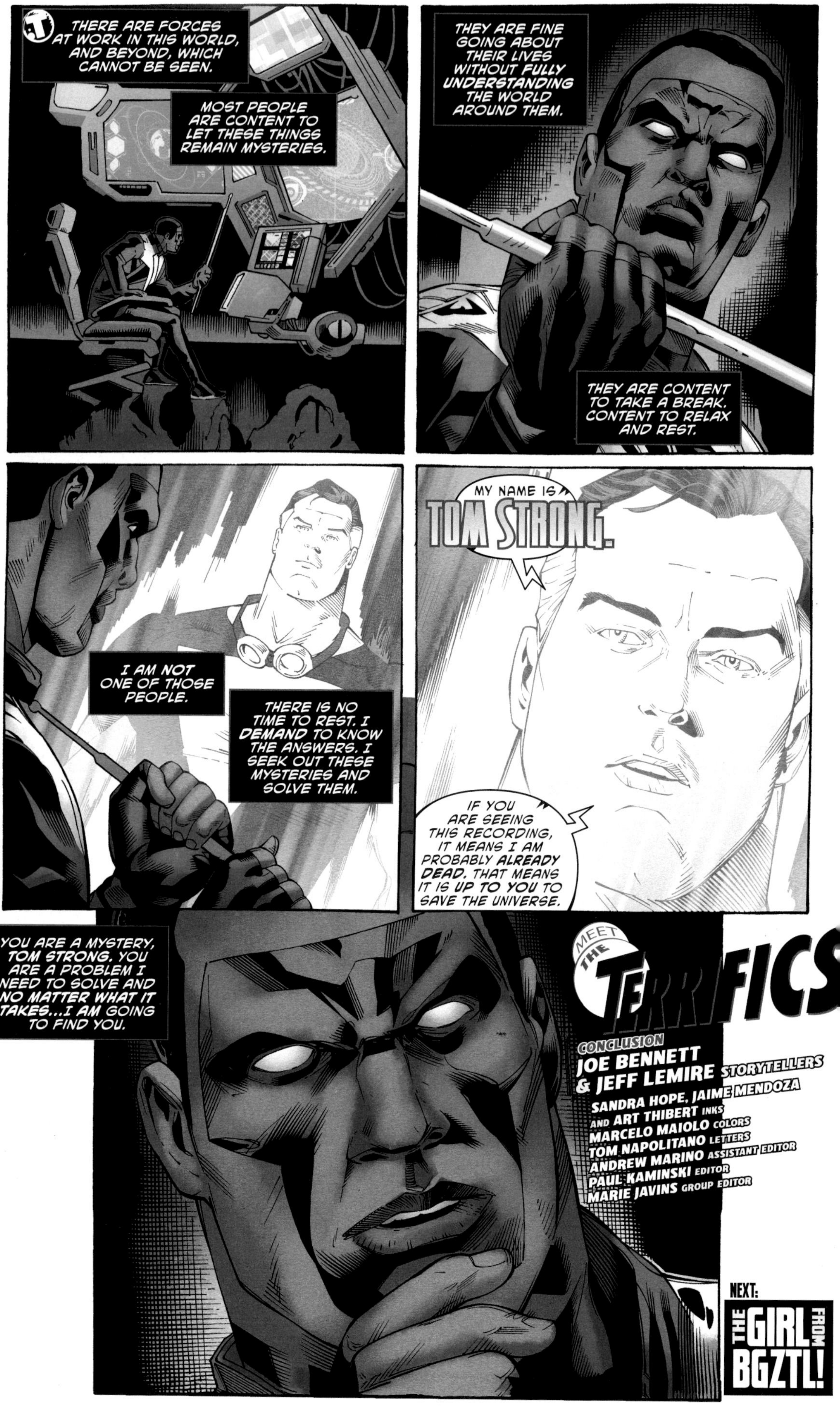

THERE ARE FORCES AT WORK IN THIS WORLD, AND BEYOND, WHICH CANNOT BE SEEN.
MOST PEOPLE ARE CONTENT TO LET THESE THINGS REMAIN MYSTERIES.
THEY ARE FINE GOING ABOUT THEIR LIVES WITHOUT FULLY UNDERSTANDING THE WORLD AROUND THEM.
THEY ARE CONTENT TO TAKE A BREAK. CONTENT TO RELAX AND REST.
I AM NOT ONE OF THOSE PEOPLE.
THERE IS NO TIME TO REST. I DEMAND TO KNOW THE ANSWERS. I SEEK OUT THESE MYSTERIES AND SOLVE THEM.
MY NAME IS TOM STRONG.
IF YOU ARE SEEING THIS RECORDING, IT MEANS I AM PROBABLY ALREADY DEAD. THAT MEANS IT IS UP TO YOU TO SAVE THE UNIVERSE.
YOU ARE A MYSTERY, TOM STRONG. YOU ARE A PROBLEM I NEED TO SOLVE AND NO MATTER WHAT IT TAKES...I AM GOING TO FIND YOU.
MEET THE TERRIFICS
CONCLUSION
JOE BENNETT & JEFF LEMIRE STORYTELLERS
SANDRA HOPE, JAIME MENDOZA AND ART THIBERT INKS
MARCELO MAIOLO COLORS
TOM NAPOLITANO LETTERS
ANDREW MARINO ASSISTANT EDITOR
PAUL KAMINSKI EDITOR
MARIE JAVINS GROUP EDITOR
NEXT:
THE GIRL FROM BGZTL!

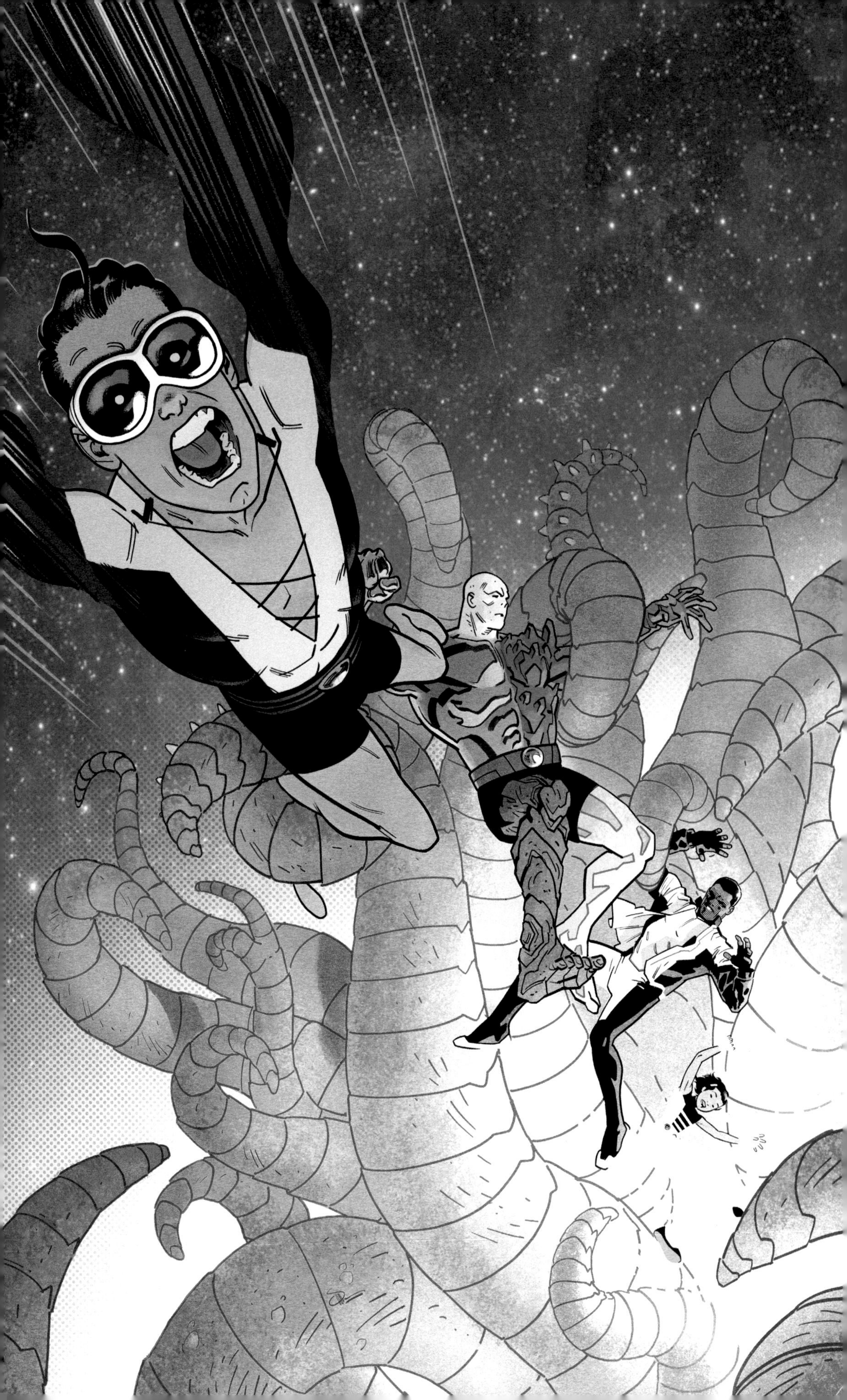

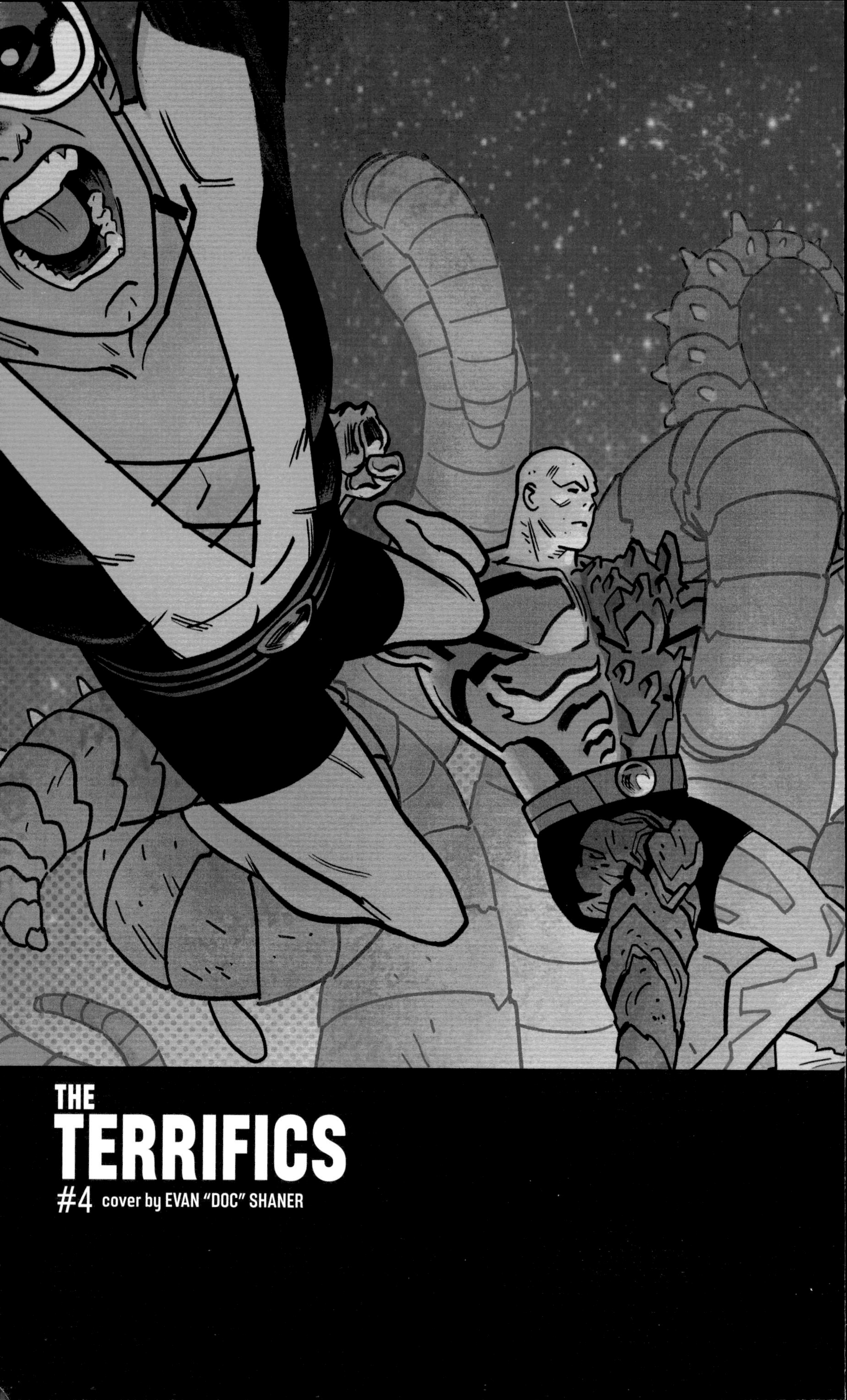

THE TERRIFICS

#4 cover by EVAN "DOC" SHANER

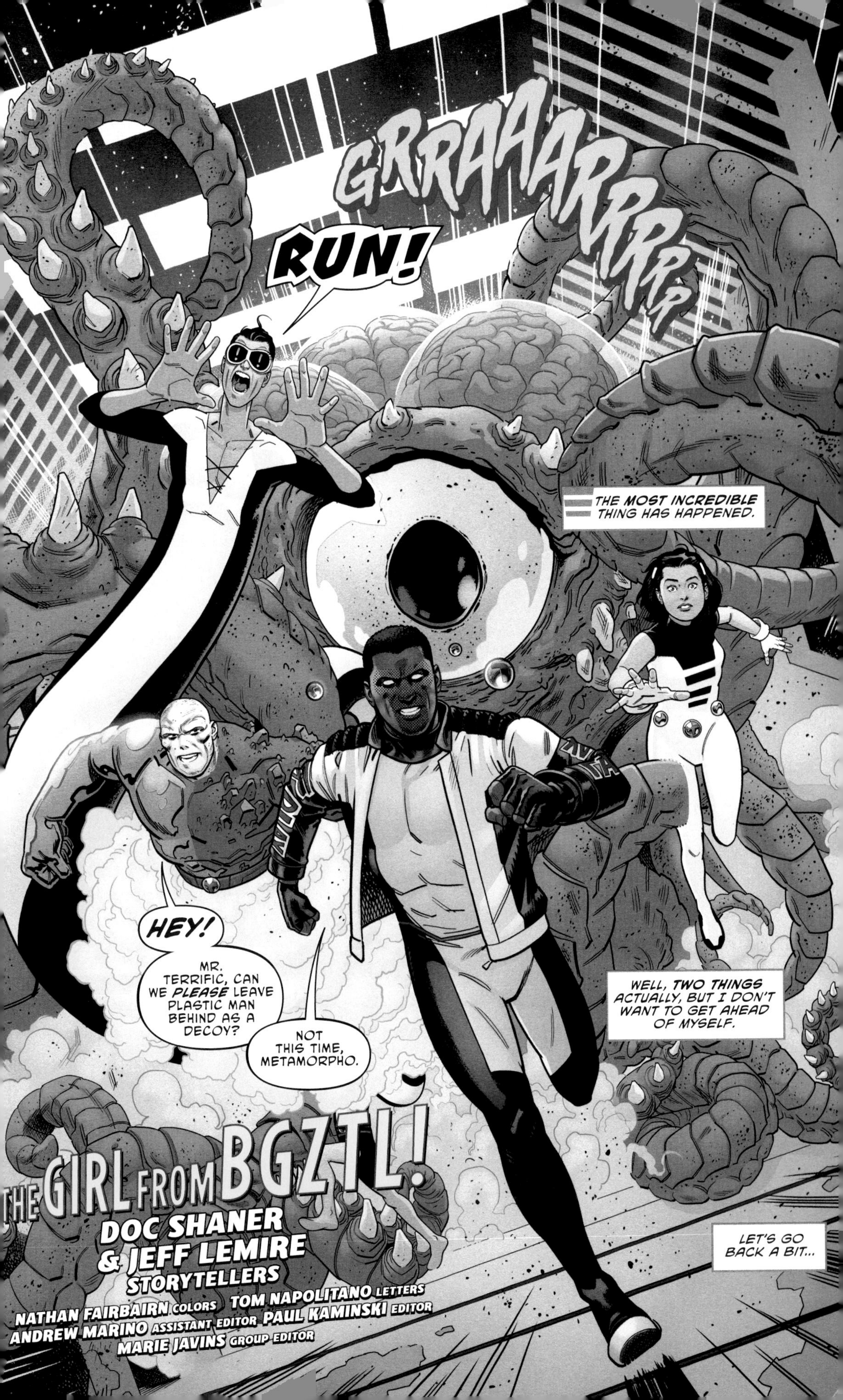

GRRAAARRRRR
RUN!
THE MOST INCREDIBLE THING HAS HAPPENED.
HEY!
MR. TERRIFIC, CAN WE PLEASE LEAVE PLASTIC MAN BEHIND AS A DECOY?
NOT THIS TIME, METAMORPHO.
WELL, TWO THINGS ACTUALLY, BUT I DON'T WANT TO GET AHEAD OF MYSELF.
THE GIRL FROM BGZTL!
DOC SHANER & JEFF LEMIRE STORYTELLERS
NATHAN FAIRBAIRN COLORS TOM NAPOLITANO LETTERS
ANDREW MARINO ASSISTANT EDITOR PAUL KAMINSKI EDITOR
MARIE JAVINS GROUP EDITOR
LET'S GO BACK A BIT...

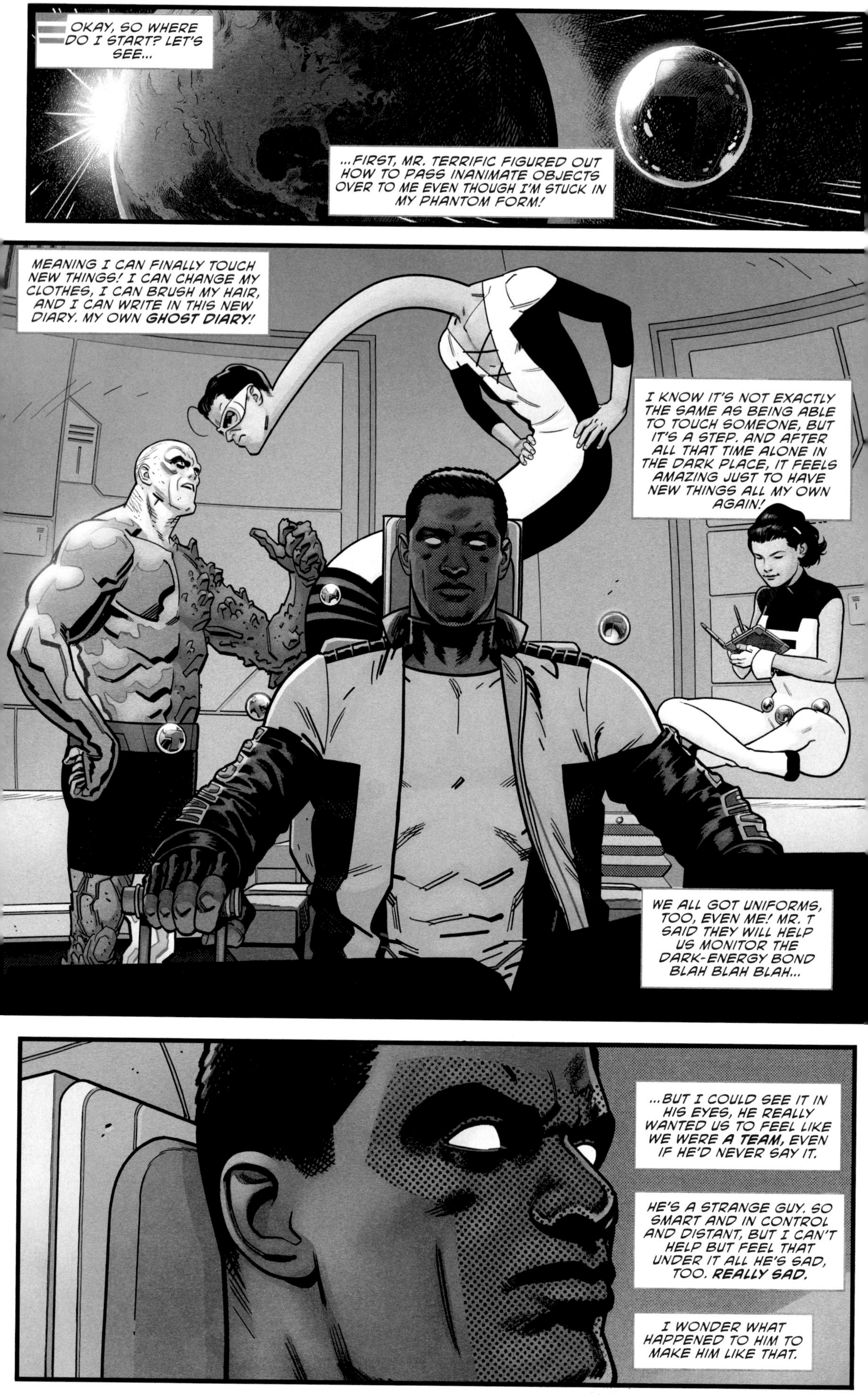
OKAY, SO WHERE DO I START? LET'S SEE...
...FIRST, MR. TERRIFIC FIGURED OUT HOW TO PASS INANIMATE OBJECTS OVER TO ME EVEN THOUGH I'M STUCK IN MY PHANTOM FORM!
MEANING I CAN FINALLY TOUCH NEW THINGS! I CAN CHANGE MY CLOTHES, I CAN BRUSH MY HAIR, AND I CAN WRITE IN THIS NEW DIARY. MY OWN GHOST DIARY!
I KNOW IT'S NOT EXACTLY THE SAME AS BEING ABLE TO TOUCH SOMEONE, BUT IT'S A STEP. AND AFTER ALL THAT TIME ALONE IN THE DARK PLACE, IT FEELS AMAZING JUST TO HAVE NEW THINGS ALL MY OWN AGAIN!
WE ALL GOT UNIFORMS, TOO, EVEN ME! MR. T SAID THEY WILL HELP US MONITOR THE DARK-ENERGY BOND BLAH BLAH BLAH...
...BUT I COULD SEE IT IN HIS EYES, HE REALLY WANTED US TO FEEL LIKE WE WERE A TEAM, EVEN IF HE'D NEVER SAY IT.
HE'S A STRANGE GUY. SO SMART AND IN CONTROL AND DISTANT, BUT I CAN'T HELP BUT FEEL THAT UNDER IT ALL HE'S SAD, TOO. REALLY SAD.
I WONDER WHAT HAPPENED TO HIM TO MAKE HIM LIKE THAT.

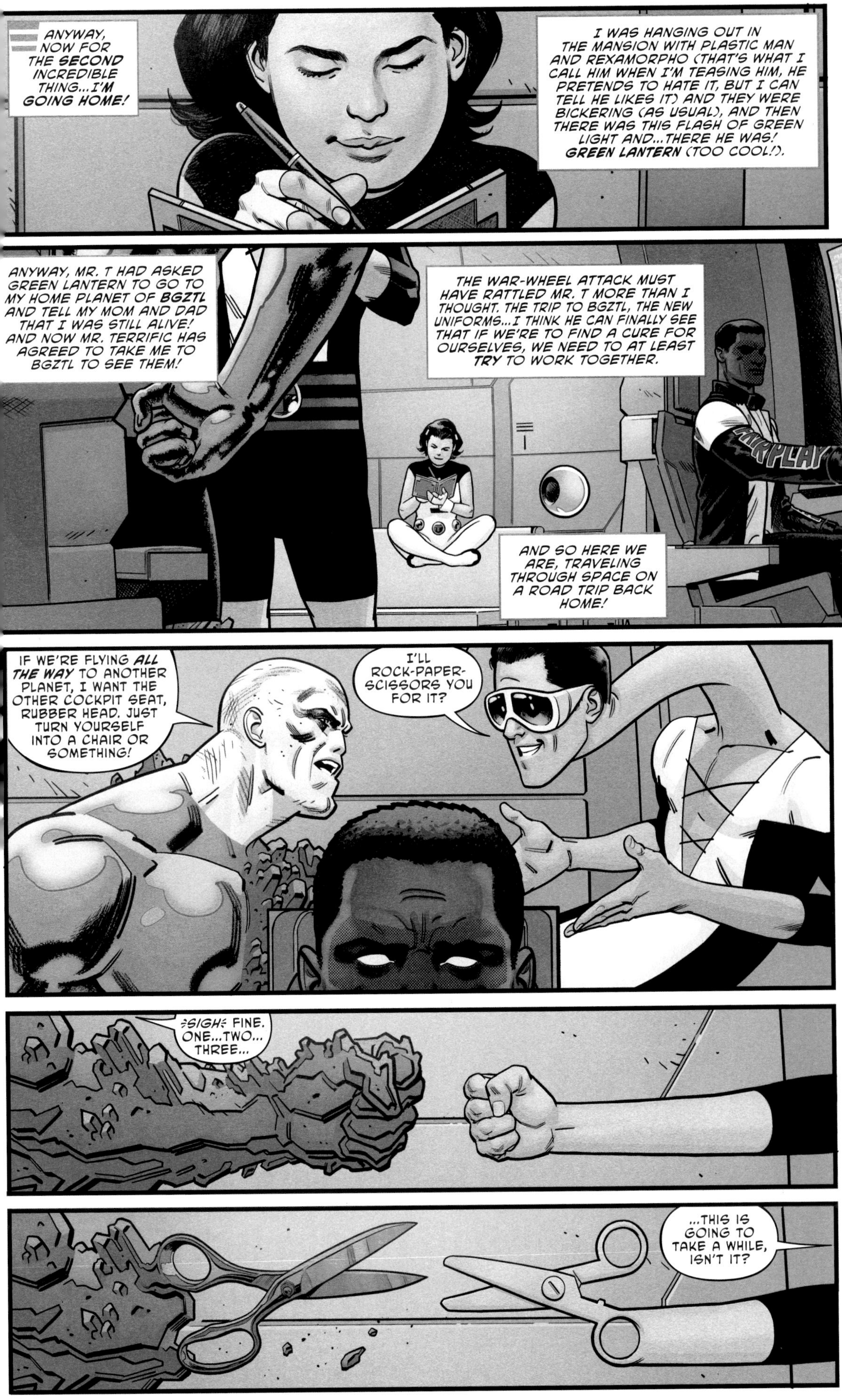

ANYWAY, NOW FOR THE SECOND INCREDIBLE THING...I'M GOING HOME!
I WAS HANGING OUT IN THE MANSION WITH PLASTIC MAN AND REXAMORPHO (THAT'S WHAT I CALL HIM WHEN I'M TEASING HIM, HE PRETENDS TO HATE IT, BUT I CAN TELL HE LIKES IT) AND THEY WERE BICKERING (AS USUAL), AND THEN THERE WAS THIS FLASH OF GREEN LIGHT AND...THERE HE WAS! GREEN LANTERN (TOO COOL!).
ANYWAY, MR. T HAD ASKED GREEN LANTERN TO GO TO MY HOME PLANET OF BGZTL AND TELL MY MOM AND DAD THAT I WAS STILL ALIVE! AND NOW MR. TERRIFIC HAS AGREED TO TAKE ME TO BGZTL TO SEE THEM!
THE WAR-WHEEL ATTACK MUST HAVE RATTLED MR. T MORE THAN I THOUGHT. THE TRIP TO BGZTL, THE NEW UNIFORMS...I THINK HE CAN FINALLY SEE THAT IF WE'RE TO FIND A CURE FOR OURSELVES, WE NEED TO AT LEAST TRY TO WORK TOGETHER.
FAIRPLAY
AND SO HERE WE ARE, TRAVELING THROUGH SPACE ON A ROAD TRIP BACK HOME!
IF WE'RE FLYING ALL THE WAY TO ANOTHER PLANET, I WANT THE OTHER COCKPIT SEAT, RUBBER HEAD. JUST TURN YOURSELF INTO A CHAIR OR SOMETHING!
I'LL ROCK-PAPER-SCISSORS YOU FOR IT?
SIGH FINE. ONE...TWO... THREE...
...THIS IS GOING TO TAKE A WHILE, ISN'T IT?

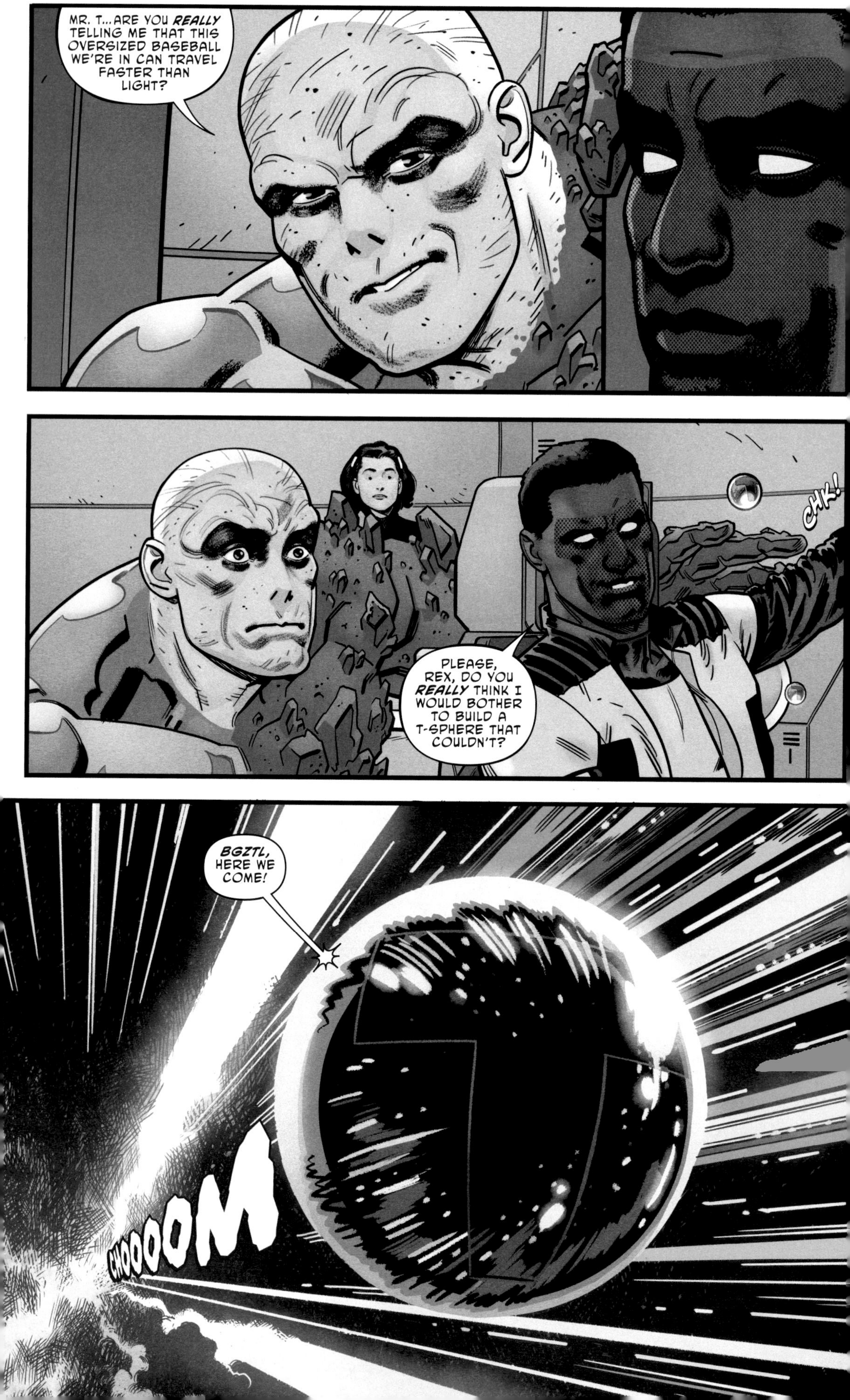
MR. T...ARE YOU REALLY TELLING ME THAT THIS OVERSIZED BASEBALL WE'RE IN CAN TRAVEL FASTER THAN LIGHT?
CHK!
PLEASE, REX, DO YOU REALLY THINK I WOULD BOTHER TO BUILD A T-SPHERE THAT COULDN'T?
BGZTL, HERE WE COME!
CHOOOOM

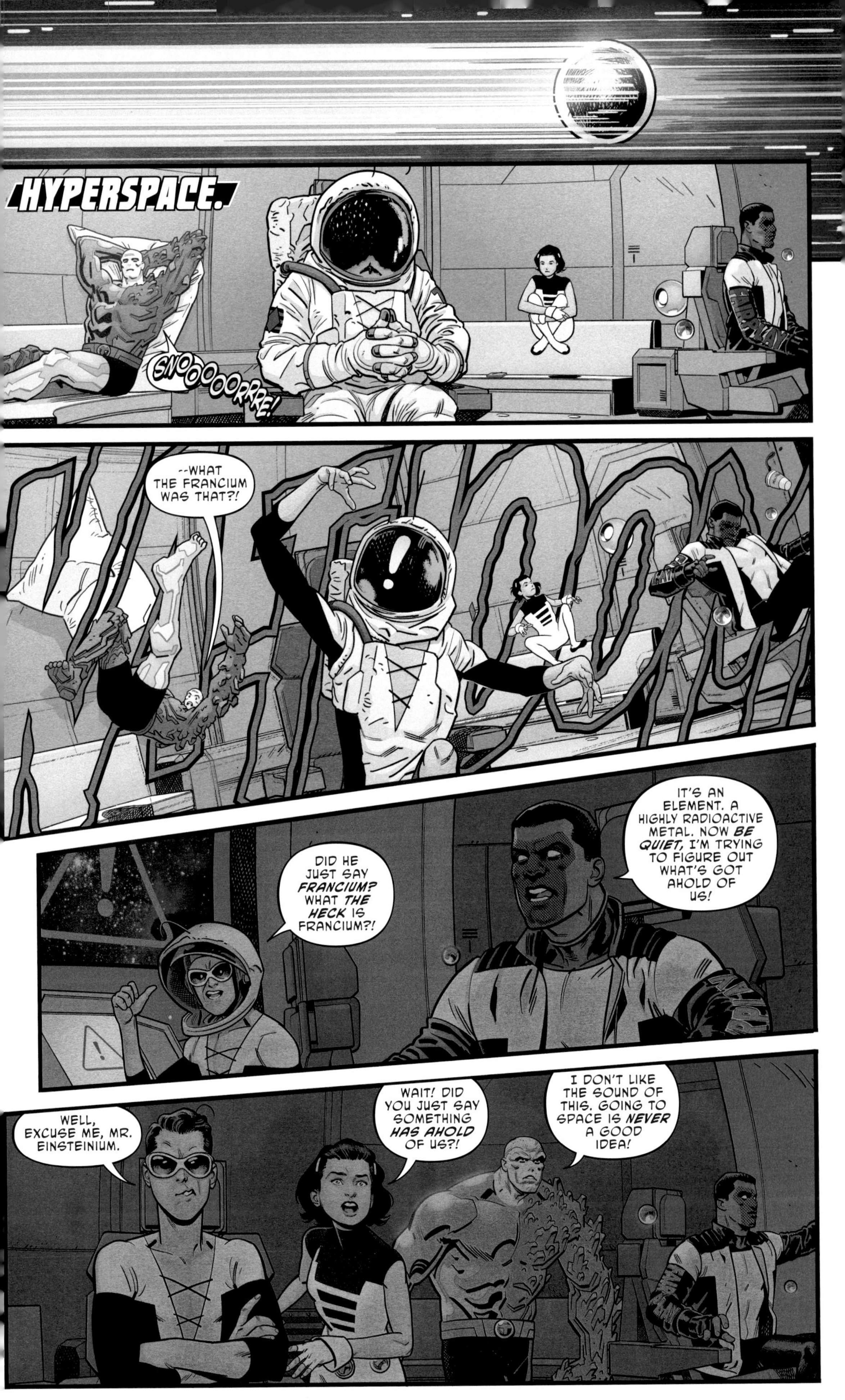
HYPERSPACE.
SNOOOOORRRE!
--WHAT THE FRANCIUM WAS THAT?!
DID HE JUST SAY FRANCIUM? WHAT THE HECK IS FRANCIUM?!
IT'S AN ELEMENT. A HIGHLY RADIOACTIVE METAL. NOW BE QUIET, I'M TRYING TO FIGURE OUT WHAT'S GOT AHOLD OF US!
WELL, EXCUSE ME, MR. EINSTEINIUM.
WAIT! DID YOU JUST SAY SOMETHING HAS AHOLD OF US?!
I DON'T LIKE THE SOUND OF THIS. GOING TO SPACE IS NEVER A GOOD IDEA!

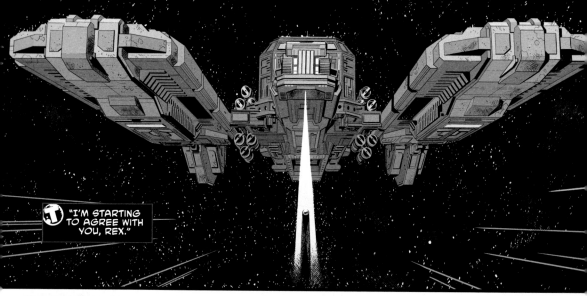

"I'M STARTING TO AGREE WITH YOU, REX."

CHOOOM

WHAT IS THAT *SMELL?!*

SPACE GARBAGE.

MAN, AM I GLAD I CAN'T SMELL ANYTHING TANGIBLE RIGHT NOW.

BASED ON MY INITIAL SCANS OF THE SHIP, MY THEORY IS THAT THIS SPACECRAFT IS ACTUALLY A "VACUUM" OF SORTS, COLLECTING DEBRIS IN SPACE AND THEN SELLING IT FOR SCRAP.

GREAT. SO HOW DO WE GET OUT OF HERE?

IT SHOULD BE NO PROBLEM. THE TRACTOR BEAM THAT PULLED US IN HAS BEEN SHUT OFF SO--

AHHH!

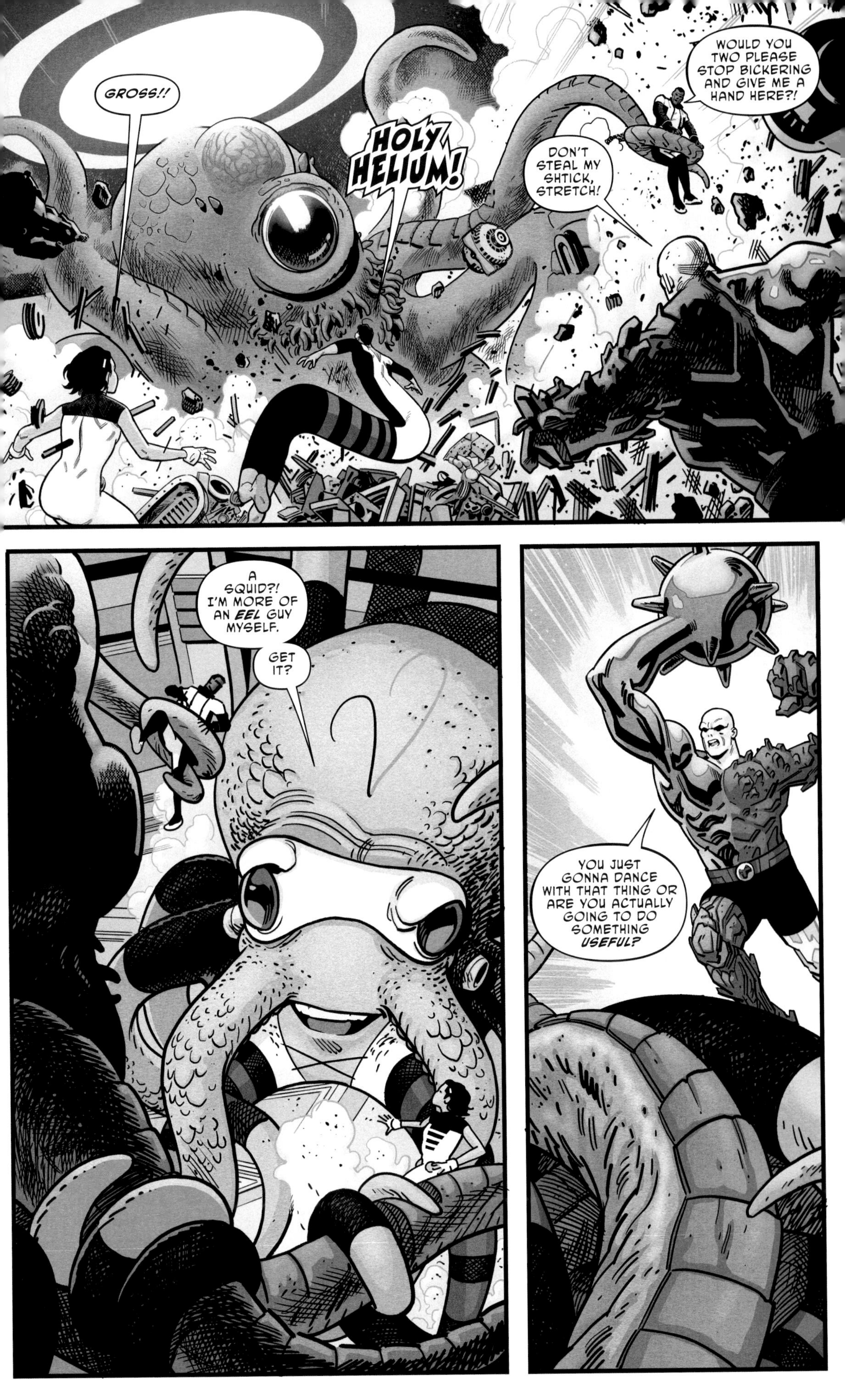
GROSS!!
HOLY HELIUM!
WOULD YOU TWO PLEASE STOP BICKERING AND GIVE ME A HAND HERE?!
DON'T STEAL MY SHTICK, STRETCH!
A SQUID?! I'M MORE OF AN *EEL* GUY MYSELF.
GET IT?
YOU JUST GONNA DANCE WITH THAT THING OR ARE YOU ACTUALLY GOING TO DO SOMETHING *USEFUL?*

WHUMP

LEMME SHOW YOU HOW IT'S DONE, SILLY PUTTY.

RAAUURGH

I TOTALLY HAD THAT THING RIGHT WHERE I WANTED IT.

UH-HUH.

UM, DO YOU GUYS *HEAR* SOMETHING?

YIKES!!

GUYS!!!

OH NO!

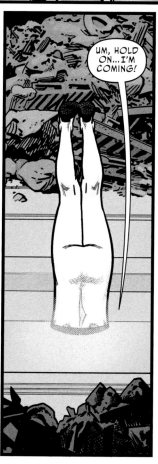

UM, HOLD ON...I'M COMING!

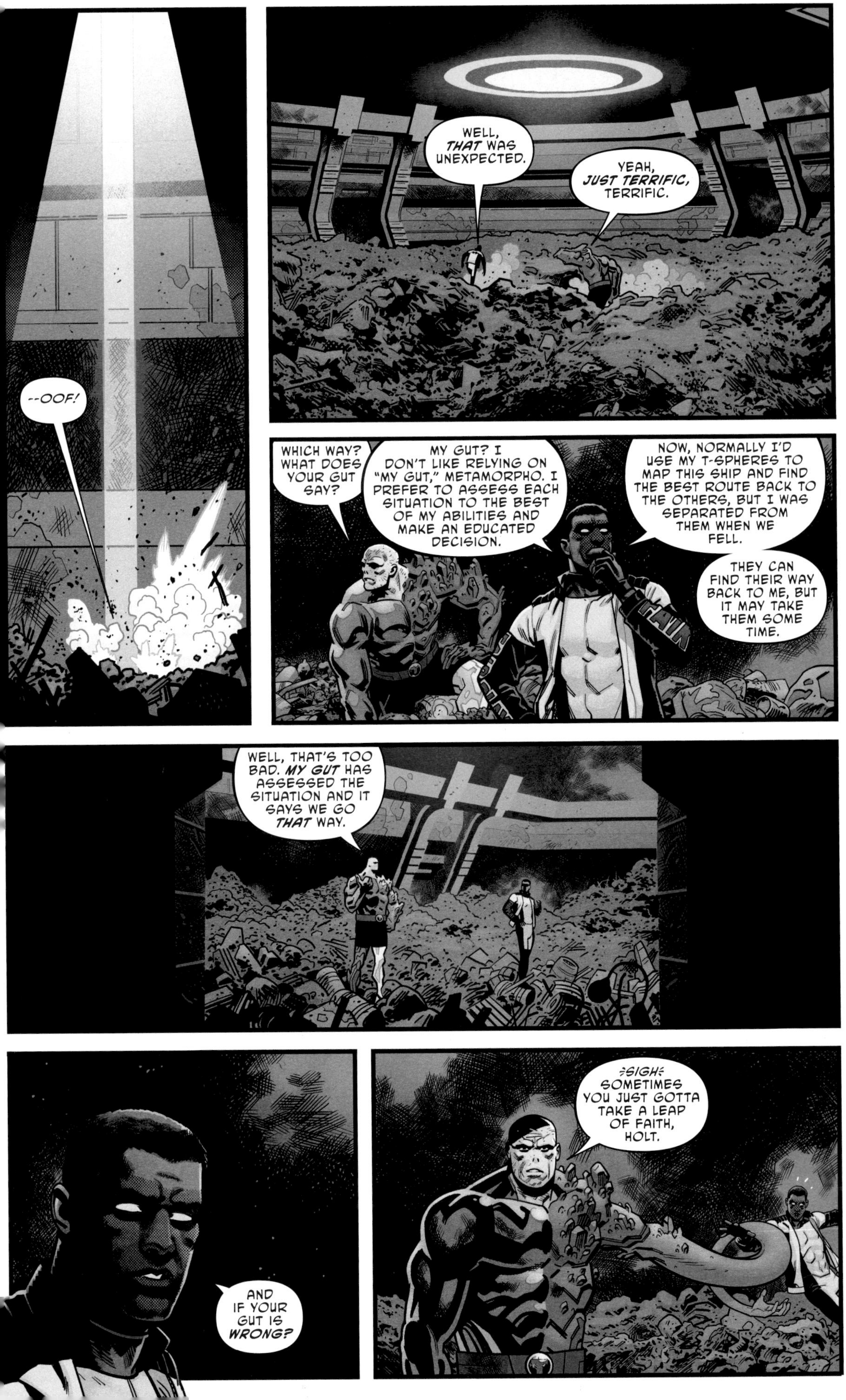
--OOF!
WELL, THAT WAS UNEXPECTED.
YEAH, JUST TERRIFIC, TERRIFIC.
WHICH WAY? WHAT DOES YOUR GUT SAY?
MY GUT? I DON'T LIKE RELYING ON "MY GUT," METAMORPHO. I PREFER TO ASSESS EACH SITUATION TO THE BEST OF MY ABILITIES AND MAKE AN EDUCATED DECISION.
NOW, NORMALLY I'D USE MY T-SPHERES TO MAP THIS SHIP AND FIND THE BEST ROUTE BACK TO THE OTHERS, BUT I WAS SEPARATED FROM THEM WHEN WE FELL.
THEY CAN FIND THEIR WAY BACK TO ME, BUT IT MAY TAKE THEM SOME TIME.
WELL, THAT'S TOO BAD. MY GUT HAS ASSESSED THE SITUATION AND IT SAYS WE GO THAT WAY.
AND IF YOUR GUT IS WRONG?
SIGH SOMETIMES YOU JUST GOTTA TAKE A LEAP OF FAITH, HOLT.

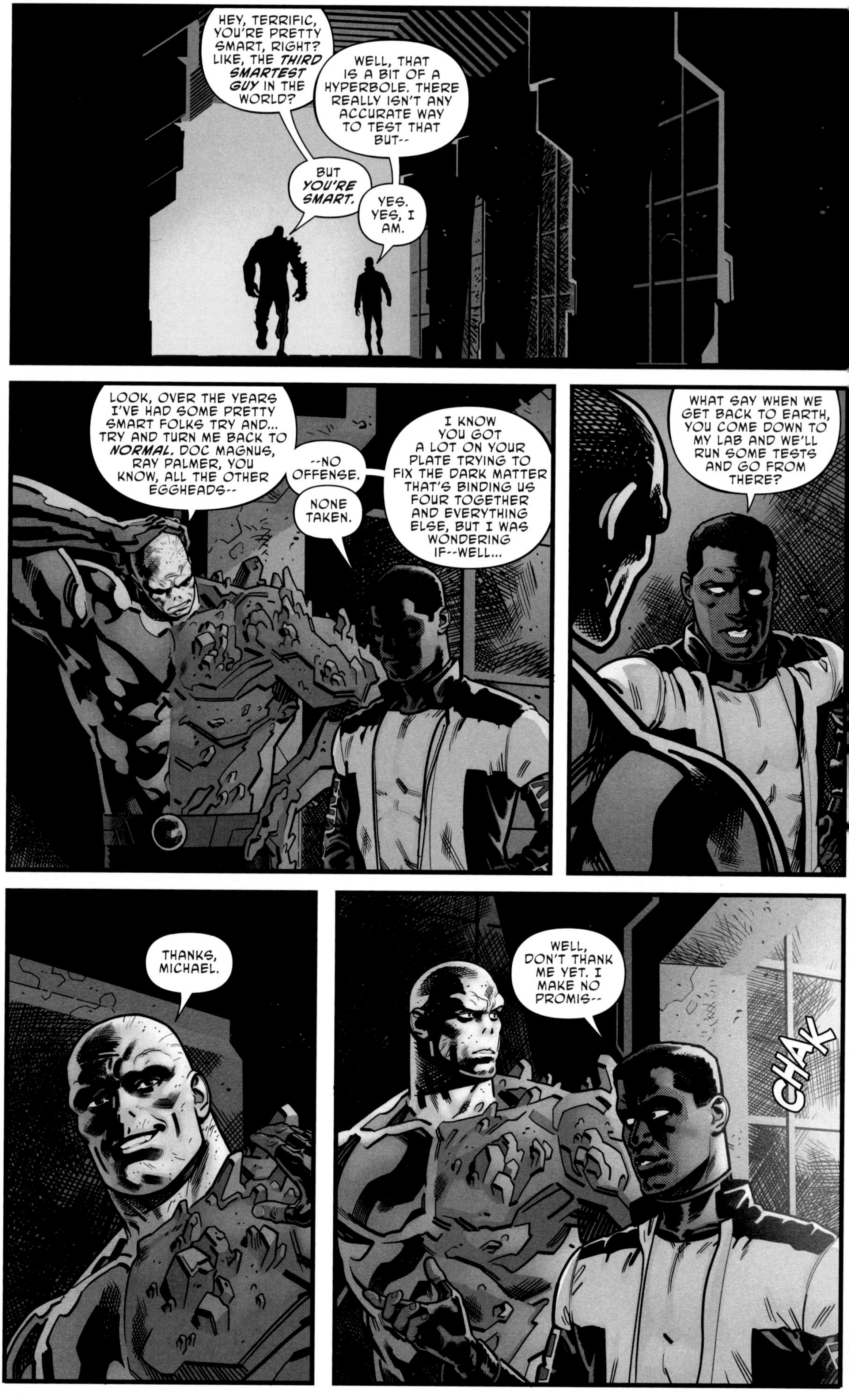
HEY, TERRIFIC, YOU'RE PRETTY SMART, RIGHT? LIKE, THE THIRD SMARTEST GUY IN THE WORLD?
WELL, THAT IS A BIT OF A HYPERBOLE. THERE REALLY ISN'T ANY ACCURATE WAY TO TEST THAT BUT--
BUT YOU'RE SMART.
YES. YES, I AM.
LOOK, OVER THE YEARS I'VE HAD SOME PRETTY SMART FOLKS TRY AND... TRY AND TURN ME BACK TO NORMAL. DOC MAGNUS, RAY PALMER, YOU KNOW, ALL THE OTHER EGGHEADS--
--NO OFFENSE.
NONE TAKEN.
I KNOW YOU GOT A LOT ON YOUR PLATE TRYING TO FIX THE DARK MATTER THAT'S BINDING US FOUR TOGETHER AND EVERYTHING ELSE, BUT I WAS WONDERING IF--WELL...
WHAT SAY WHEN WE GET BACK TO EARTH, YOU COME DOWN TO MY LAB AND WE'LL RUN SOME TESTS AND GO FROM THERE?
THANKS, MICHAEL.
WELL, DON'T THANK ME YET. I MAKE NO PROMIS--
CHAK

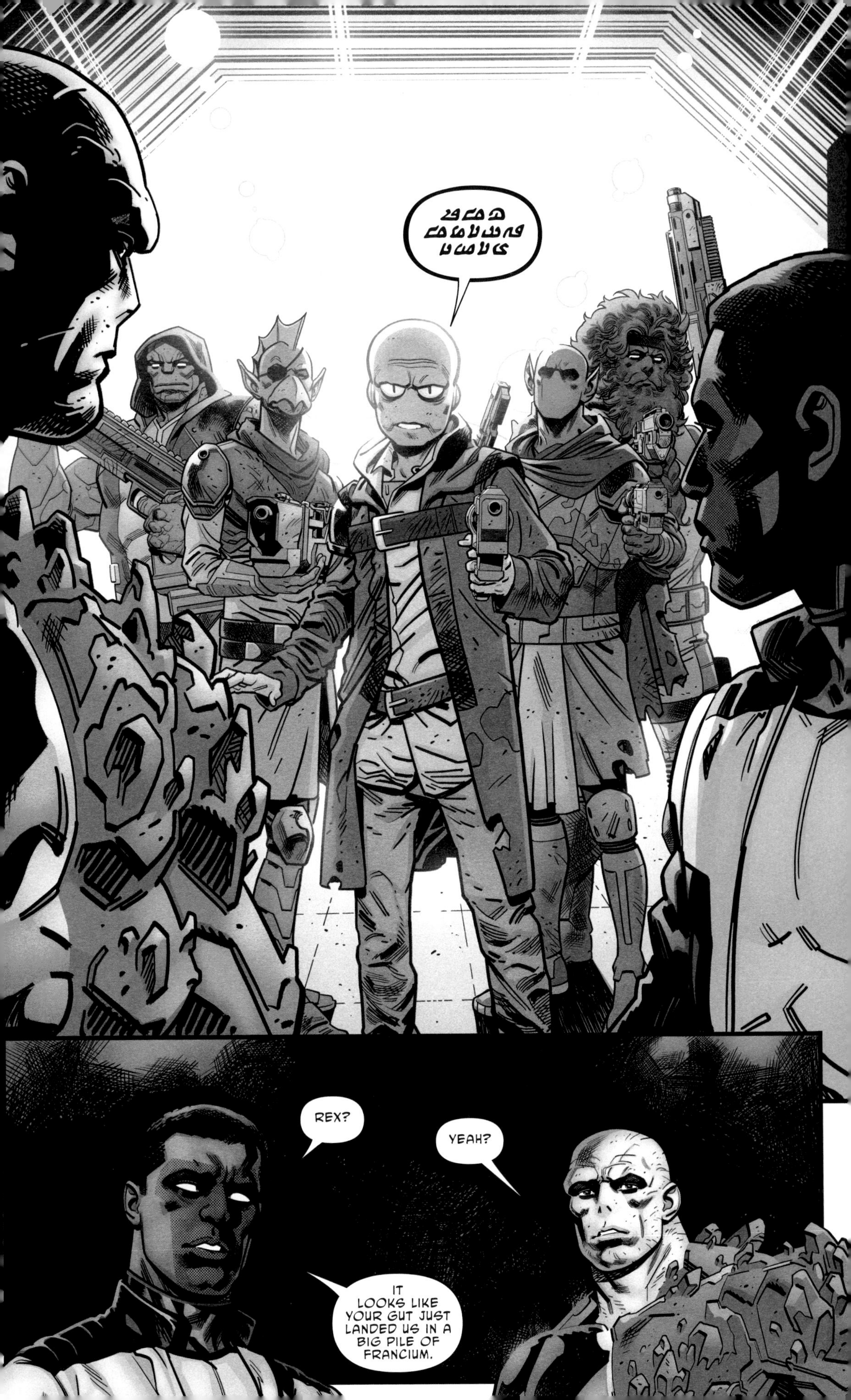
REX?
YEAH?
IT LOOKS LIKE YOUR GUT JUST LANDED US IN A BIG PILE OF FRANCIUM.

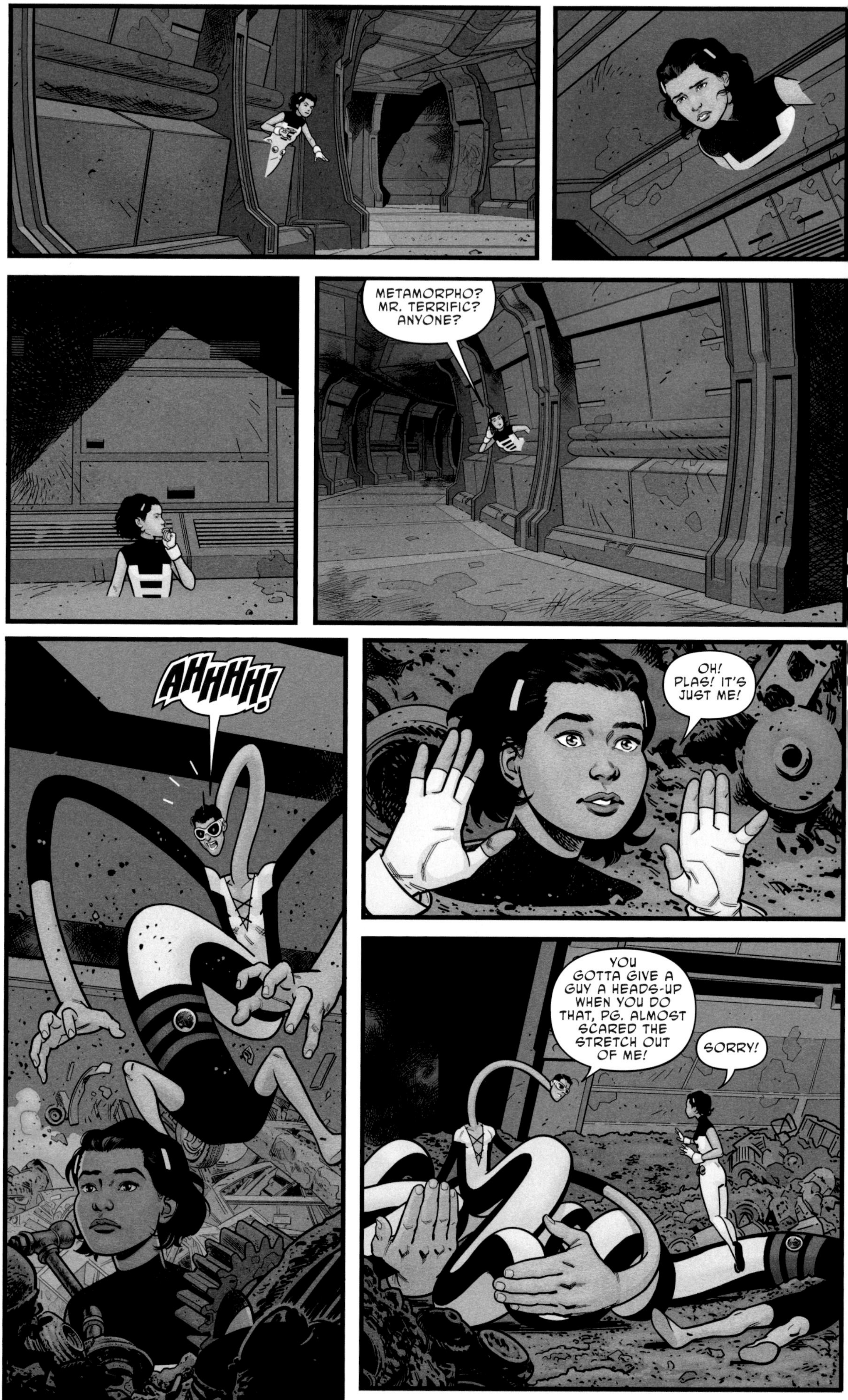
METAMORPHO? MR. TERRIFIC? ANYONE?
AHHHH!
OH! PLAS! IT'S JUST ME!
YOU GOTTA GIVE A GUY A HEADS-UP WHEN YOU DO THAT, PG. ALMOST SCARED THE STRETCH OUT OF ME!
SORRY!

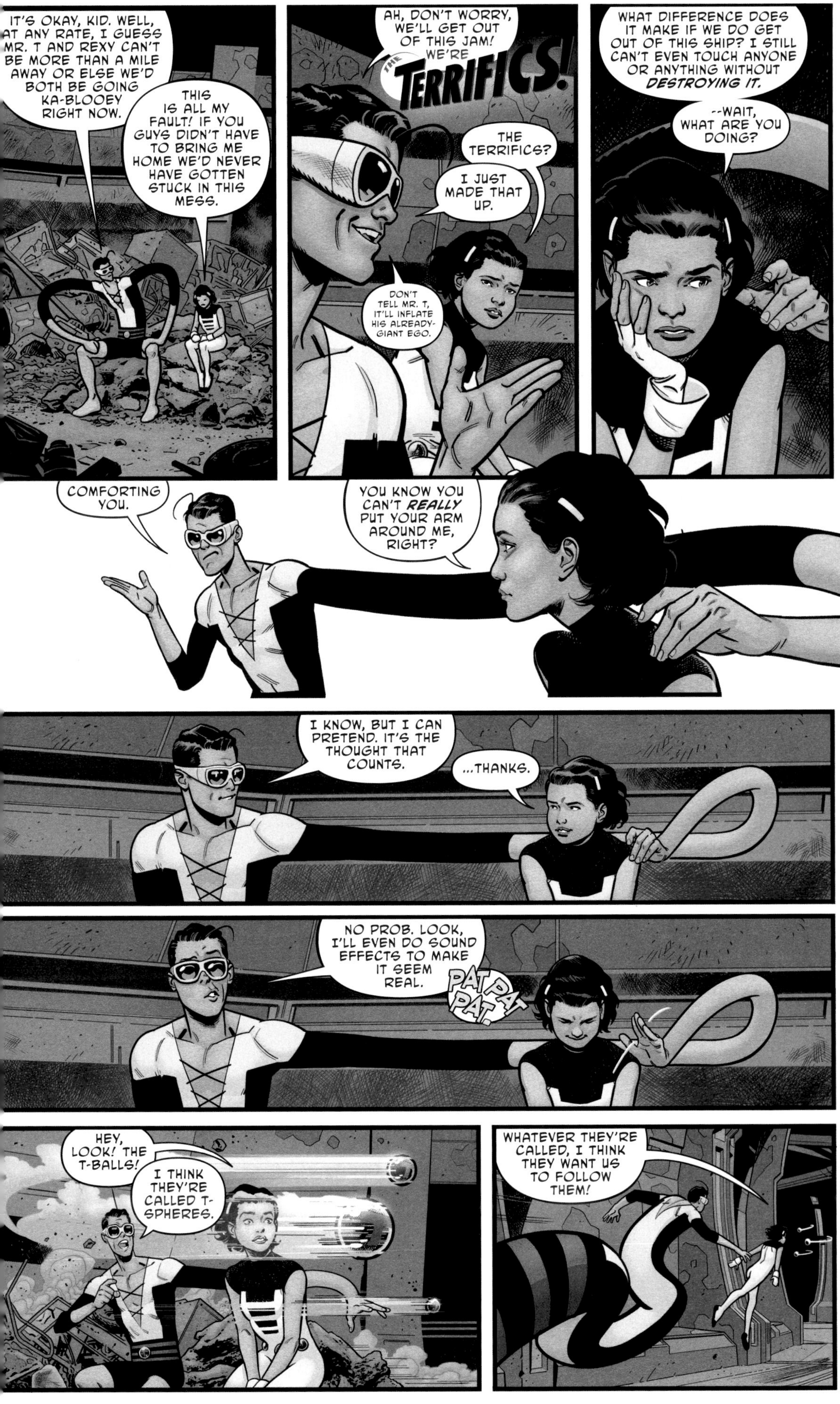
IT'S OKAY, KID. WELL, AT ANY RATE, I GUESS MR. T AND REXY CAN'T BE MORE THAN A MILE AWAY OR ELSE WE'D BOTH BE GOING KA-BLOOEY RIGHT NOW.
THIS IS ALL MY FAULT! IF YOU GUYS DIDN'T HAVE TO BRING ME HOME WE'D NEVER HAVE GOTTEN STUCK IN THIS MESS.
AH, DON'T WORRY, WE'LL GET OUT OF THIS JAM! WE'RE THE TERRIFICS!
THE TERRIFICS?
I JUST MADE THAT UP.
DON'T TELL MR. T, IT'LL INFLATE HIS ALREADY-GIANT EGO.
WHAT DIFFERENCE DOES IT MAKE IF WE DO GET OUT OF THIS SHIP? I STILL CAN'T EVEN TOUCH ANYONE OR ANYTHING WITHOUT DESTROYING IT.
--WAIT, WHAT ARE YOU DOING?
COMFORTING YOU.
YOU KNOW YOU CAN'T REALLY PUT YOUR ARM AROUND ME, RIGHT?
I KNOW, BUT I CAN PRETEND. IT'S THE THOUGHT THAT COUNTS.
...THANKS.
NO PROB. LOOK, I'LL EVEN DO SOUND EFFECTS TO MAKE IT SEEM REAL.
PAT PAT PAT
HEY, LOOK! THE T-BALLS!
I THINK THEY'RE CALLED T-SPHERES.
WHATEVER THEY'RE CALLED, I THINK THEY WANT US TO FOLLOW THEM!

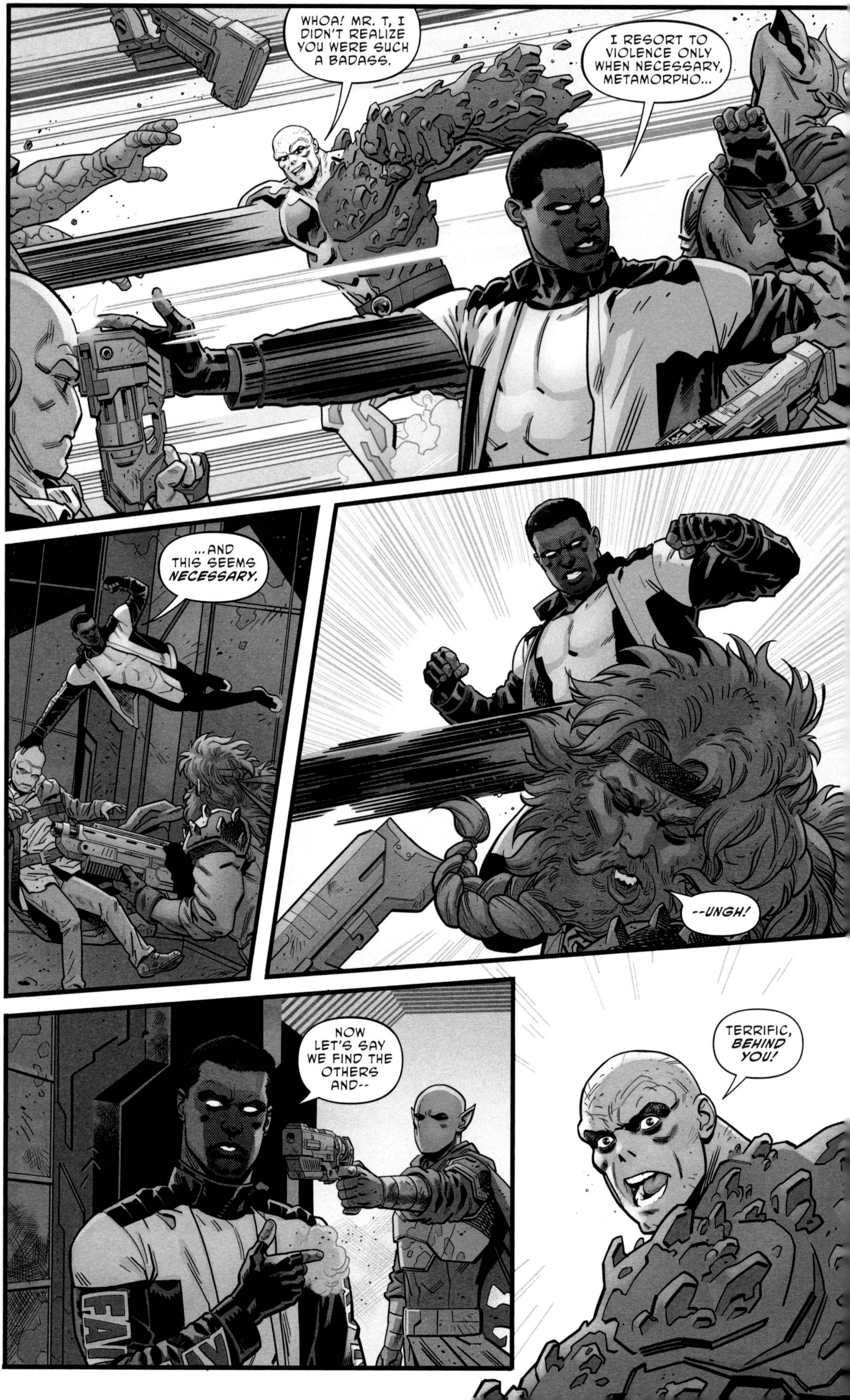
WHOA! MR. T, I DIDN'T REALIZE YOU WERE SUCH A BADASS.
I RESORT TO VIOLENCE ONLY WHEN NECESSARY, METAMORPHO...
...AND THIS SEEMS *NECESSARY.*
--UNGH!
NOW LET'S SAY WE FIND THE OTHERS AND--
TERRIFIC, *BEHIND YOU!*

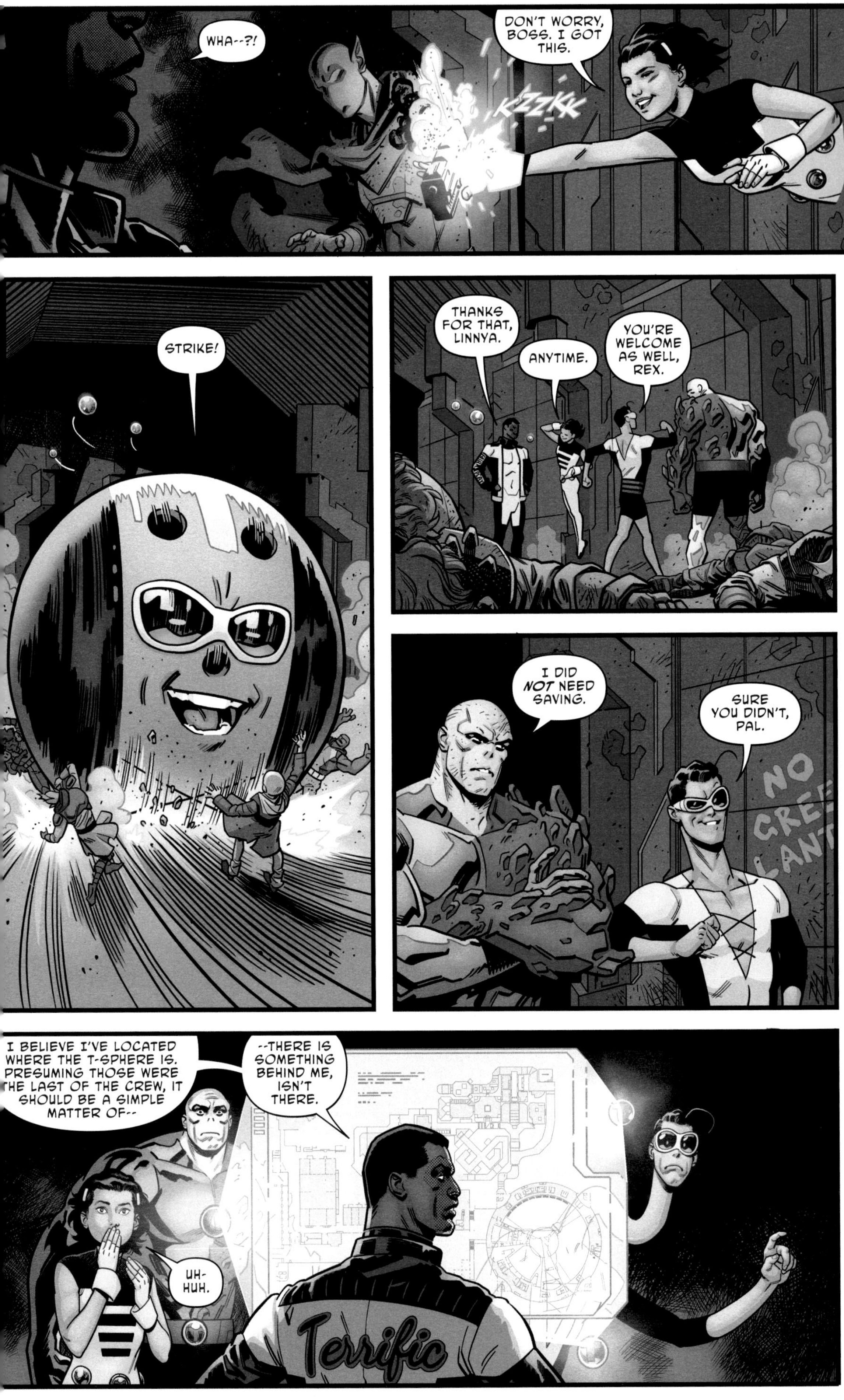

WHA--?!
DON'T WORRY, BOSS. I GOT THIS.
KZZKK
STRIKE!
THANKS FOR THAT, LINNYA.
ANYTIME.
YOU'RE WELCOME AS WELL, REX.
I DID *NOT* NEED SAVING.
SURE YOU DIDN'T, PAL.
I BELIEVE I'VE LOCATED WHERE THE T-SPHERE IS. PRESUMING THOSE WERE THE LAST OF THE CREW, IT SHOULD BE A SIMPLE MATTER OF--
--THERE IS SOMETHING BEHIND ME, ISN'T THERE.
UH-HUH.
Terrific

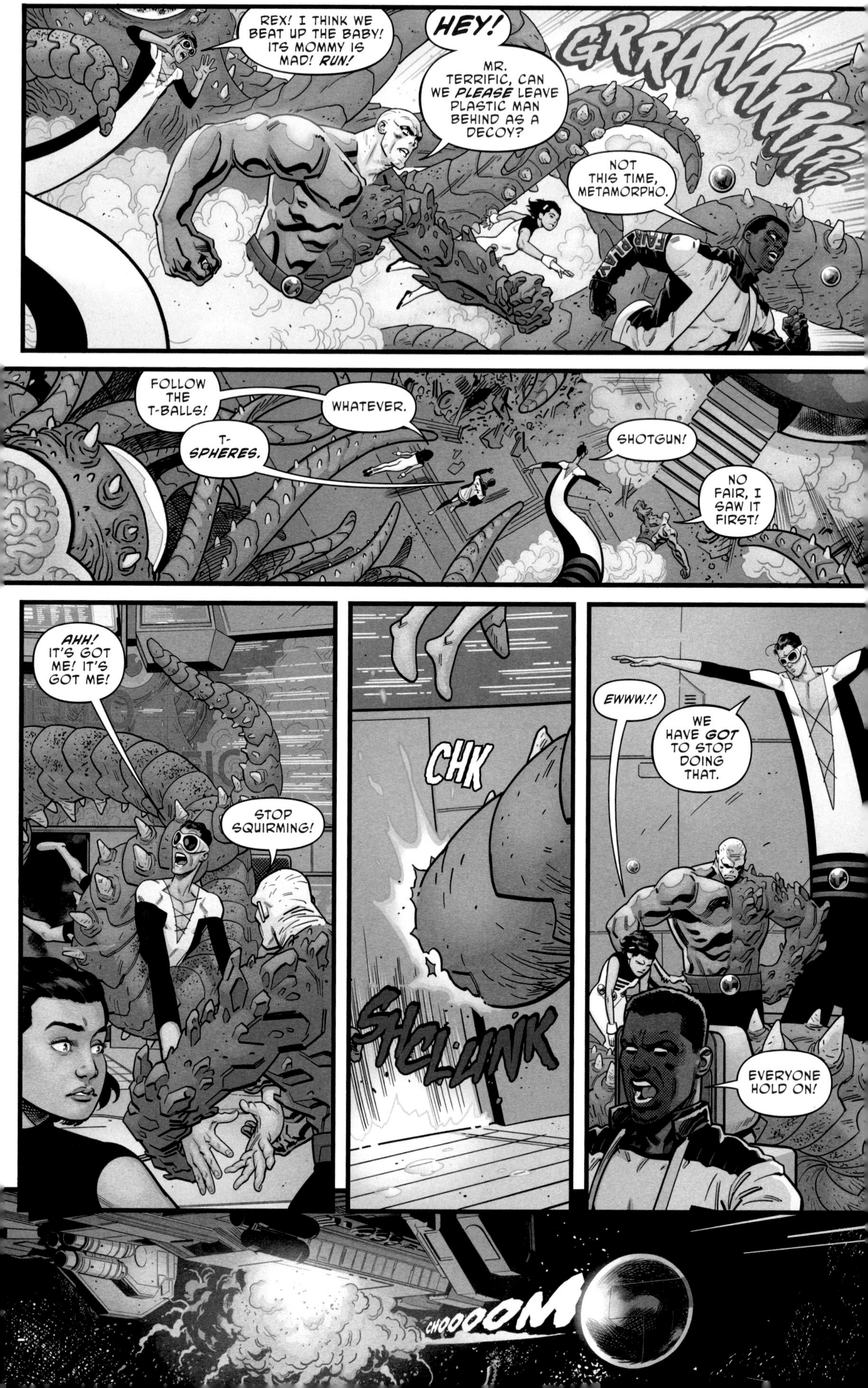
REX! I THINK WE BEAT UP THE BABY! ITS MOMMY IS MAD! RUN!
HEY!
MR. TERRIFIC, CAN WE PLEASE LEAVE PLASTIC MAN BEHIND AS A DECOY?
GRRAAARRR
NOT THIS TIME, METAMORPHO.
FAIR PLAY
FOLLOW THE T-BALLS!
WHATEVER.
T-SPHERES.
SHOTGUN!
NO FAIR, I SAW IT FIRST!
AHH! IT'S GOT ME! IT'S GOT ME!
STOP SQUIRMING!
CHK
SHCLUNK
EWWW!!
WE HAVE GOT TO STOP DOING THAT.
EVERYONE HOLD ON!
CHOOOOOM

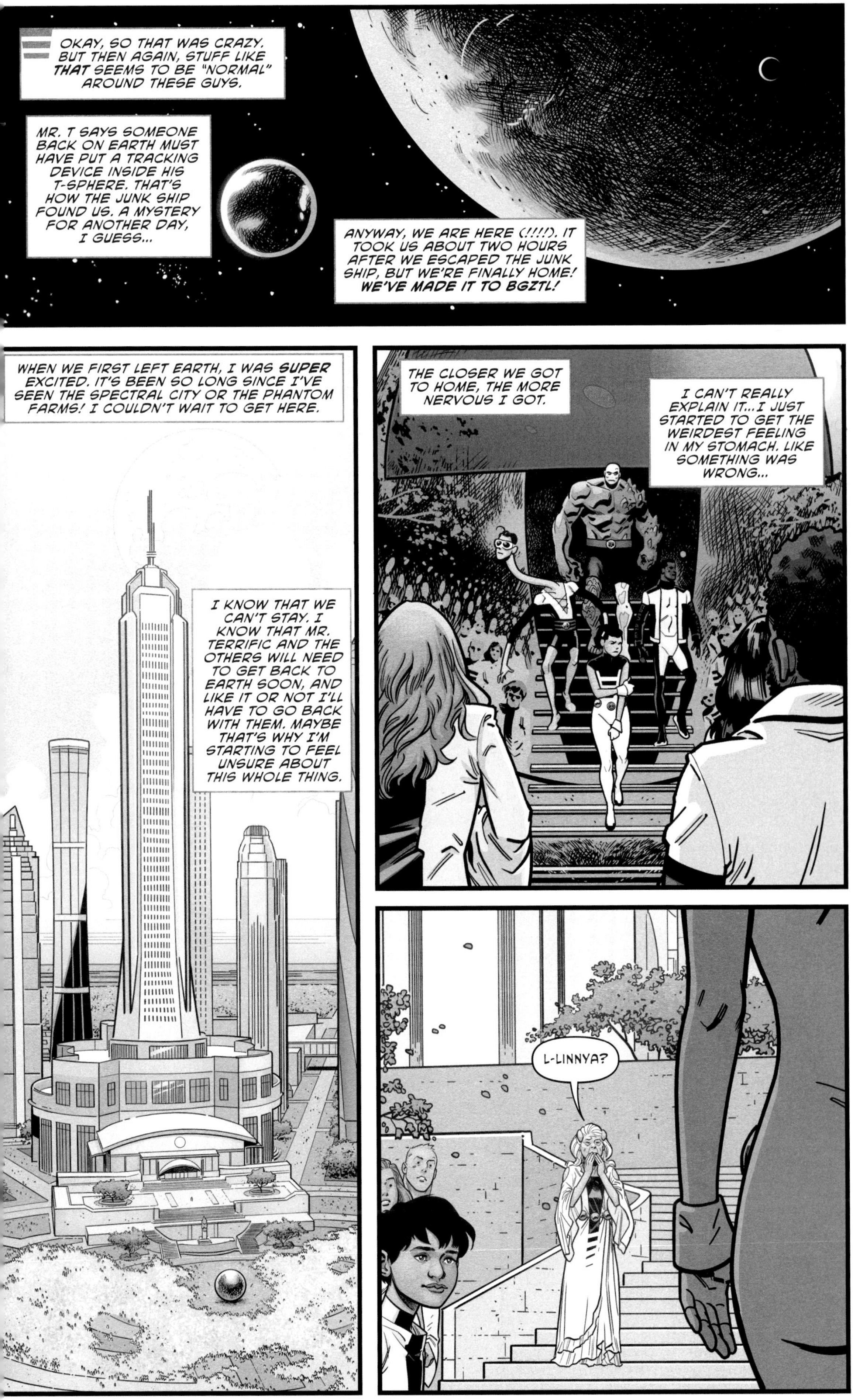
OKAY, SO THAT WAS CRAZY. BUT THEN AGAIN, STUFF LIKE THAT SEEMS TO BE "NORMAL" AROUND THESE GUYS.
MR. T SAYS SOMEONE BACK ON EARTH MUST HAVE PUT A TRACKING DEVICE INSIDE HIS T-SPHERE. THAT'S HOW THE JUNK SHIP FOUND US. A MYSTERY FOR ANOTHER DAY, I GUESS...
ANYWAY, WE ARE HERE (!!!!). IT TOOK US ABOUT TWO HOURS AFTER WE ESCAPED THE JUNK SHIP, BUT WE'RE FINALLY HOME! WE'VE MADE IT TO BGZTL!
WHEN WE FIRST LEFT EARTH, I WAS SUPER EXCITED. IT'S BEEN SO LONG SINCE I'VE SEEN THE SPECTRAL CITY OR THE PHANTOM FARMS! I COULDN'T WAIT TO GET HERE.
I KNOW THAT WE CAN'T STAY. I KNOW THAT MR. TERRIFIC AND THE OTHERS WILL NEED TO GET BACK TO EARTH SOON, AND LIKE IT OR NOT I'LL HAVE TO GO BACK WITH THEM. MAYBE THAT'S WHY I'M STARTING TO FEEL UNSURE ABOUT THIS WHOLE THING.
THE CLOSER WE GOT TO HOME, THE MORE NERVOUS I GOT.
I CAN'T REALLY EXPLAIN IT...I JUST STARTED TO GET THE WEIRDEST FEELING IN MY STOMACH. LIKE SOMETHING WAS WRONG...
L-LINNYA?

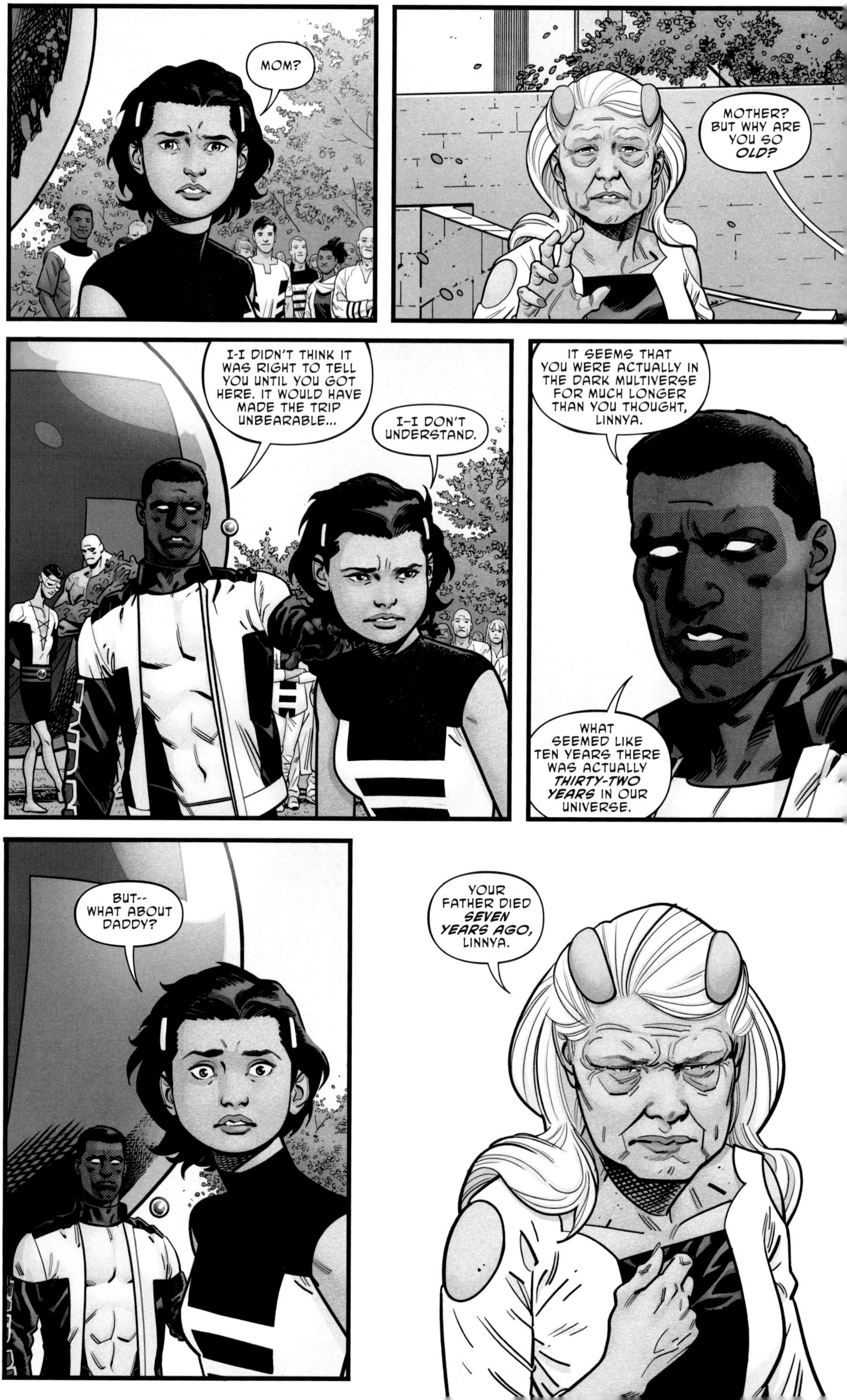
MOM?
MOTHER? BUT WHY ARE YOU SO *OLD?*
I-I DIDN'T THINK IT WAS RIGHT TO TELL YOU UNTIL YOU GOT HERE. IT WOULD HAVE MADE THE TRIP UNBEARABLE...
I-I DON'T UNDERSTAND.
IT SEEMS THAT YOU WERE ACTUALLY IN THE DARK MULTIVERSE FOR MUCH LONGER THAN YOU THOUGHT, LINNYA.
WHAT SEEMED LIKE TEN YEARS THERE WAS ACTUALLY *THIRTY-TWO YEARS* IN OUR UNIVERSE.
BUT-- WHAT ABOUT DADDY?
YOUR FATHER DIED *SEVEN YEARS AGO,* LINNYA.

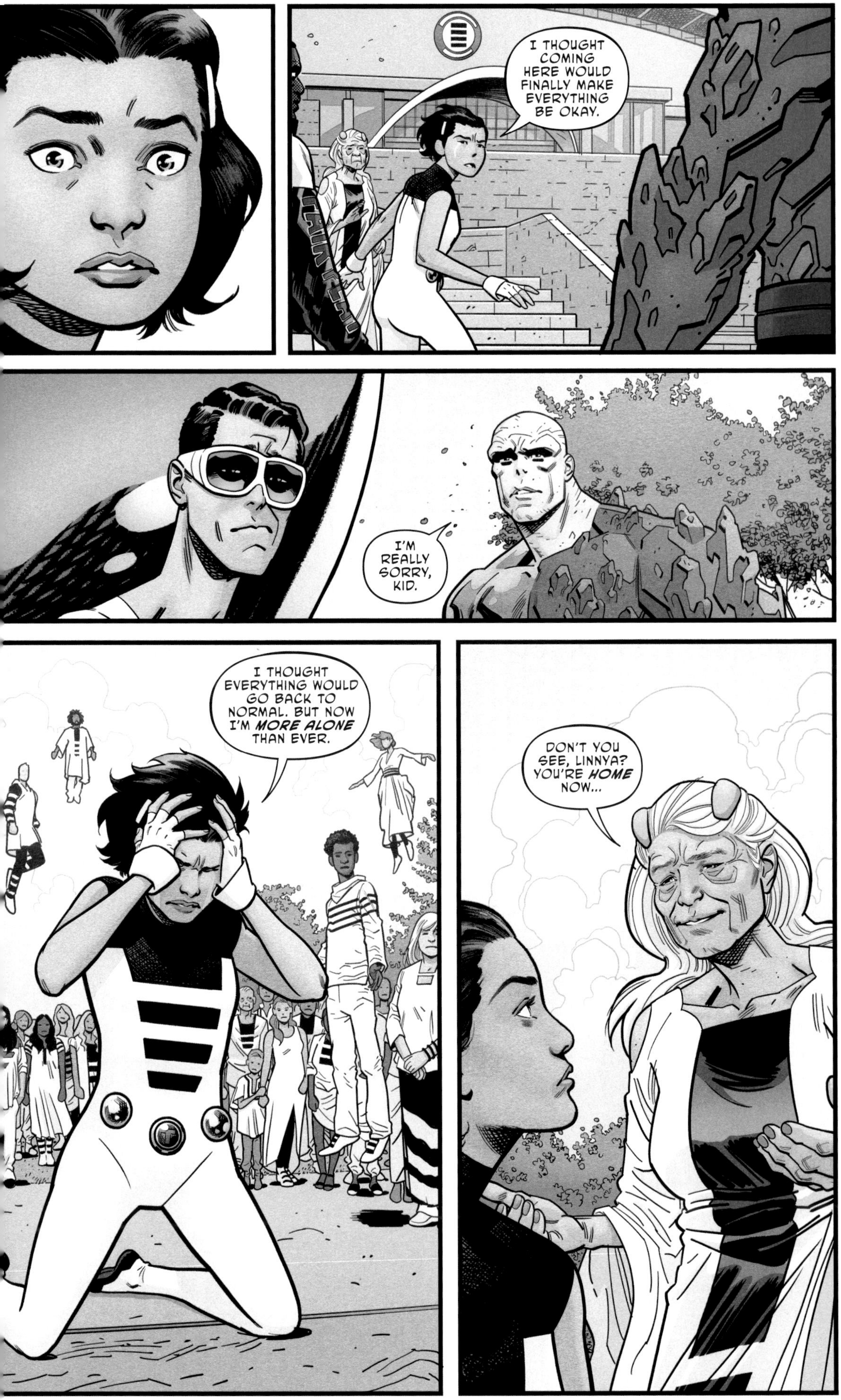
I THOUGHT COMING HERE WOULD FINALLY MAKE EVERYTHING BE OKAY.
I'M REALLY SORRY, KID.
I THOUGHT EVERYTHING WOULD GO BACK TO NORMAL. BUT NOW I'M *MORE ALONE* THAN EVER.
DON'T YOU SEE, LINNYA? YOU'RE *HOME* NOW...

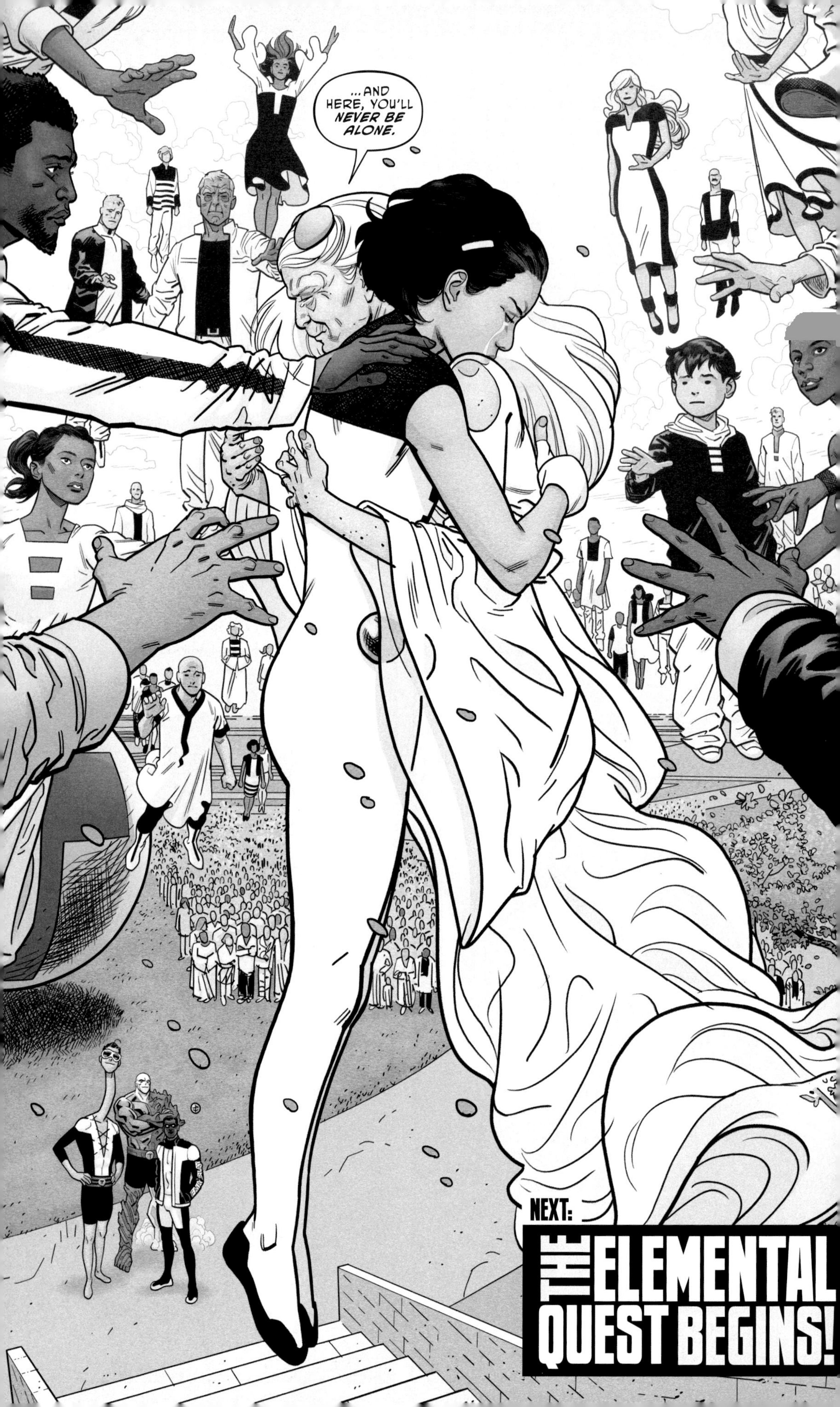
...AND HERE, YOU'LL NEVER BE ALONE.
NEXT:
THE ELEMENTAL QUEST BEGINS!

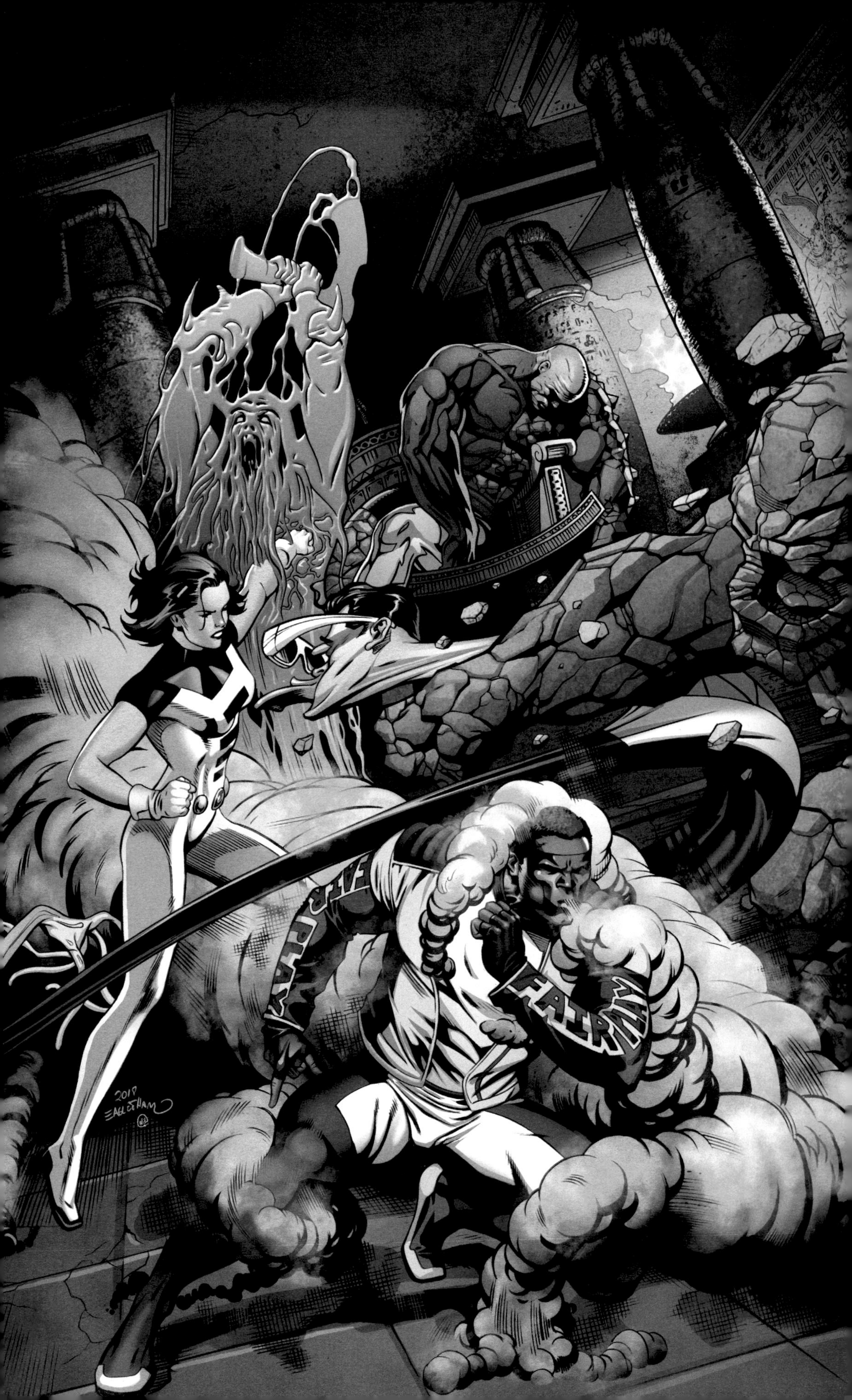
FAIRPLAY

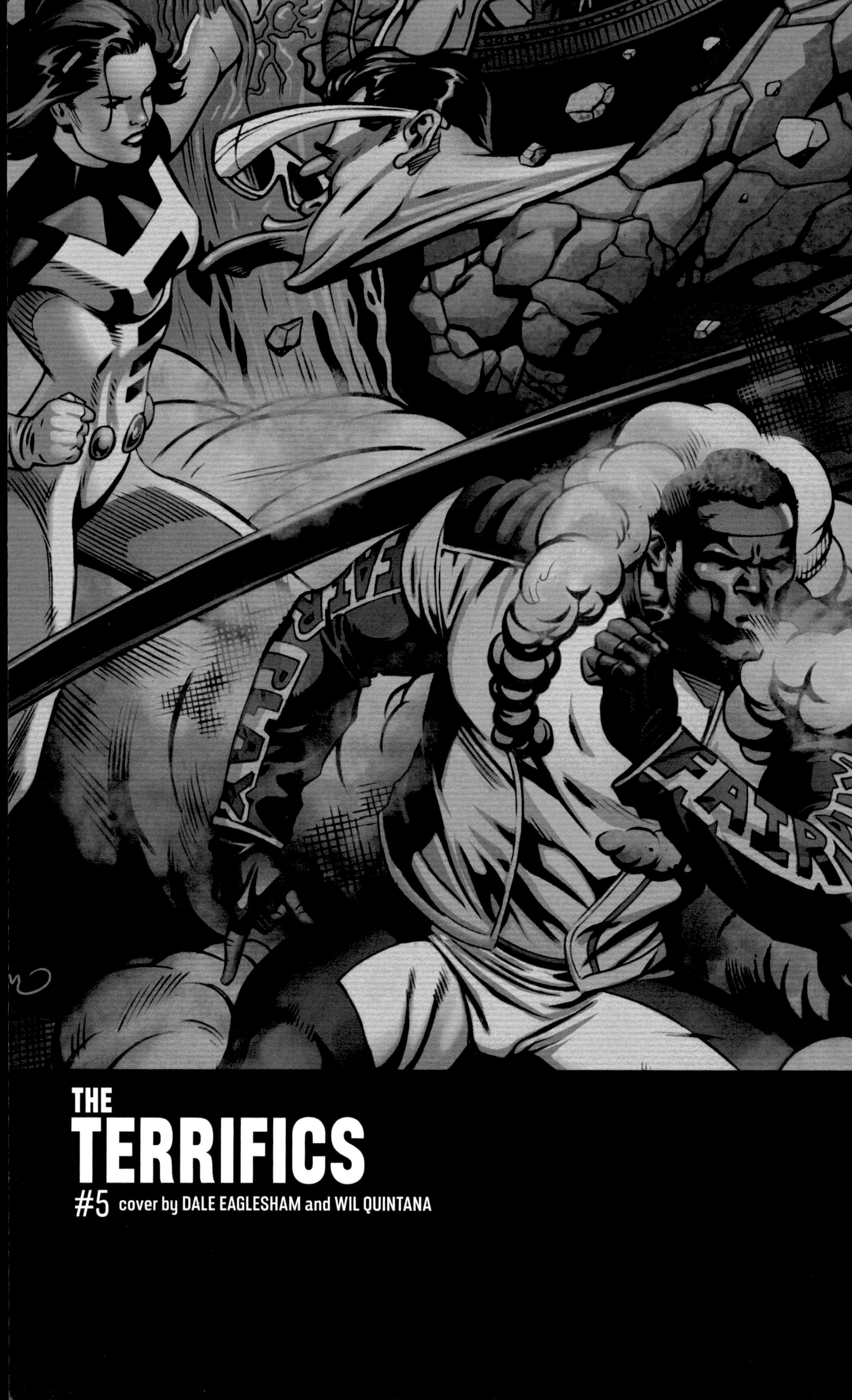
FAIR
PLAY

THE TERRIFICS

#5 cover by DALE EAGLESHAM and WIL QUINTANA

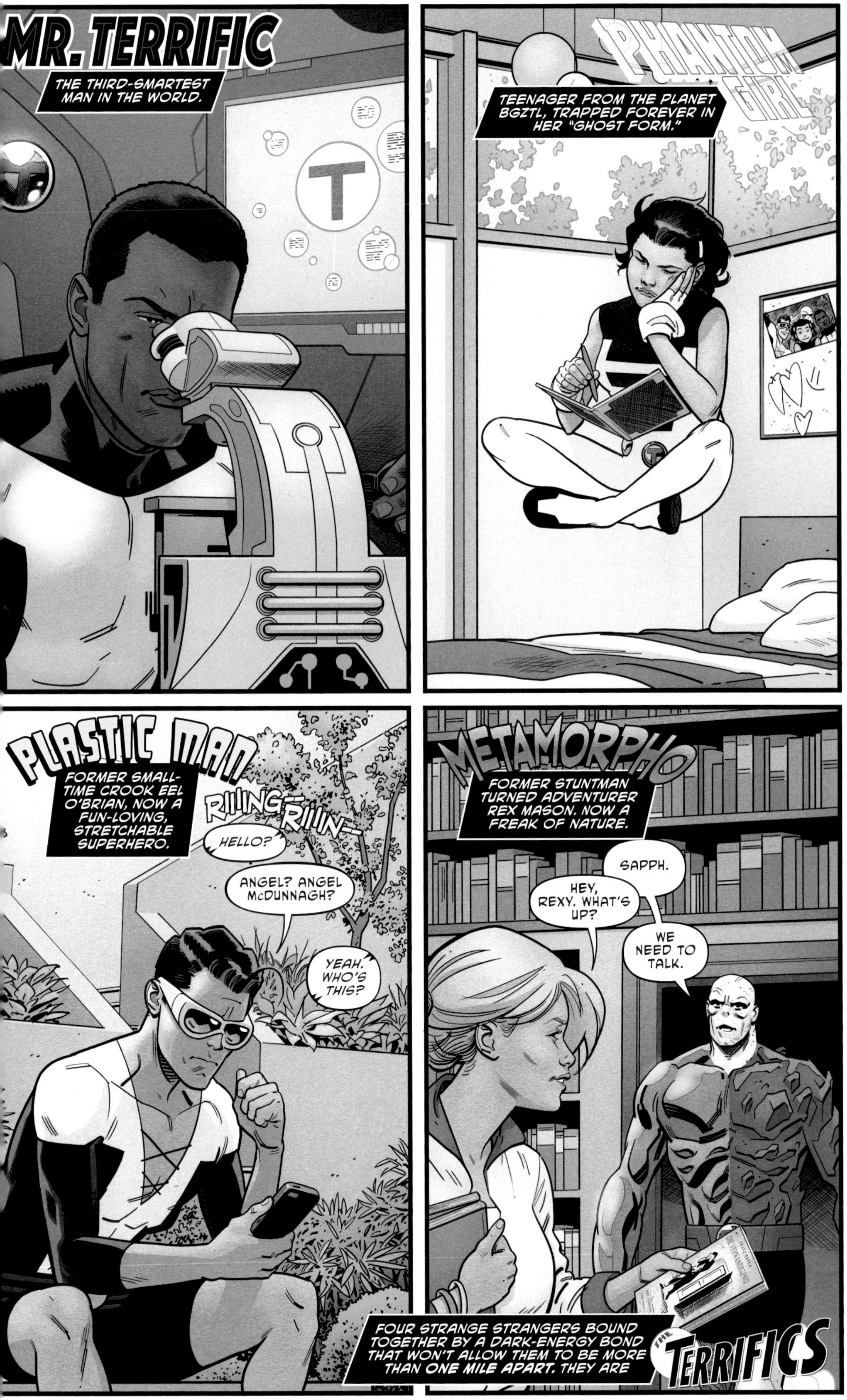

MR. TERRIFIC
THE THIRD-SMARTEST MAN IN THE WORLD.
PHANTOM GIRL
TEENAGER FROM THE PLANET BGZTL, TRAPPED FOREVER IN HER "GHOST FORM."
PLASTIC MAN
FORMER SMALL-TIME CROOK EEL O'BRIAN, NOW A FUN-LOVING, STRETCHABLE SUPERHERO.
RIIING-RIIIN--
HELLO?
ANGEL? ANGEL McDUNNAGH?
YEAH. WHO'S THIS?
METAMORPHO
FORMER STUNTMAN TURNED ADVENTURER REX MASON. NOW A FREAK OF NATURE.
SAPPH.
HEY, REXY. WHAT'S UP?
WE NEED TO TALK.
FOUR STRANGE STRANGERS BOUND TOGETHER BY A DARK-ENERGY BOND THAT WON'T ALLOW THEM TO BE MORE THAN ONE MILE APART. THEY ARE
THE TERRIFICS

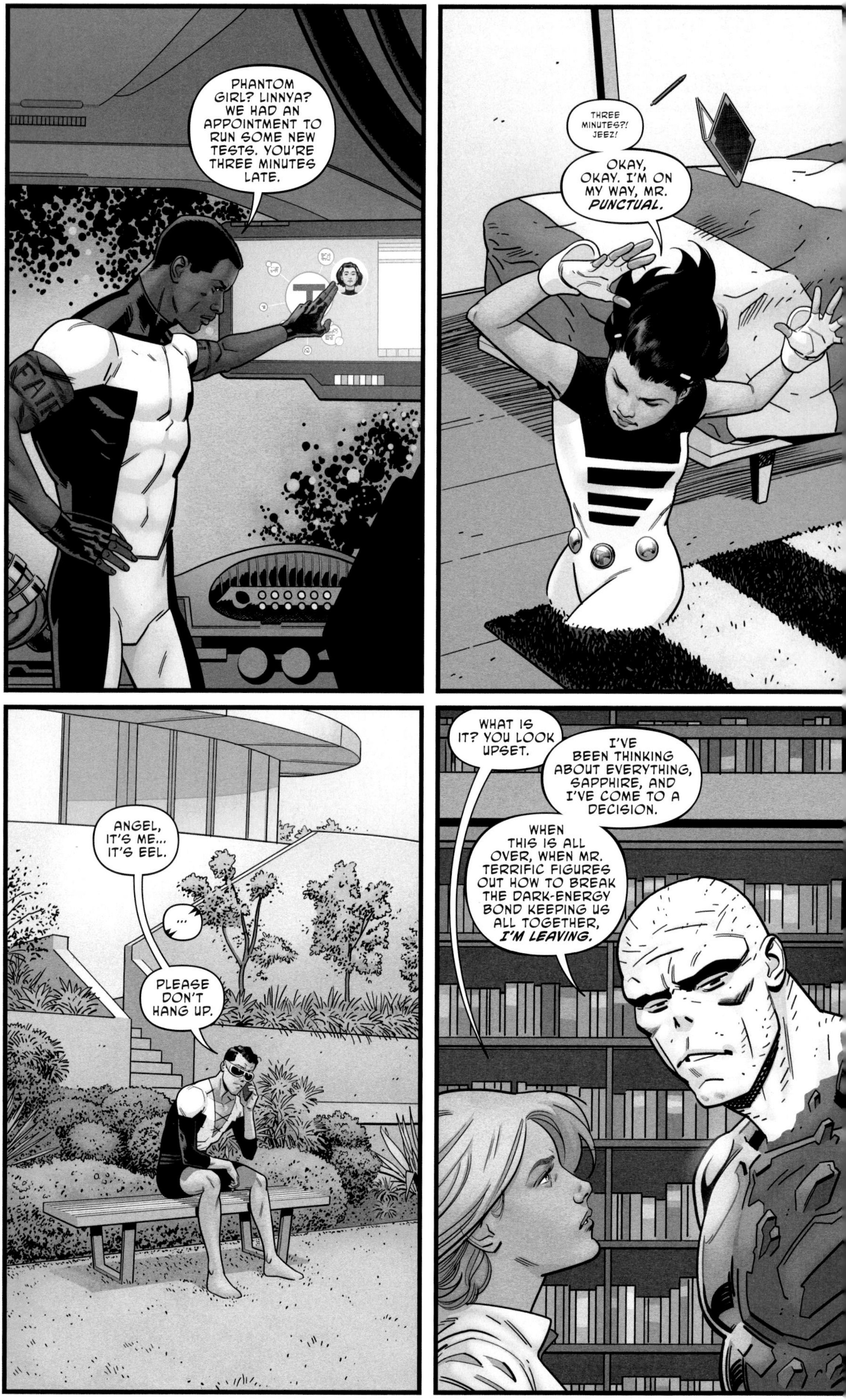
PHANTOM GIRL? LINNYA? WE HAD AN APPOINTMENT TO RUN SOME NEW TESTS. YOU'RE THREE MINUTES LATE.
THREE MINUTES?! JEEZ!
OKAY, OKAY. I'M ON MY WAY, MR. *PUNCTUAL.*
ANGEL, IT'S ME... IT'S EEL.
...
PLEASE DON'T HANG UP.
WHAT IS IT? YOU LOOK UPSET.
I'VE BEEN THINKING ABOUT EVERYTHING, SAPPHIRE, AND I'VE COME TO A DECISION.
WHEN THIS IS ALL OVER, WHEN MR. TERRIFIC FIGURES OUT HOW TO BREAK THE DARK-ENERGY BOND KEEPING US ALL TOGETHER, *I'M LEAVING.*

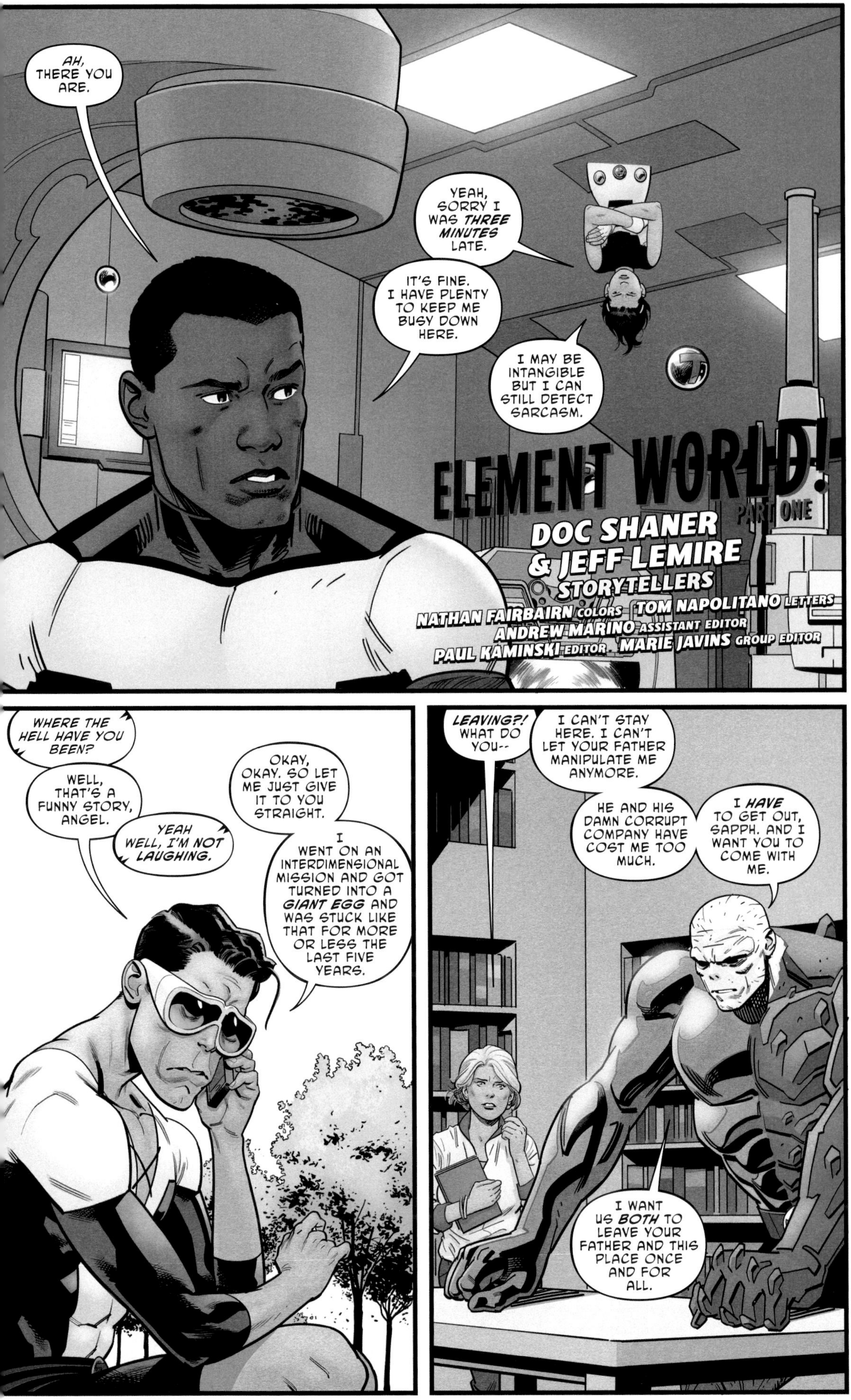
AH, THERE YOU ARE.
YEAH, SORRY I WAS THREE MINUTES LATE.
IT'S FINE. I HAVE PLENTY TO KEEP ME BUSY DOWN HERE.
I MAY BE INTANGIBLE BUT I CAN STILL DETECT SARCASM.
ELEMENT WORLD! PART ONE
DOC SHANER & JEFF LEMIRE STORYTELLERS
NATHAN FAIRBAIRN COLORS TOM NAPOLITANO LETTERS
ANDREW MARINO ASSISTANT EDITOR
PAUL KAMINSKI EDITOR MARIE JAVINS GROUP EDITOR
WHERE THE HELL HAVE YOU BEEN?
WELL, THAT'S A FUNNY STORY, ANGEL.
YEAH WELL, I'M NOT LAUGHING.
OKAY, OKAY. SO LET ME JUST GIVE IT TO YOU STRAIGHT.
I WENT ON AN INTERDIMENSIONAL MISSION AND GOT TURNED INTO A GIANT EGG AND WAS STUCK LIKE THAT FOR MORE OR LESS THE LAST FIVE YEARS.
LEAVING?! WHAT DO YOU--
I CAN'T STAY HERE. I CAN'T LET YOUR FATHER MANIPULATE ME ANYMORE.
HE AND HIS DAMN CORRUPT COMPANY HAVE COST ME TOO MUCH.
I HAVE TO GET OUT, SAPPH. AND I WANT YOU TO COME WITH ME.
I WANT US BOTH TO LEAVE YOUR FATHER AND THIS PLACE ONCE AND FOR ALL.

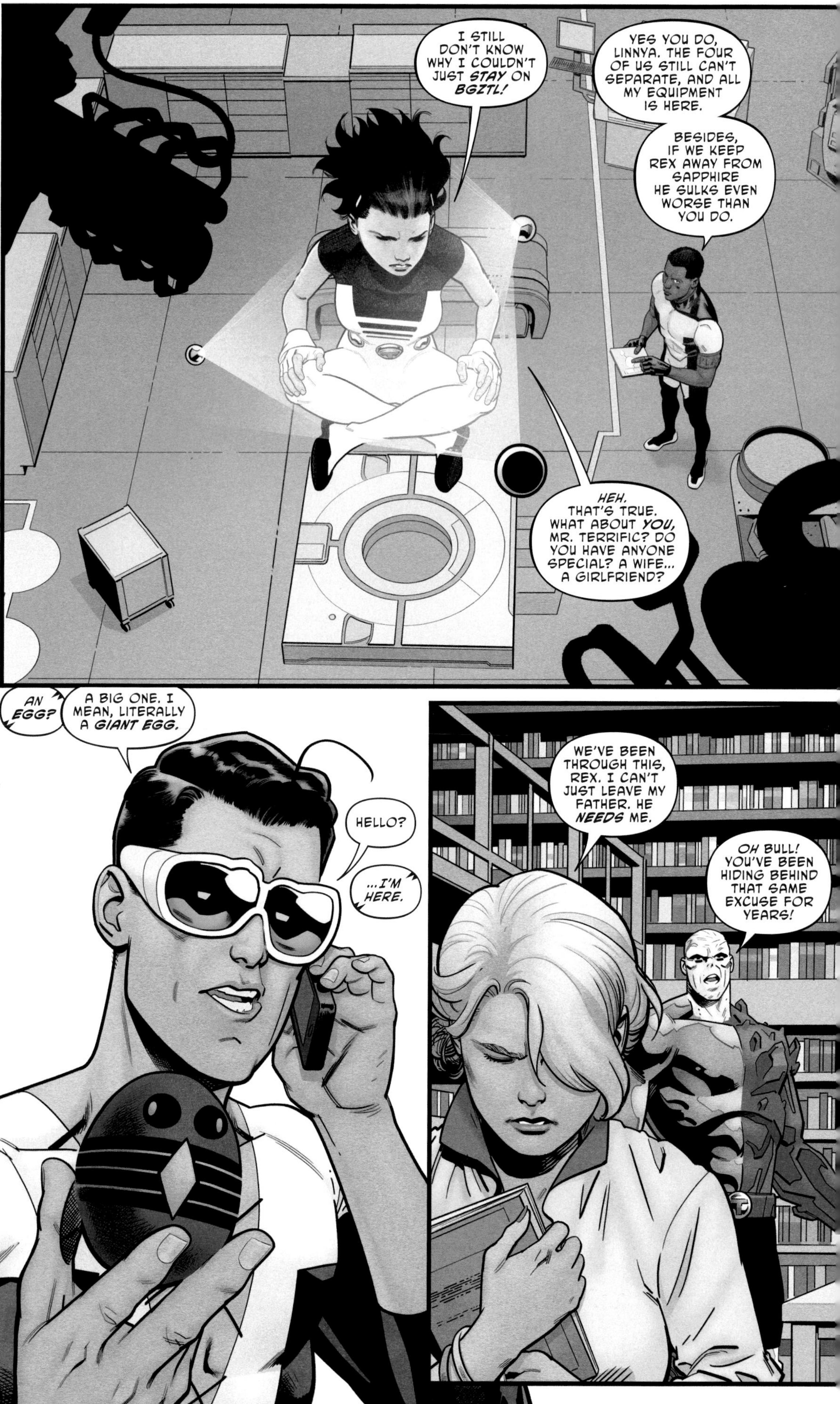
I STILL DON'T KNOW WHY I COULDN'T JUST STAY ON BGZTL!
YES YOU DO, LINNYA. THE FOUR OF US STILL CAN'T SEPARATE, AND ALL MY EQUIPMENT IS HERE.
BESIDES, IF WE KEEP REX AWAY FROM SAPPHIRE HE SULKS EVEN WORSE THAN YOU DO.
HEH. THAT'S TRUE. WHAT ABOUT YOU, MR. TERRIFIC? DO YOU HAVE ANYONE SPECIAL? A WIFE... A GIRLFRIEND?
AN EGG?
A BIG ONE. I MEAN, LITERALLY A GIANT EGG.
HELLO?
...I'M HERE.
WE'VE BEEN THROUGH THIS, REX. I CAN'T JUST LEAVE MY FATHER. HE NEEDS ME.
OH BULL! YOU'VE BEEN HIDING BEHIND THAT SAME EXCUSE FOR YEARS!

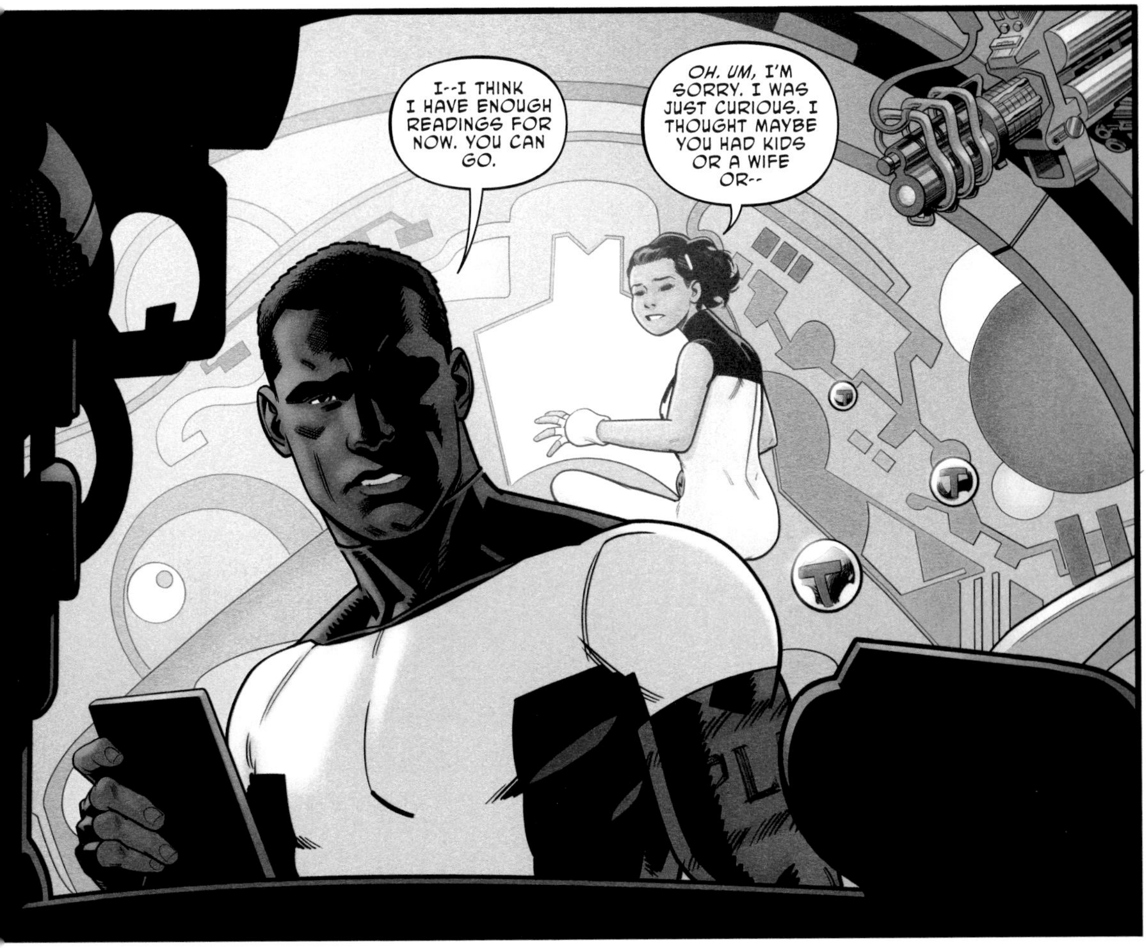
I--I THINK I HAVE ENOUGH READINGS FOR NOW. YOU CAN GO.
OH. UM, I'M SORRY. I WAS JUST CURIOUS. I THOUGHT MAYBE YOU HAD KIDS OR A WIFE OR--

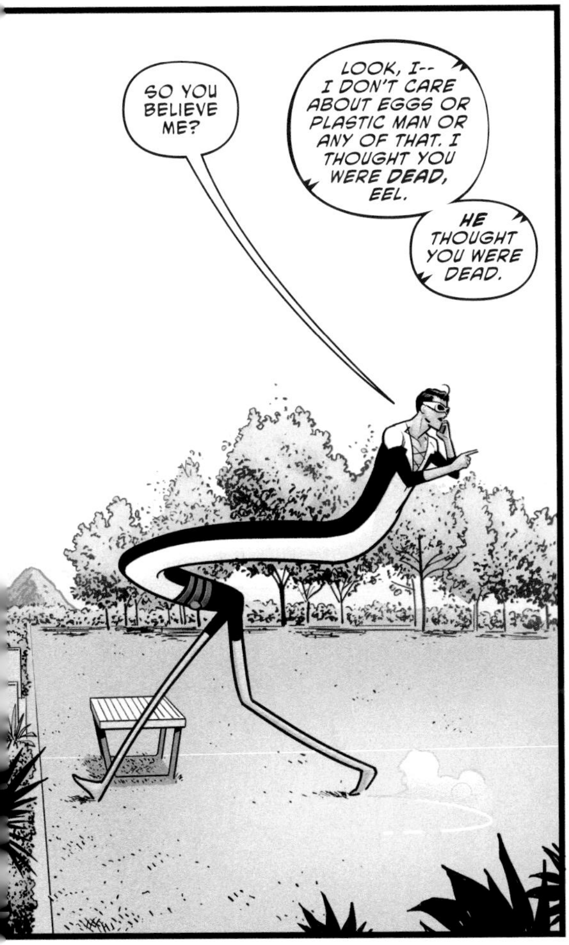
LOOK, I-- I DON'T CARE ABOUT EGGS OR PLASTIC MAN OR ANY OF THAT. I THOUGHT YOU WERE DEAD, EEL.
SO YOU BELIEVE ME?
HE THOUGHT YOU WERE DEAD.

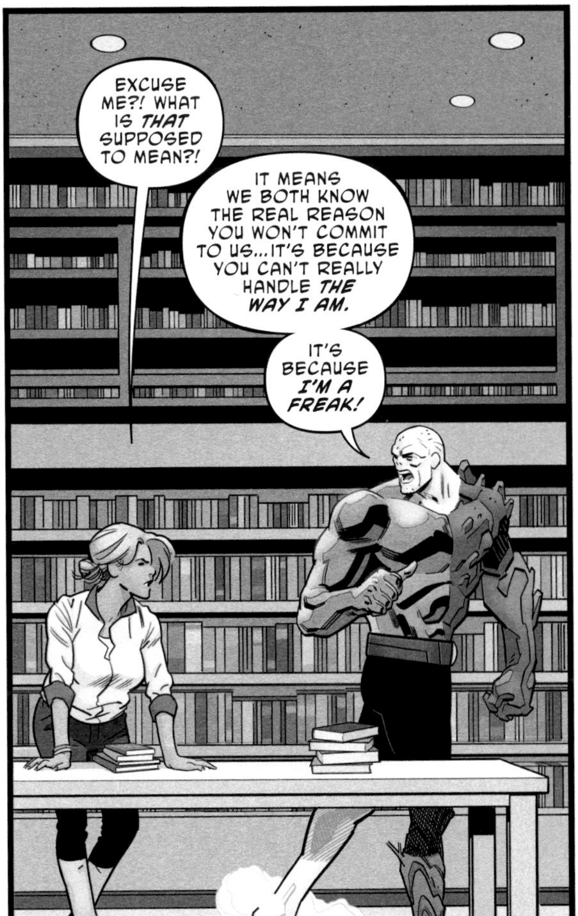
EXCUSE ME?! WHAT IS THAT SUPPOSED TO MEAN?!
IT MEANS WE BOTH KNOW THE REAL REASON YOU WON'T COMMIT TO US...IT'S BECAUSE YOU CAN'T REALLY HANDLE THE WAY I AM.
IT'S BECAUSE I'M A FREAK!

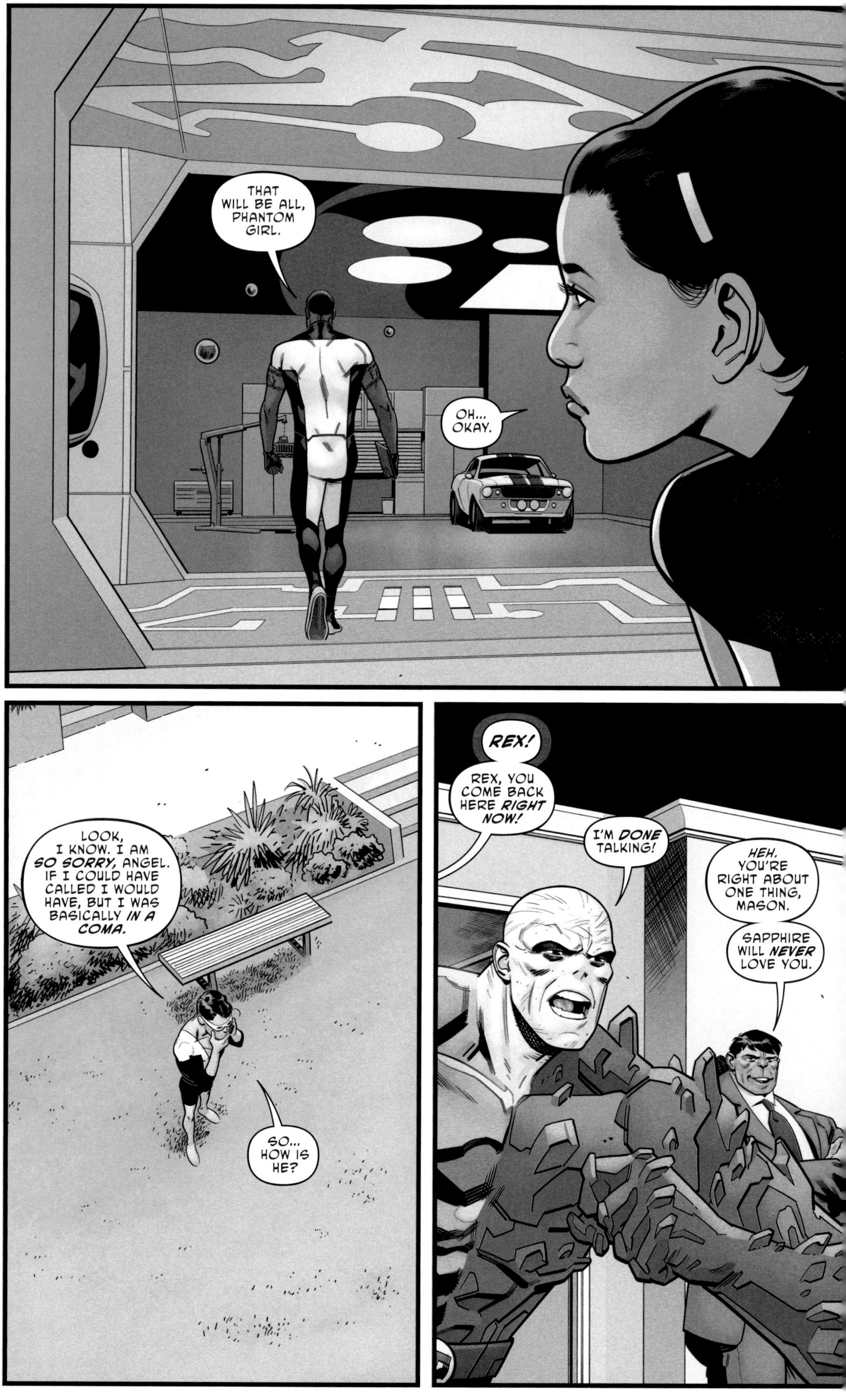
THAT WILL BE ALL, PHANTOM GIRL.
OH... OKAY.
LOOK, I KNOW. I AM *SO SORRY,* ANGEL. IF I COULD HAVE CALLED I WOULD HAVE, BUT I WAS BASICALLY *IN A COMA.*
SO... HOW IS HE?
REX!
REX, YOU COME BACK HERE *RIGHT NOW!*
I'M *DONE* TALKING!
HEH. YOU'RE RIGHT ABOUT ONE THING, MASON.
SAPPHIRE WILL *NEVER* LOVE YOU.

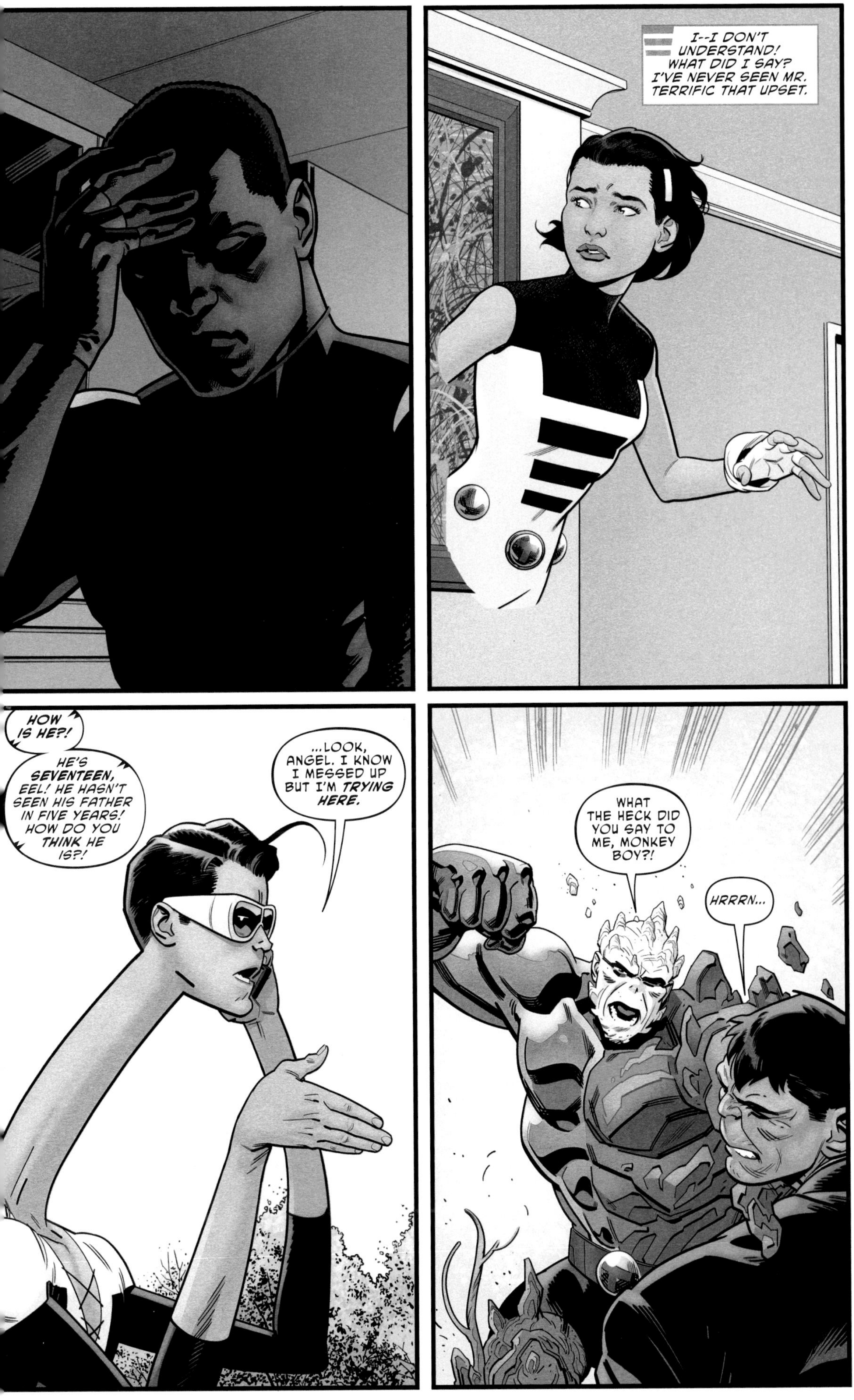
I--I DON'T UNDERSTAND! WHAT DID I SAY? I'VE NEVER SEEN MR. TERRIFIC THAT UPSET.
HOW IS HE?!
HE'S SEVENTEEN, EEL! HE HASN'T SEEN HIS FATHER IN FIVE YEARS! HOW DO YOU THINK HE IS?!
...LOOK, ANGEL. I KNOW I MESSED UP BUT I'M TRYING HERE.
WHAT THE HECK DID YOU SAY TO ME, MONKEY BOY?!
HRRRN...

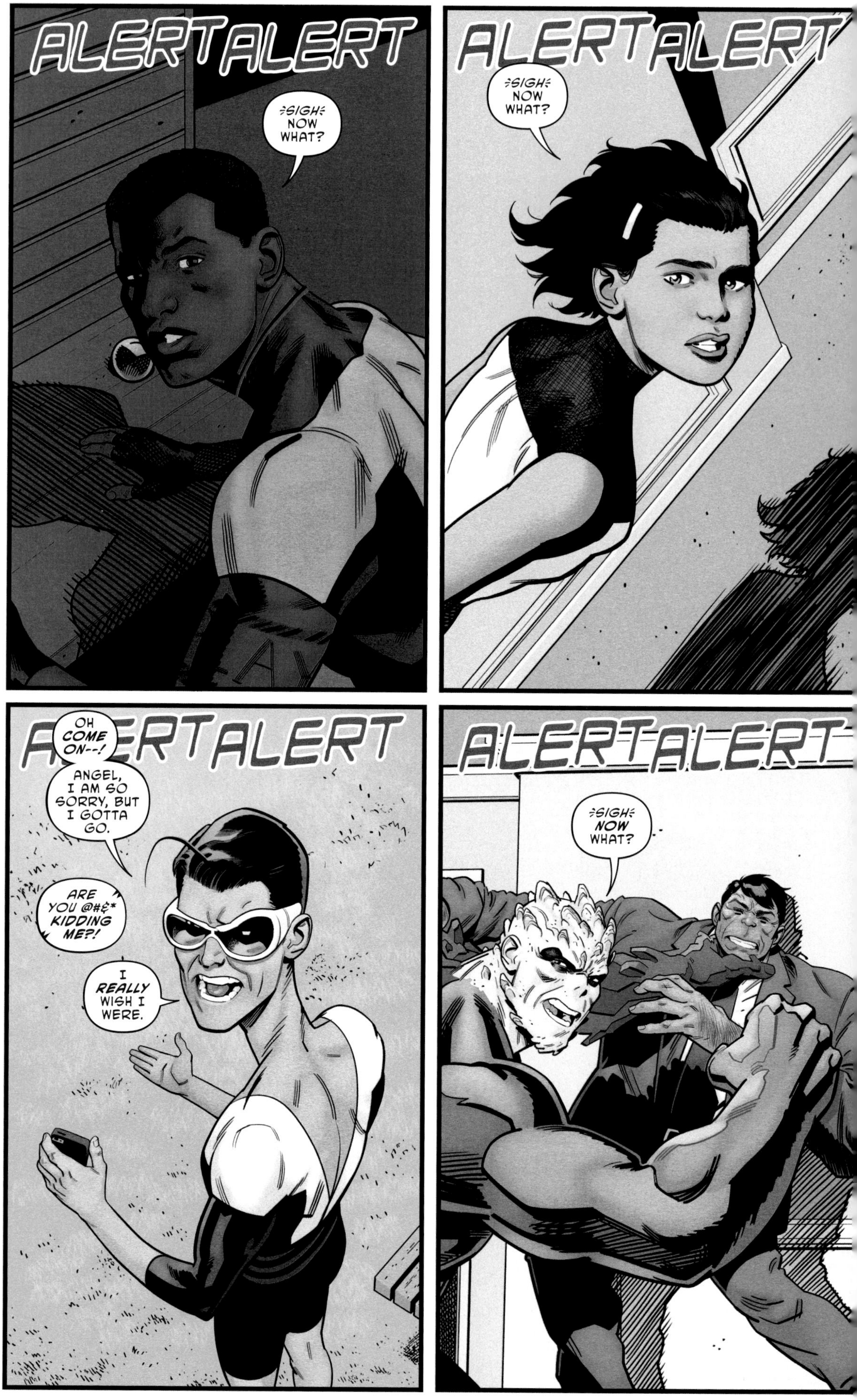
ALERT ALERT
SIGH NOW WHAT?
ALERT ALERT
SIGH NOW WHAT?
ERT ALERT
OH COME ON--!
ANGEL, I AM SO SORRY, BUT I GOTTA GO.
ARE YOU @#&* KIDDING ME?!
I REALLY WISH I WERE.
ALERT ALERT
SIGH NOW WHAT?

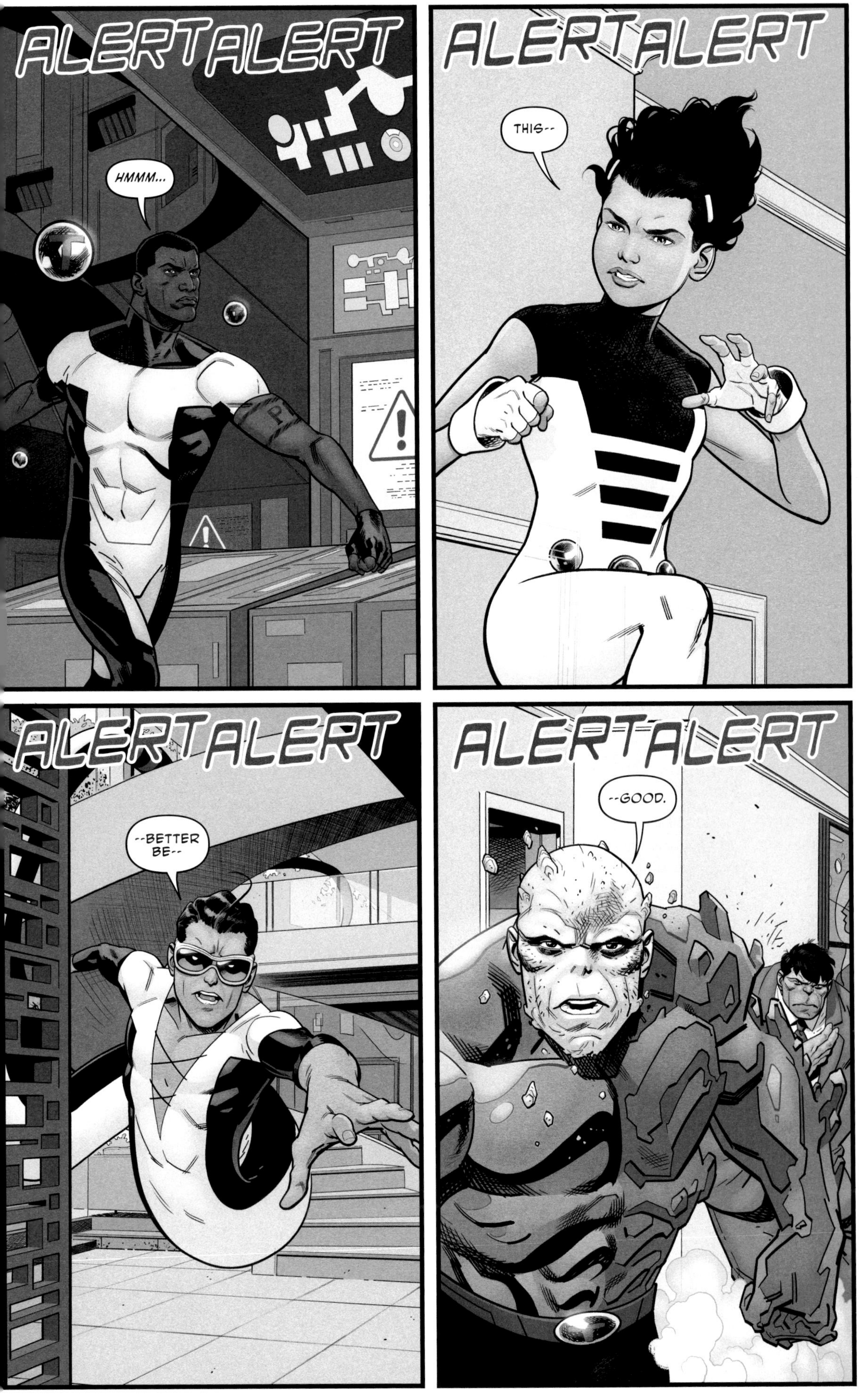
ALERTALERT
HMMM...
ALERTALERT
THIS--
ALERTALERT
--BETTER BE--
ALERTALERT
--GOOD.

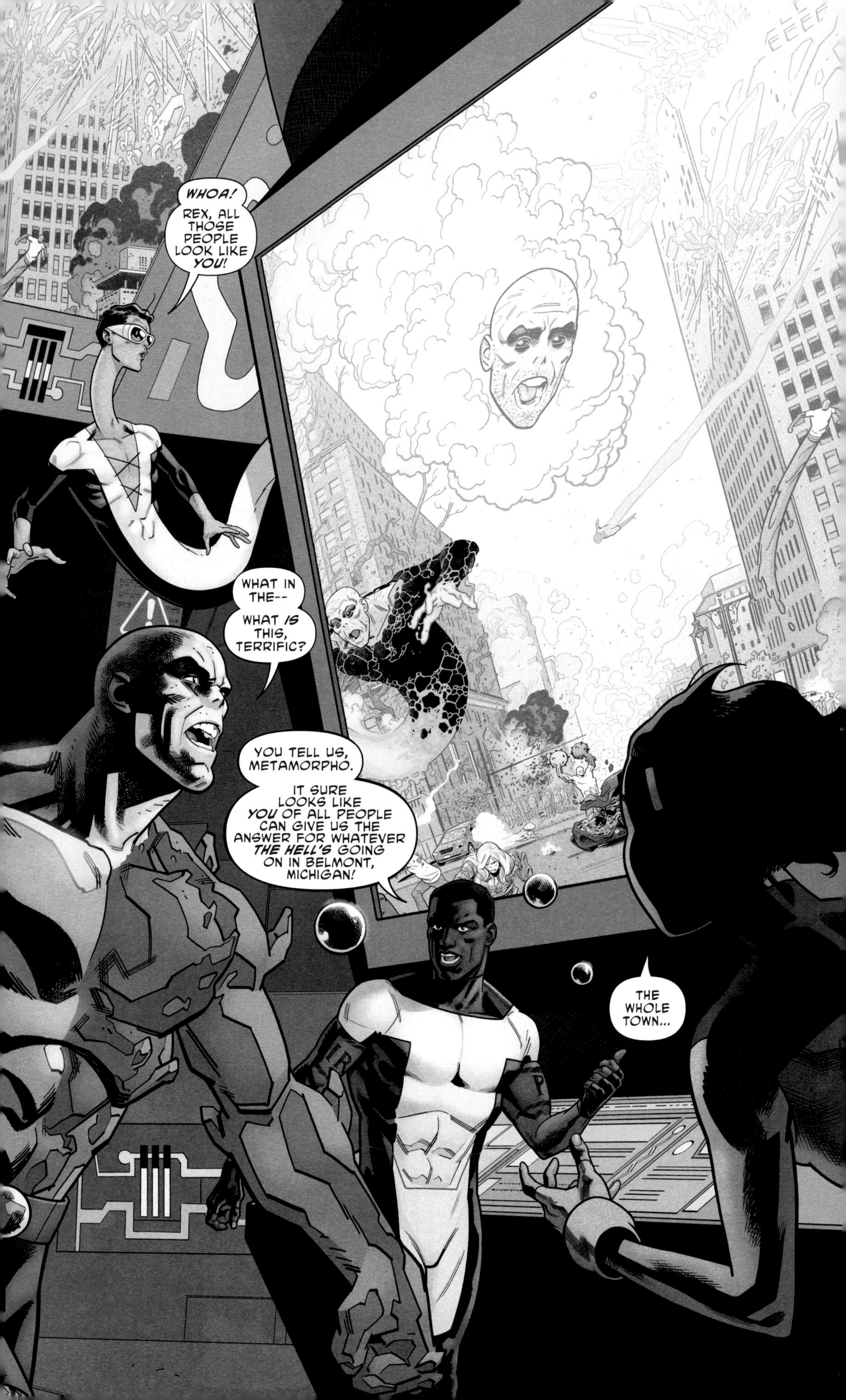
WHOA!
REX, ALL THOSE PEOPLE LOOK LIKE YOU!
WHAT IN THE--
WHAT IS THIS, TERRIFIC?
YOU TELL US, METAMORPHO.
IT SURE LOOKS LIKE YOU OF ALL PEOPLE CAN GIVE US THE ANSWER FOR WHATEVER THE HELL'S GOING ON IN BELMONT, MICHIGAN!
THE WHOLE TOWN...

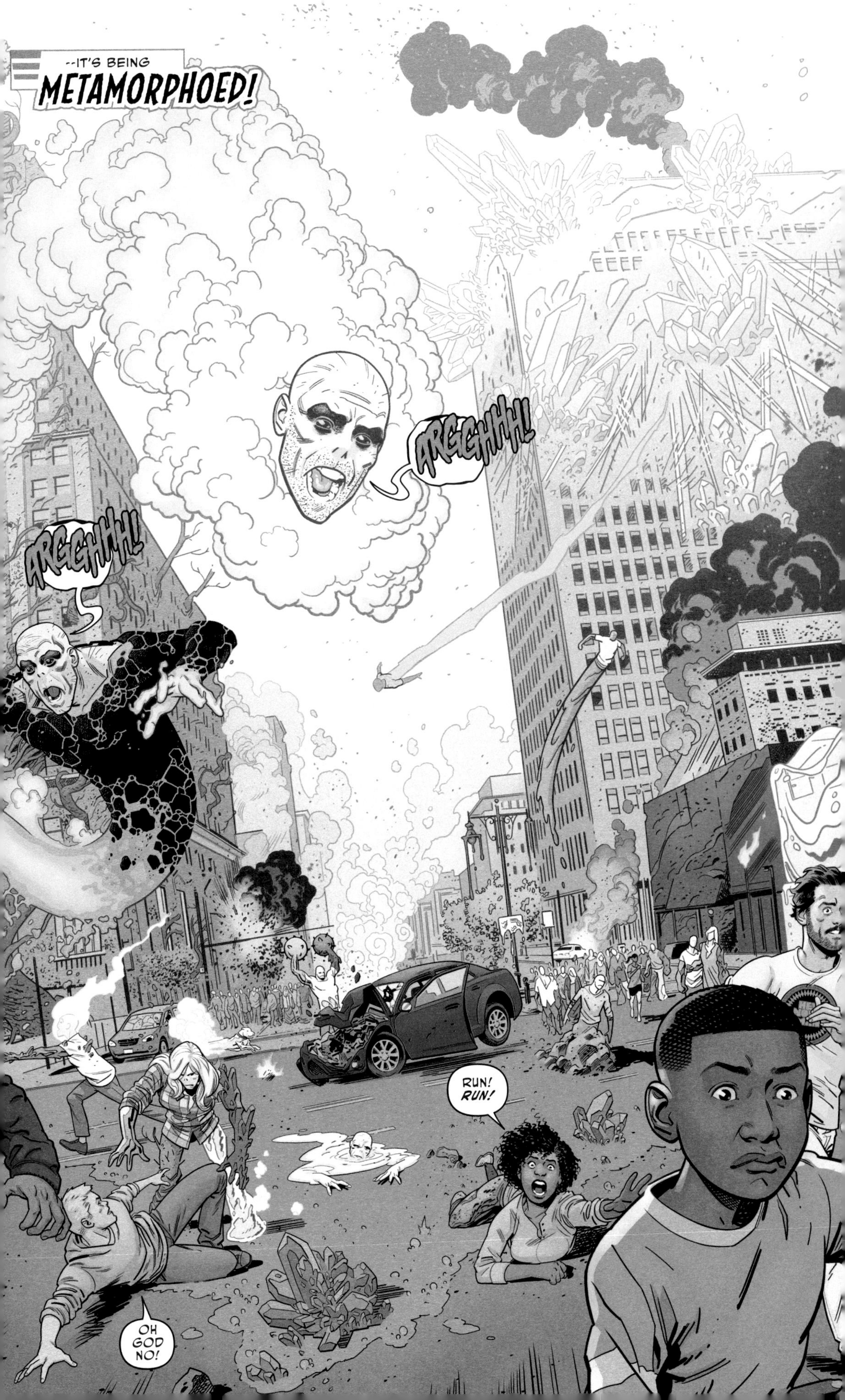
--IT'S BEING
METAMORPHOED!
ARGGHHH!
ARGGHHH!
RUN! RUN!
OH GOD NO!

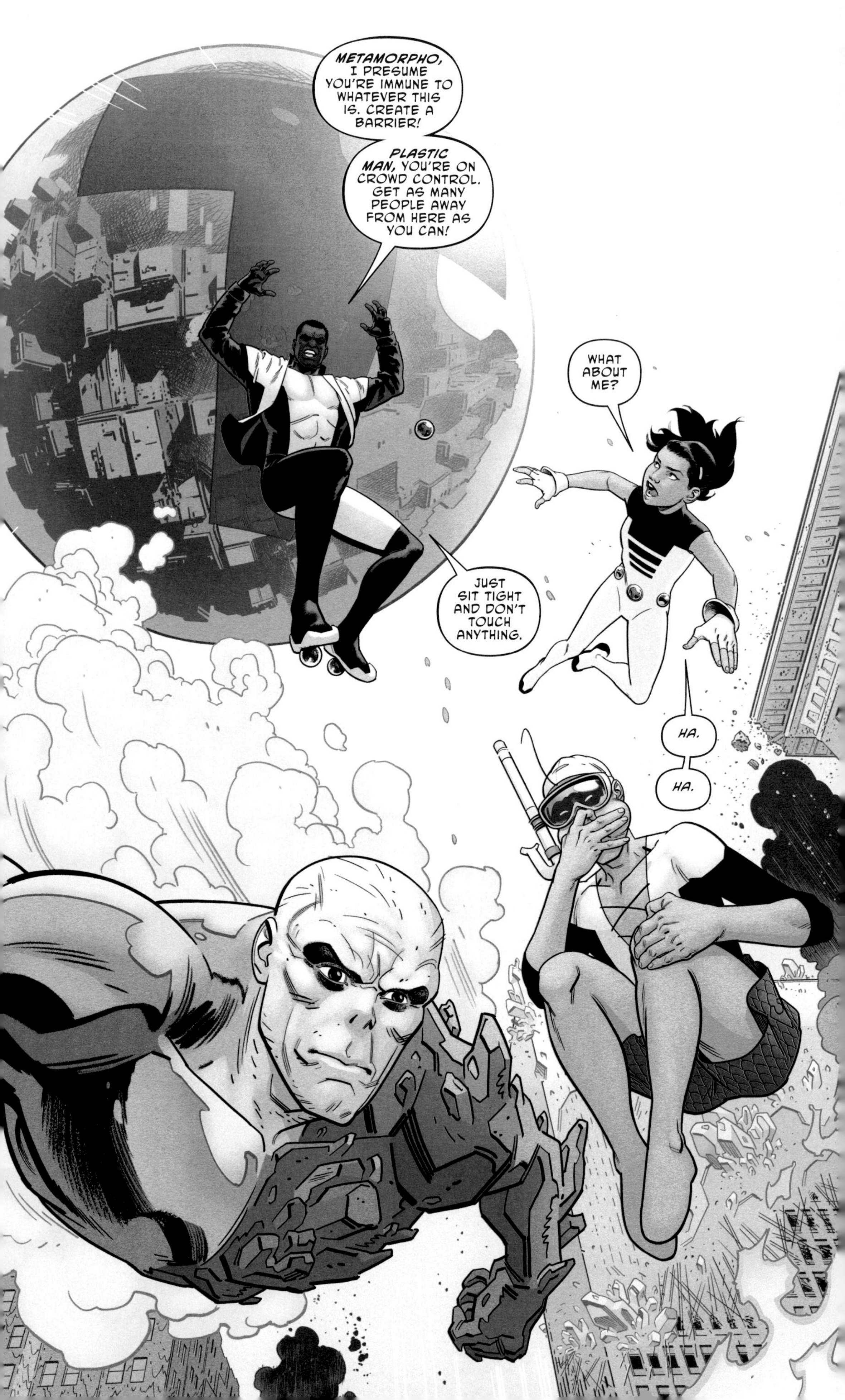
METAMORPHO, I PRESUME YOU'RE IMMUNE TO WHATEVER THIS IS. CREATE A BARRIER!
PLASTIC MAN, YOU'RE ON CROWD CONTROL. GET AS MANY PEOPLE AWAY FROM HERE AS YOU CAN!
WHAT ABOUT ME?
JUST SIT TIGHT AND DON'T TOUCH ANYTHING.
HA.
HA.

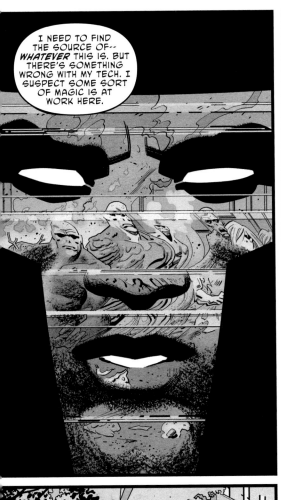

I NEED TO FIND THE SOURCE OF-- *WHATEVER* THIS IS. BUT THERE'S SOMETHING WRONG WITH MY TECH. I SUSPECT SOME SORT OF MAGIC IS AT WORK HERE.

IS THAT--AN *ELEMENT DOG*?!

ARK! ARK!

MAGIC?!

WHAT DID YOU DO *NOW,* REX?

ME?! I *DIDN'T DO ANYTHING!*

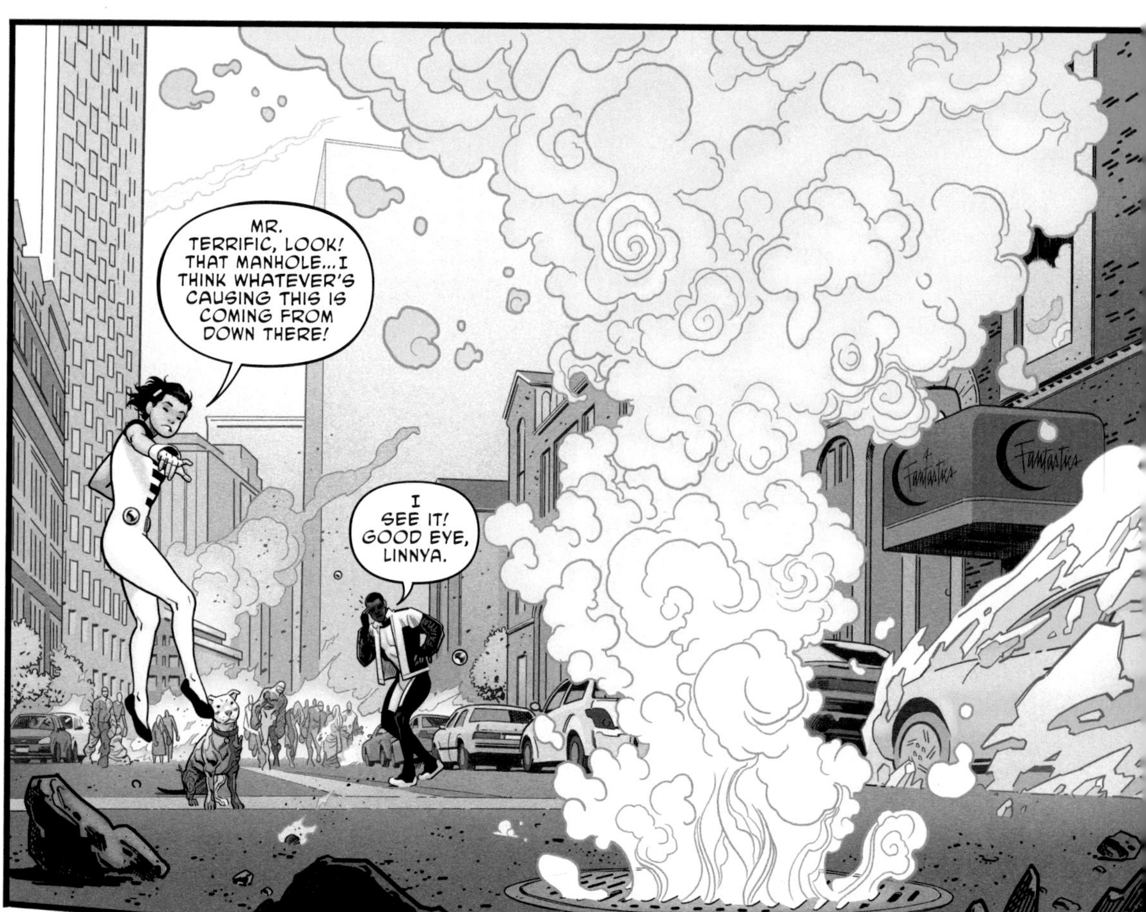
MR. TERRIFIC, LOOK! THAT MANHOLE...I THINK WHATEVER'S CAUSING THIS IS COMING FROM DOWN THERE!
I SEE IT! GOOD EYE, LINNYA.
Fantastics

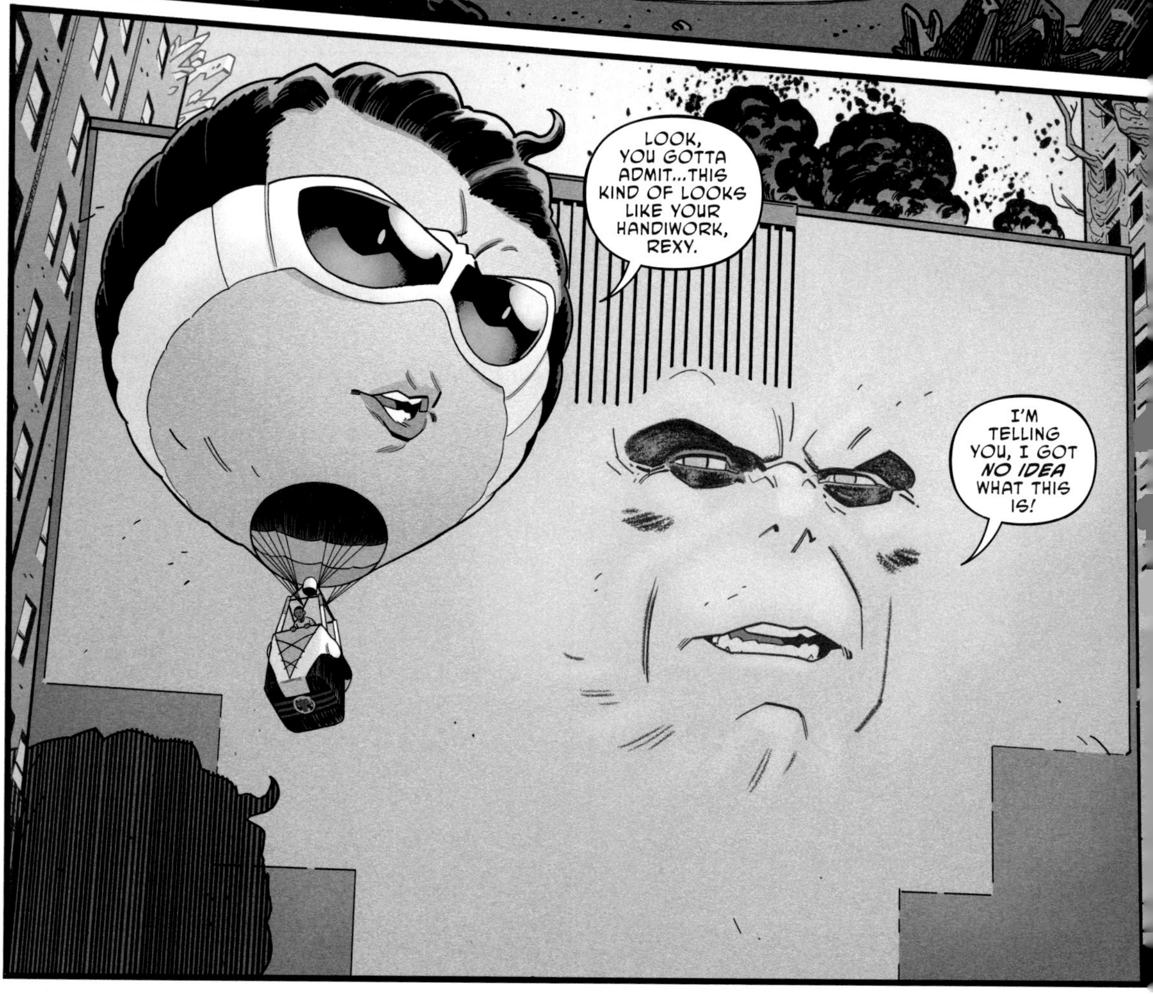
LOOK, YOU GOTTA ADMIT...THIS KIND OF LOOKS LIKE YOUR HANDIWORK, REXY.
I'M TELLING YOU, I GOT *NO IDEA* WHAT THIS IS!

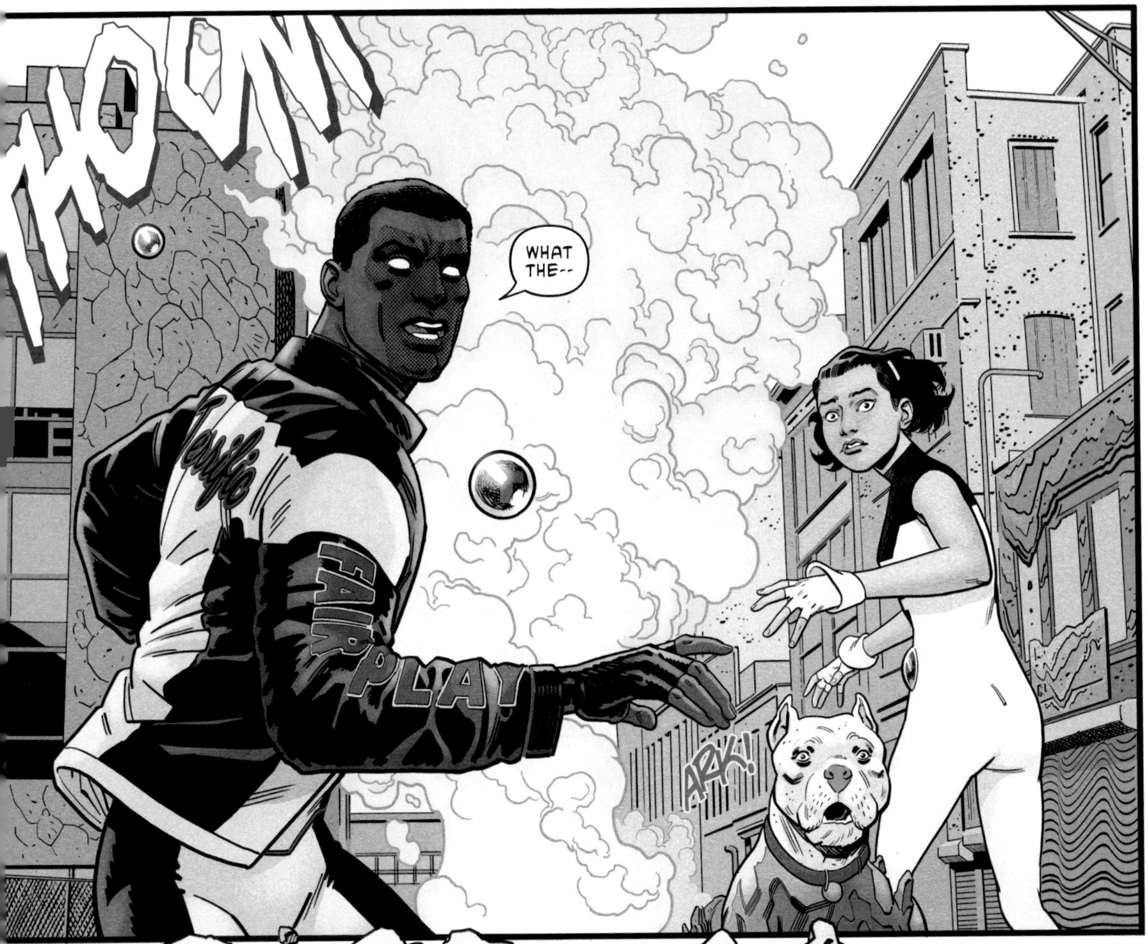
THOOM
WHAT THE--
FAIR PLAY
ARK!
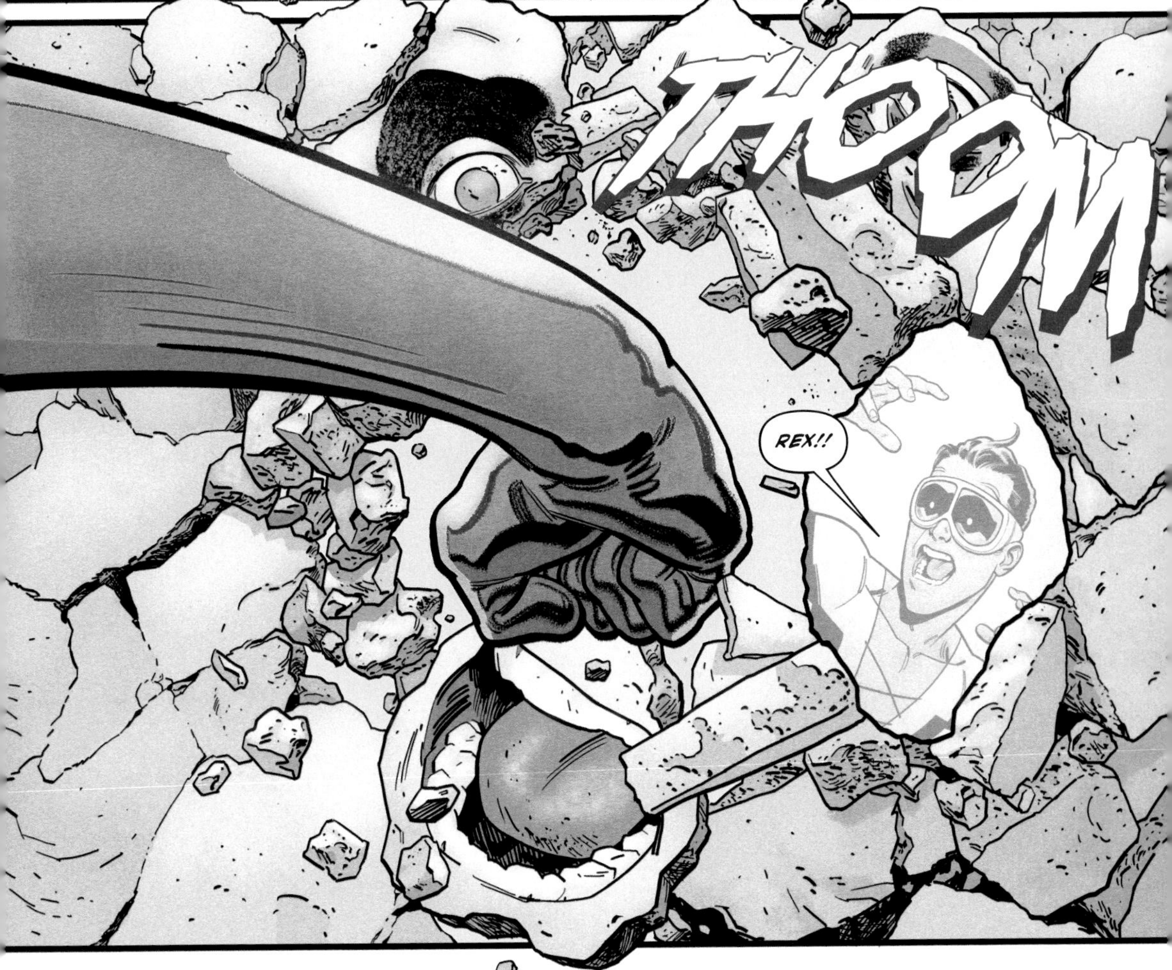
THOOM
REX!!

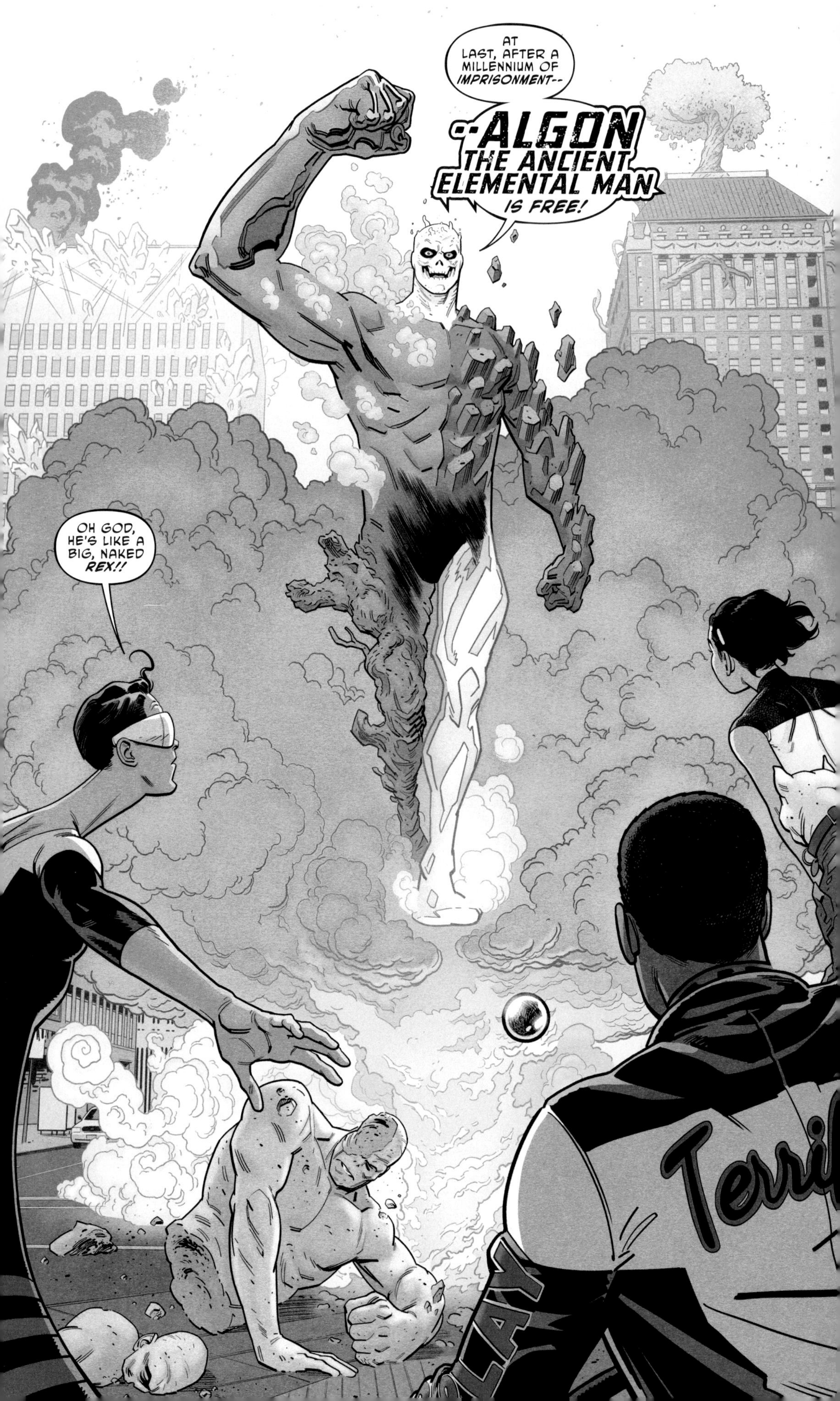
AT LAST, AFTER A MILLENNIUM OF IMPRISONMENT--
--ALGON THE ANCIENT ELEMENTAL MAN IS FREE!
OH GOD, HE'S LIKE A BIG, NAKED REX!!
Terri
PLAY

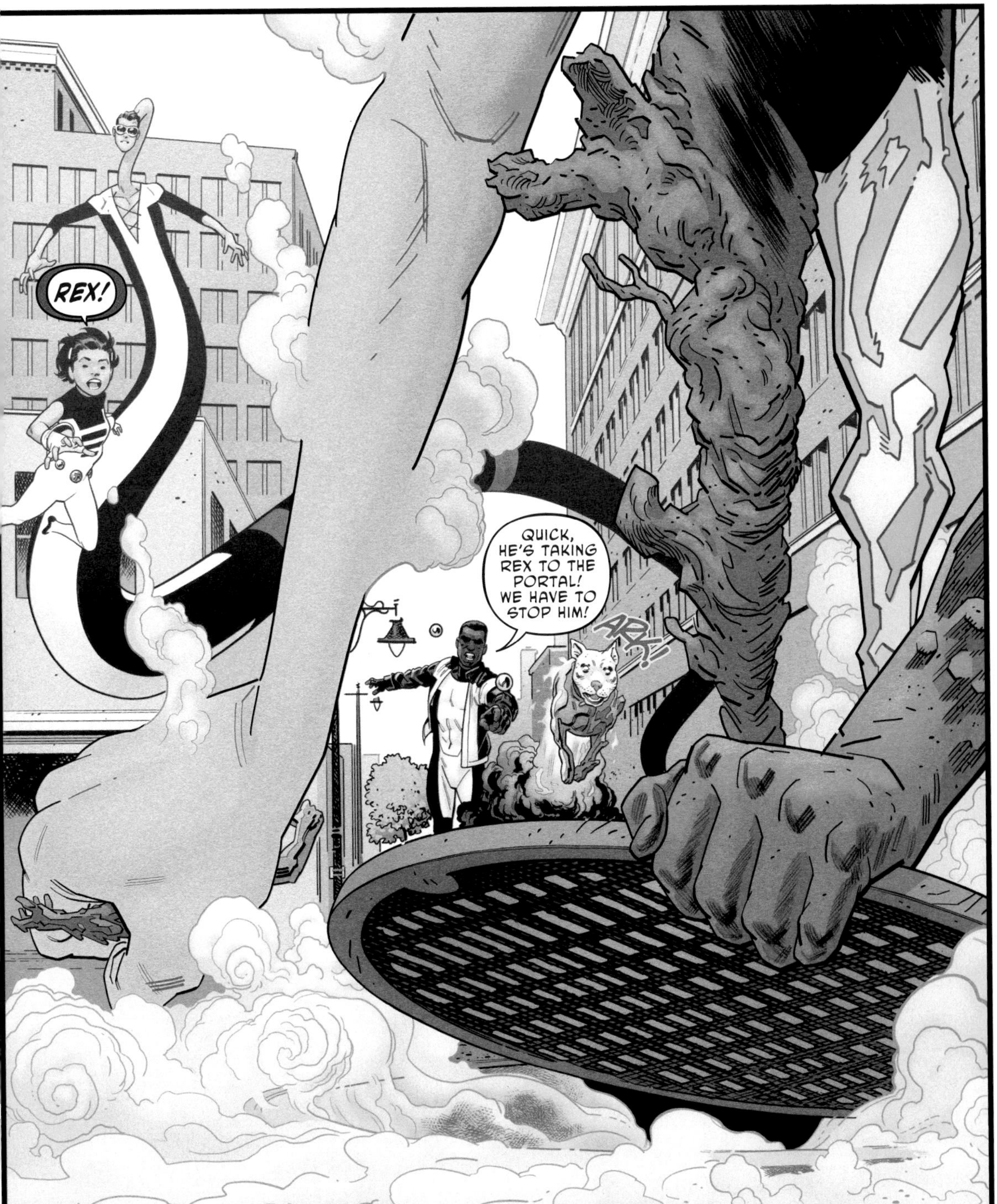
REX!
QUICK, HE'S TAKING REX TO THE PORTAL! WE HAVE TO STOP HIM!
ARF!

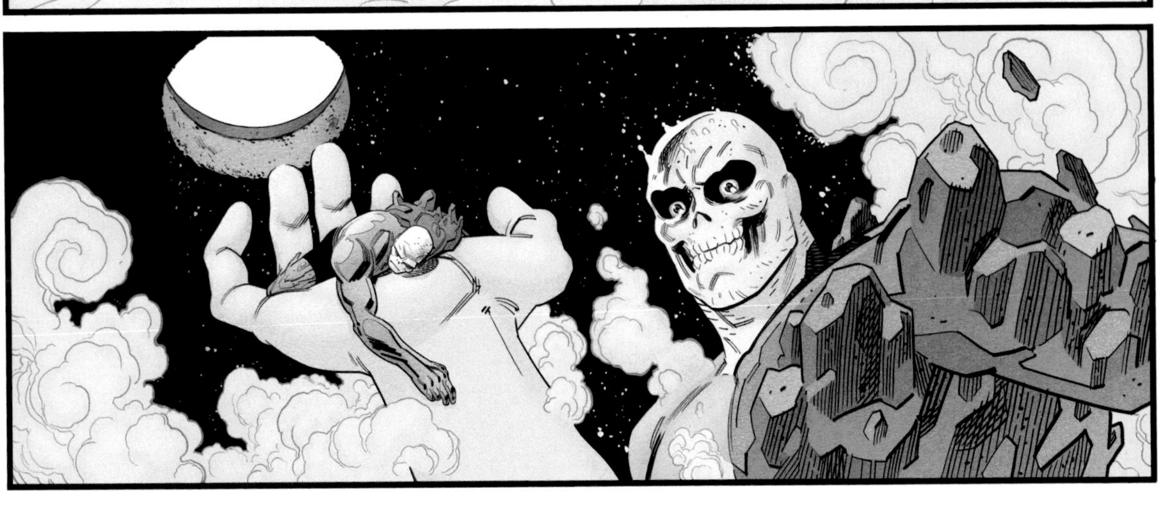

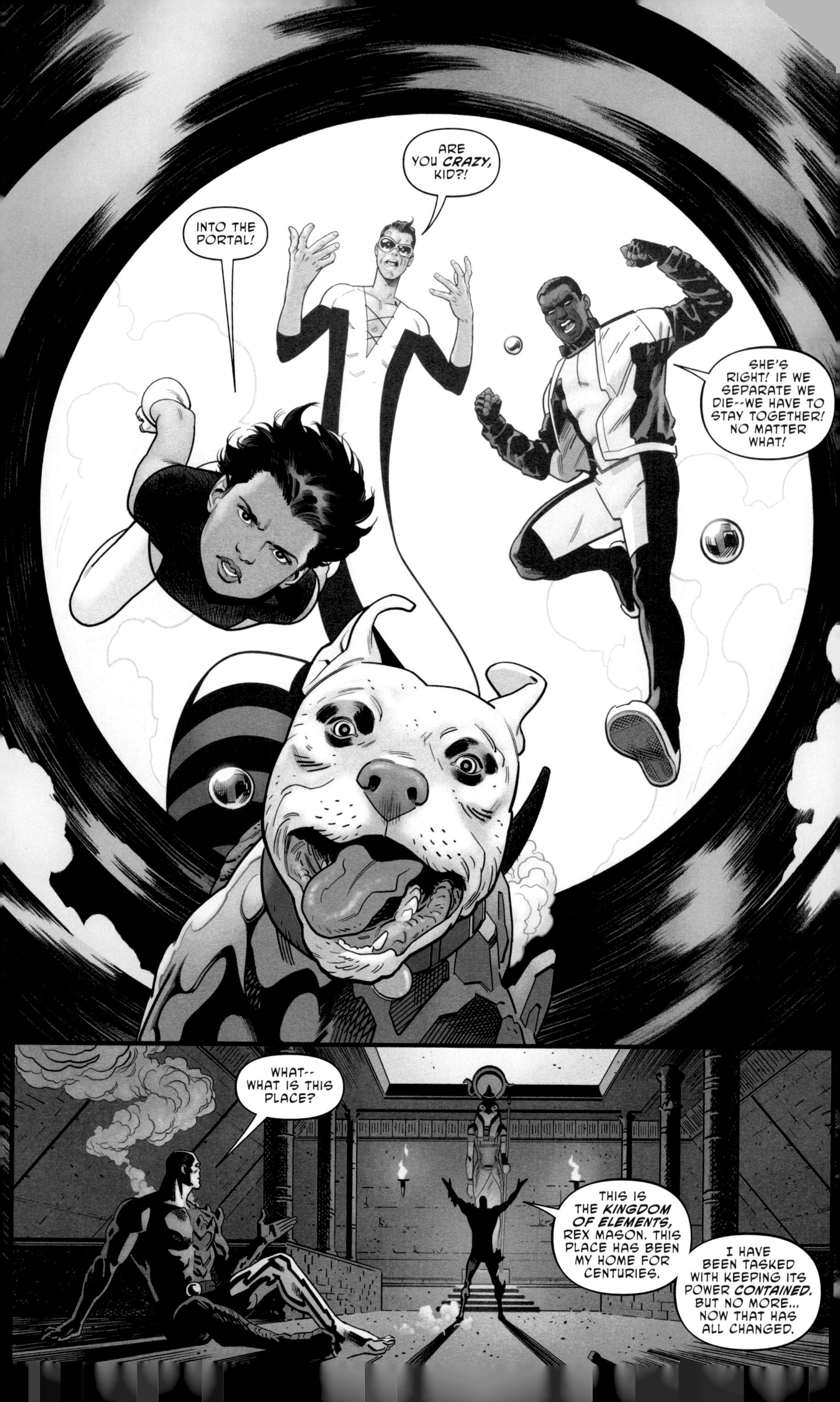
INTO THE PORTAL!
ARE YOU CRAZY, KID?!
SHE'S RIGHT! IF WE SEPARATE WE DIE--WE HAVE TO STAY TOGETHER! NO MATTER WHAT!
WHAT-- WHAT IS THIS PLACE?
THIS IS THE KINGDOM OF ELEMENTS, REX MASON. THIS PLACE HAS BEEN MY HOME FOR CENTURIES.
I HAVE BEEN TASKED WITH KEEPING ITS POWER CONTAINED. BUT NO MORE... NOW THAT HAS ALL CHANGED.

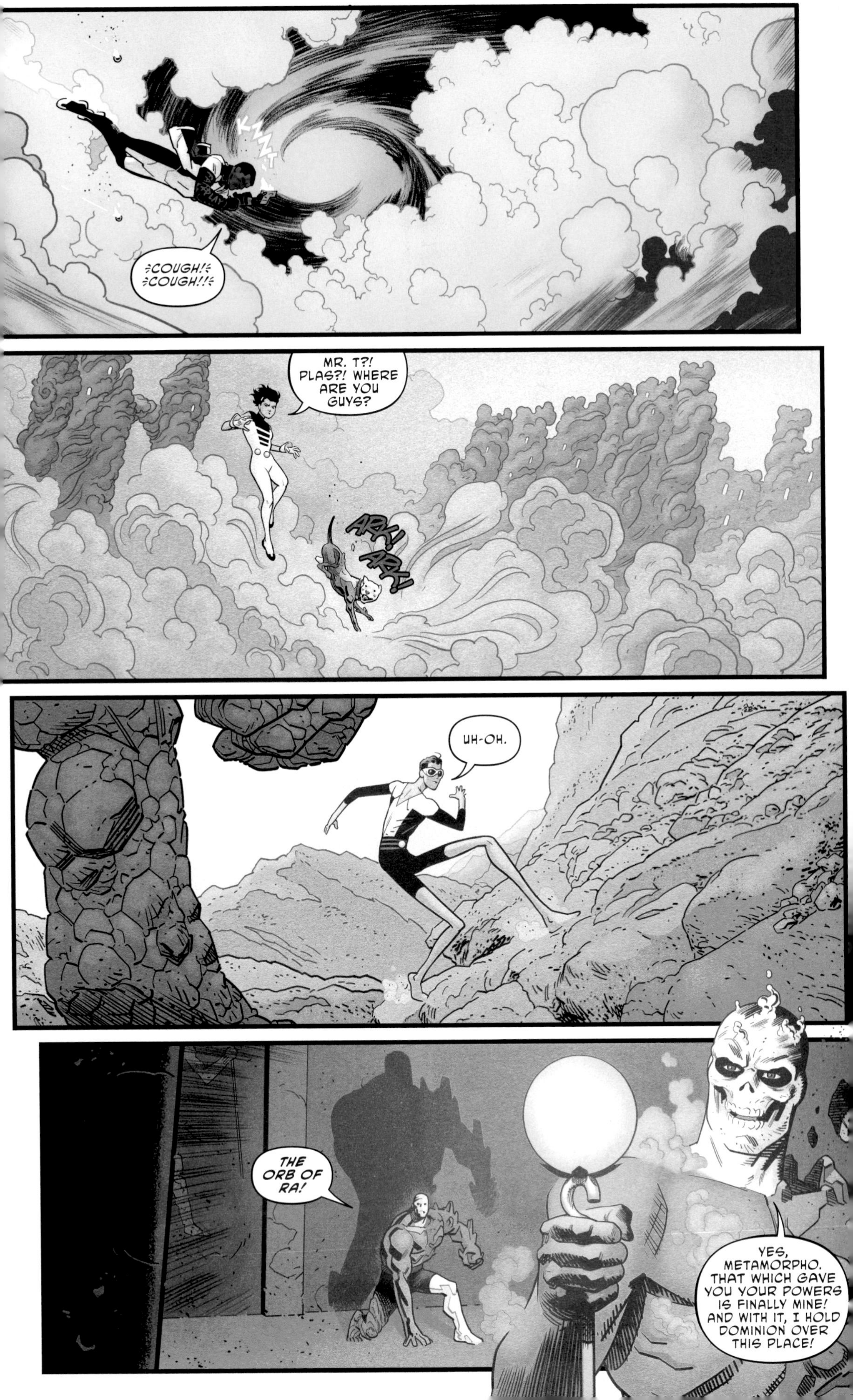
KZZZT
¡COUGH!¡ ¡COUGH!!¡
MR. T?! PLAS?! WHERE ARE YOU GUYS?
ARK! ARK!
UH-OH.
THE ORB OF RA!
YES, METAMORPHO. THAT WHICH GAVE YOU YOUR POWERS IS FINALLY MINE! AND WITH IT, I HOLD DOMINION OVER THIS PLACE!

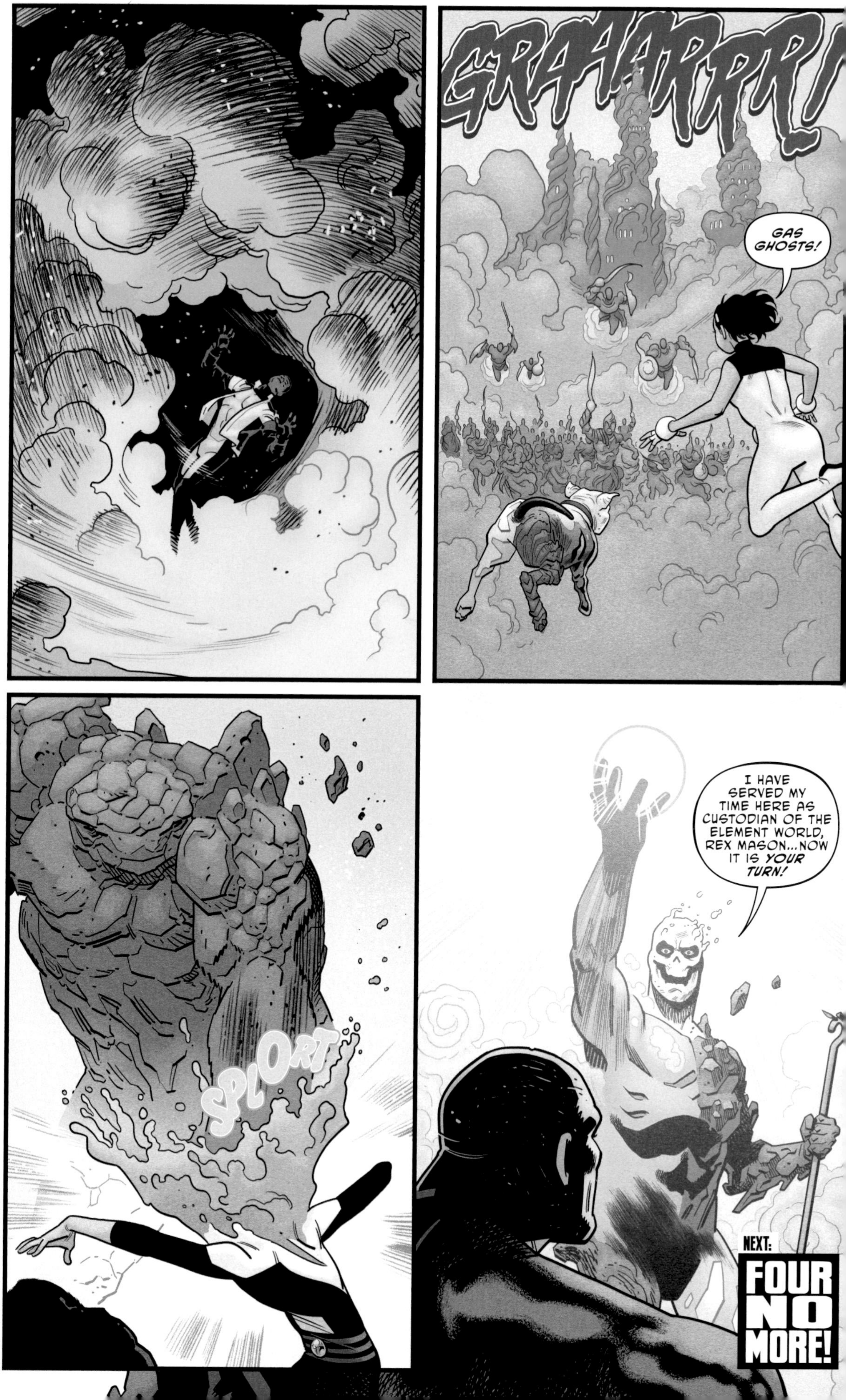
GRAAARRR!
GAS GHOSTS!
SPLORT
I HAVE SERVED MY TIME HERE AS CUSTODIAN OF THE ELEMENT WORLD, REX MASON...NOW IT IS *YOUR TURN!*
NEXT:
FOUR NO MORE!

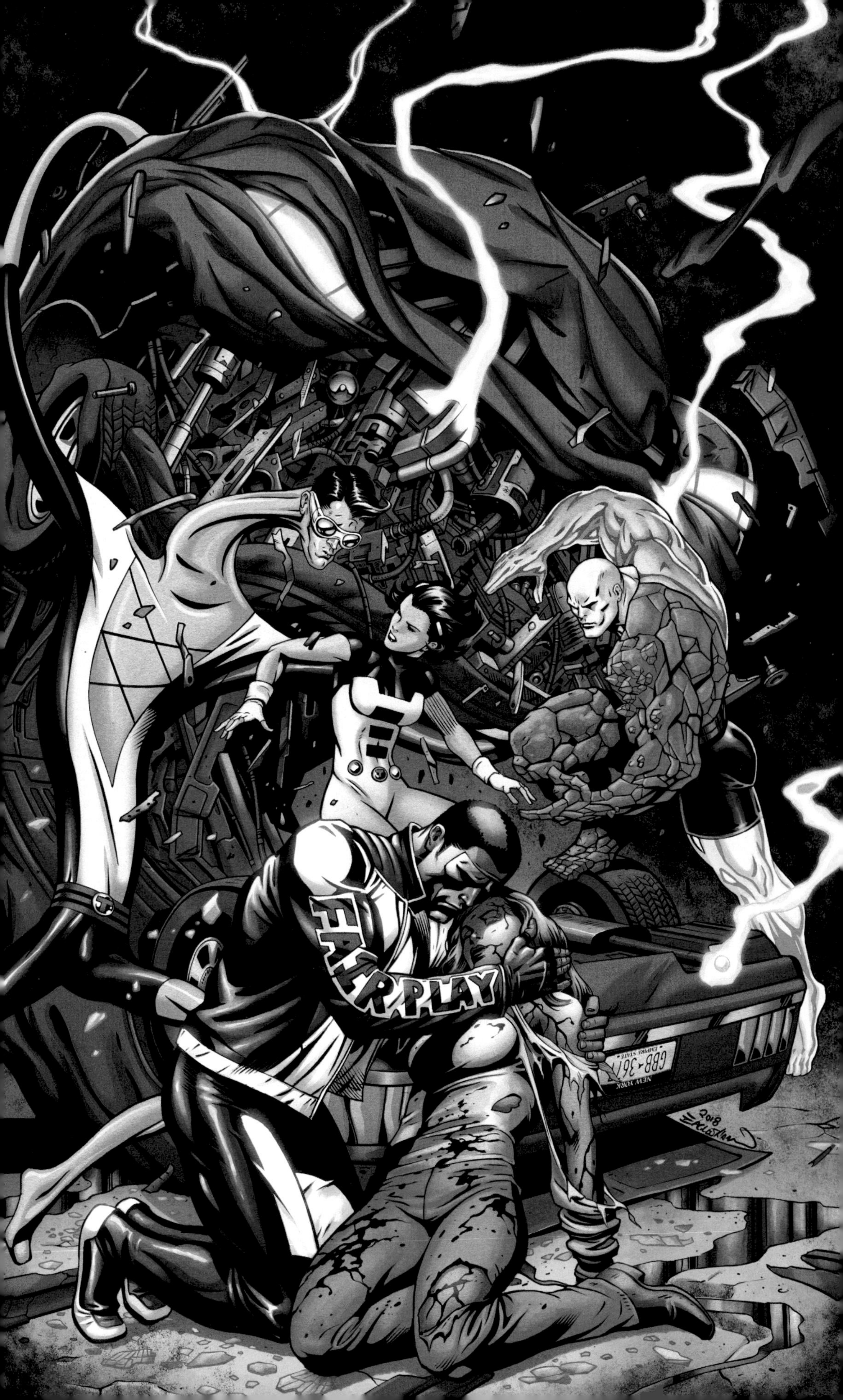
FAIR PLAY
EMPIRE STATE
NEW YORK

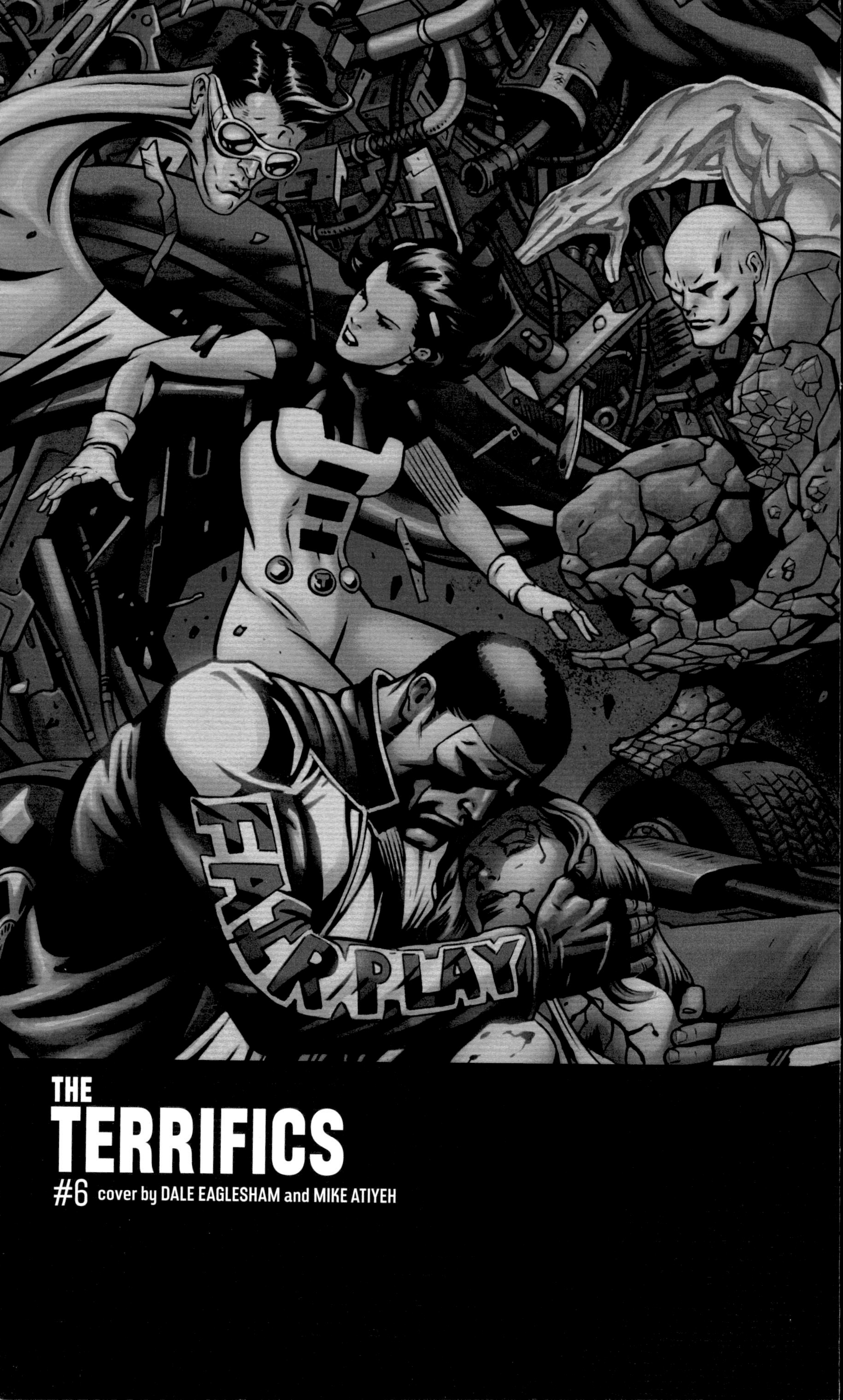
FAIR PLAY

THE
TERRIFICS
#6 cover by DALE EAGLESHAM and MIKE ATIYEH

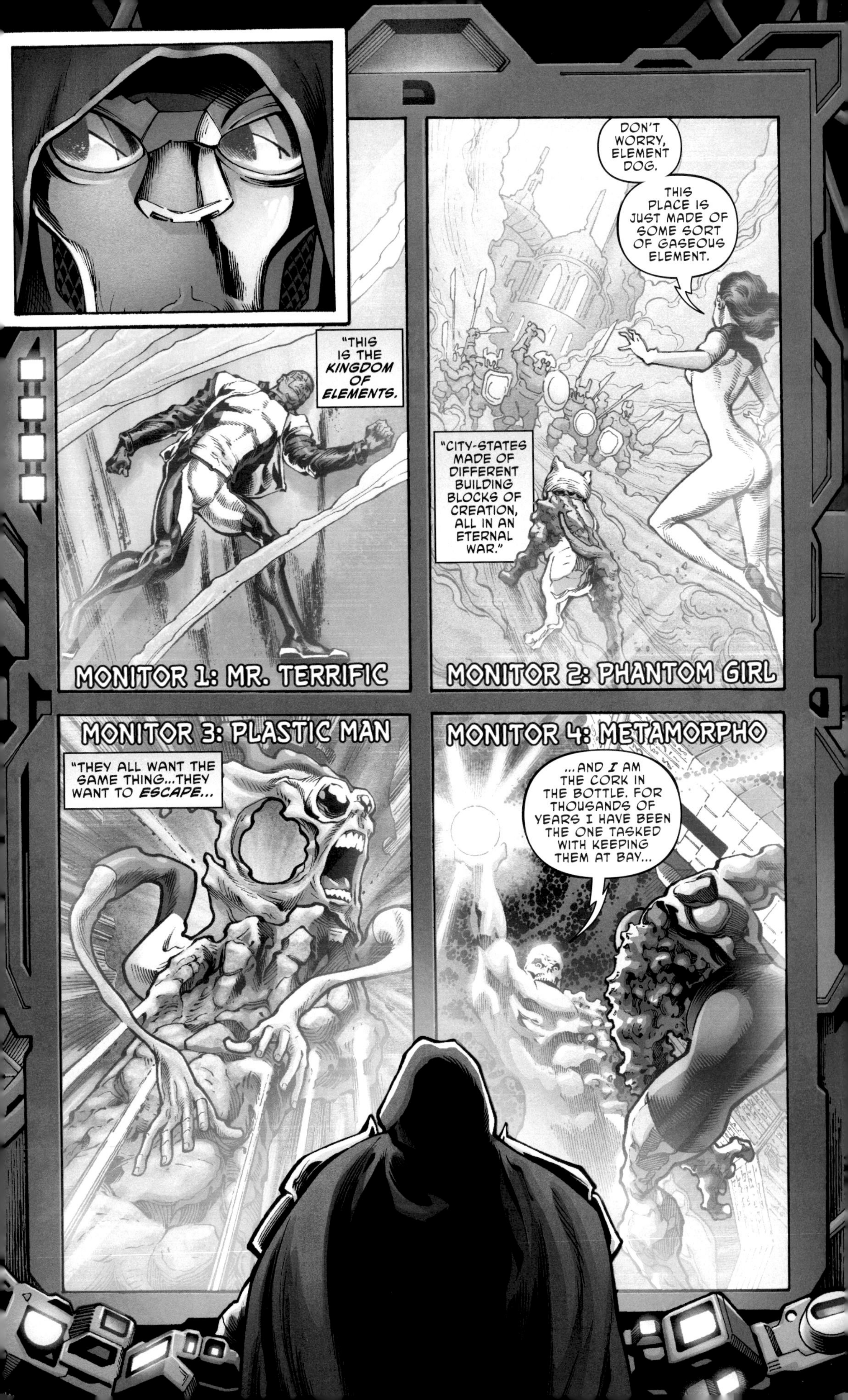
"THIS IS THE KINGDOM OF ELEMENTS.
MONITOR 1: MR. TERRIFIC
DON'T WORRY, ELEMENT DOG.
THIS PLACE IS JUST MADE OF SOME SORT OF GASEOUS ELEMENT.
"CITY-STATES MADE OF DIFFERENT BUILDING BLOCKS OF CREATION, ALL IN AN ETERNAL WAR."
MONITOR 2: PHANTOM GIRL
MONITOR 3: PLASTIC MAN
"THEY ALL WANT THE SAME THING...THEY WANT TO ESCAPE...
MONITOR 4: METAMORPHO
...AND I AM THE CORK IN THE BOTTLE. FOR THOUSANDS OF YEARS I HAVE BEEN THE ONE TASKED WITH KEEPING THEM AT BAY...

MICHAEL... MICHAEL, YOU HAVE TO *WAKE UP.*

--UNGH.

JOE BENNETT & JEFF LEMIRE STORYTELLERS

SANDRA HOPE AND MATT SANTORELLI INKS
HI-FI COLORS   TOM NAPOLITANO LETTERS

THEY CAN'T HURT U--*OUCH!*

SHOOM

DALE EAGLESHAM AND MIKE ATIYEH COVER
ANDREW MARINO ASSISTANT EDITOR
PAUL KAMINSKI EDITOR   MARIE JAVINS GROUP EDITOR

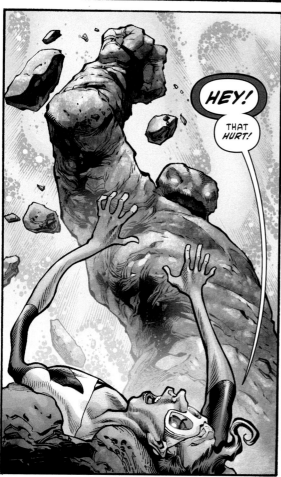

HEY!

THAT *HURT!*

...BUT NOW *YOU* WILL TAKE MY PLACE, METAMORPHO!

YOU WILL BE STUCK HERE AND *I* WILL BE *FREE.*

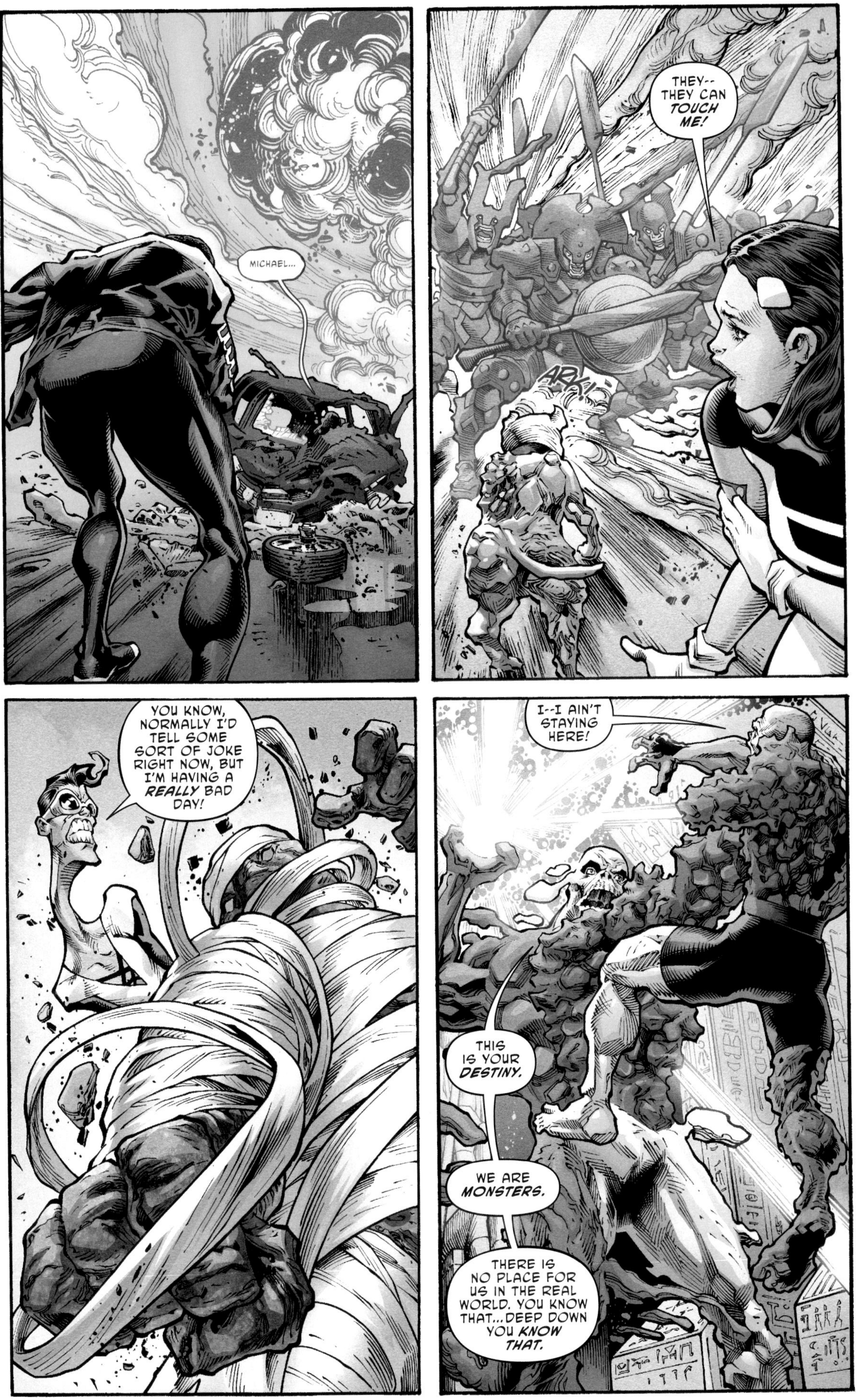
MICHAEL...
THEY-- THEY CAN TOUCH ME!
ARK!
YOU KNOW, NORMALLY I'D TELL SOME SORT OF JOKE RIGHT NOW, BUT I'M HAVING A REALLY BAD DAY!
I--I AIN'T STAYING HERE!
THIS IS YOUR DESTINY.
WE ARE MONSTERS.
THERE IS NO PLACE FOR US IN THE REAL WORLD. YOU KNOW THAT...DEEP DOWN YOU KNOW THAT.

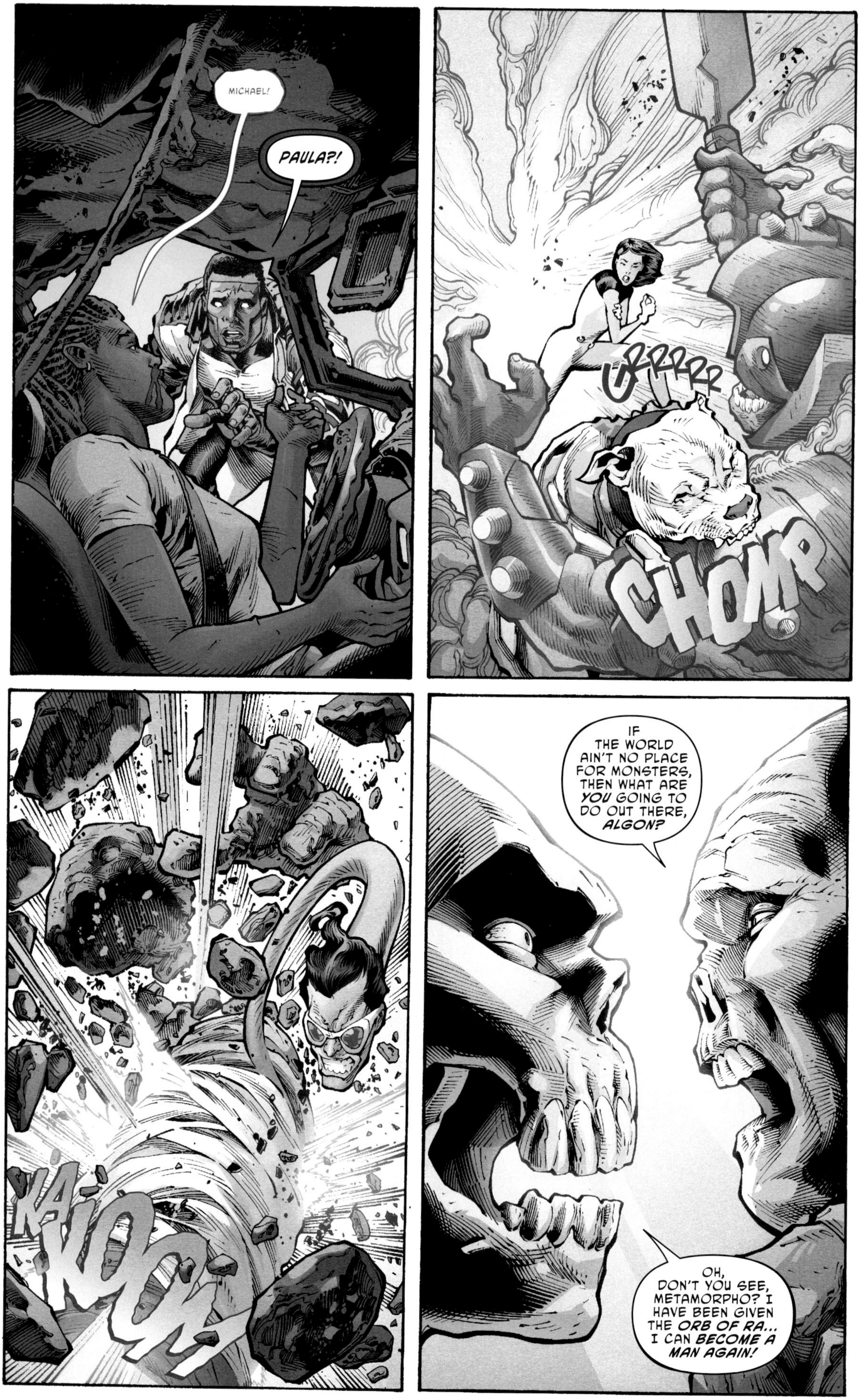
MICHAEL!
PAULA?!
GRRRRR
CHOMP
KA
IF THE WORLD AIN'T NO PLACE FOR MONSTERS, THEN WHAT ARE *YOU* GOING TO DO OUT THERE, *ALGON?*
OH, DON'T YOU SEE, METAMORPHO? I HAVE BEEN GIVEN THE *ORB OF RA*... I CAN *BECOME A MAN AGAIN!*

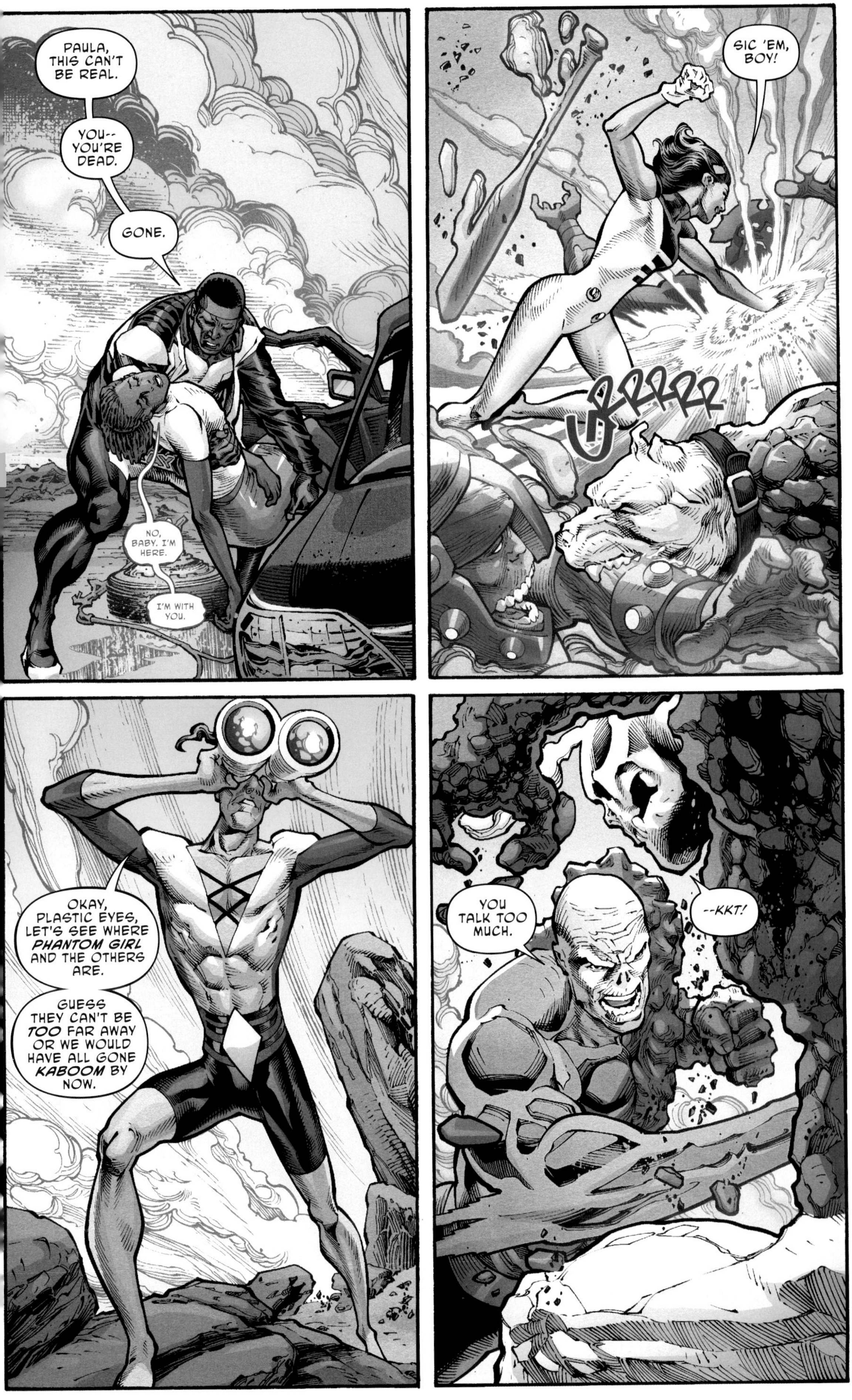
PAULA, THIS CAN'T BE REAL.
YOU-- YOU'RE DEAD.
GONE.
NO, BABY. I'M HERE.
I'M WITH YOU.
SIC 'EM, BOY!
GRRRRR
OKAY, PLASTIC EYES, LET'S SEE WHERE *PHANTOM GIRL* AND THE OTHERS ARE.
GUESS THEY CAN'T BE *TOO* FAR AWAY OR WE WOULD HAVE ALL GONE *KABOOM* BY NOW.
YOU TALK TOO MUCH.
--KKT!

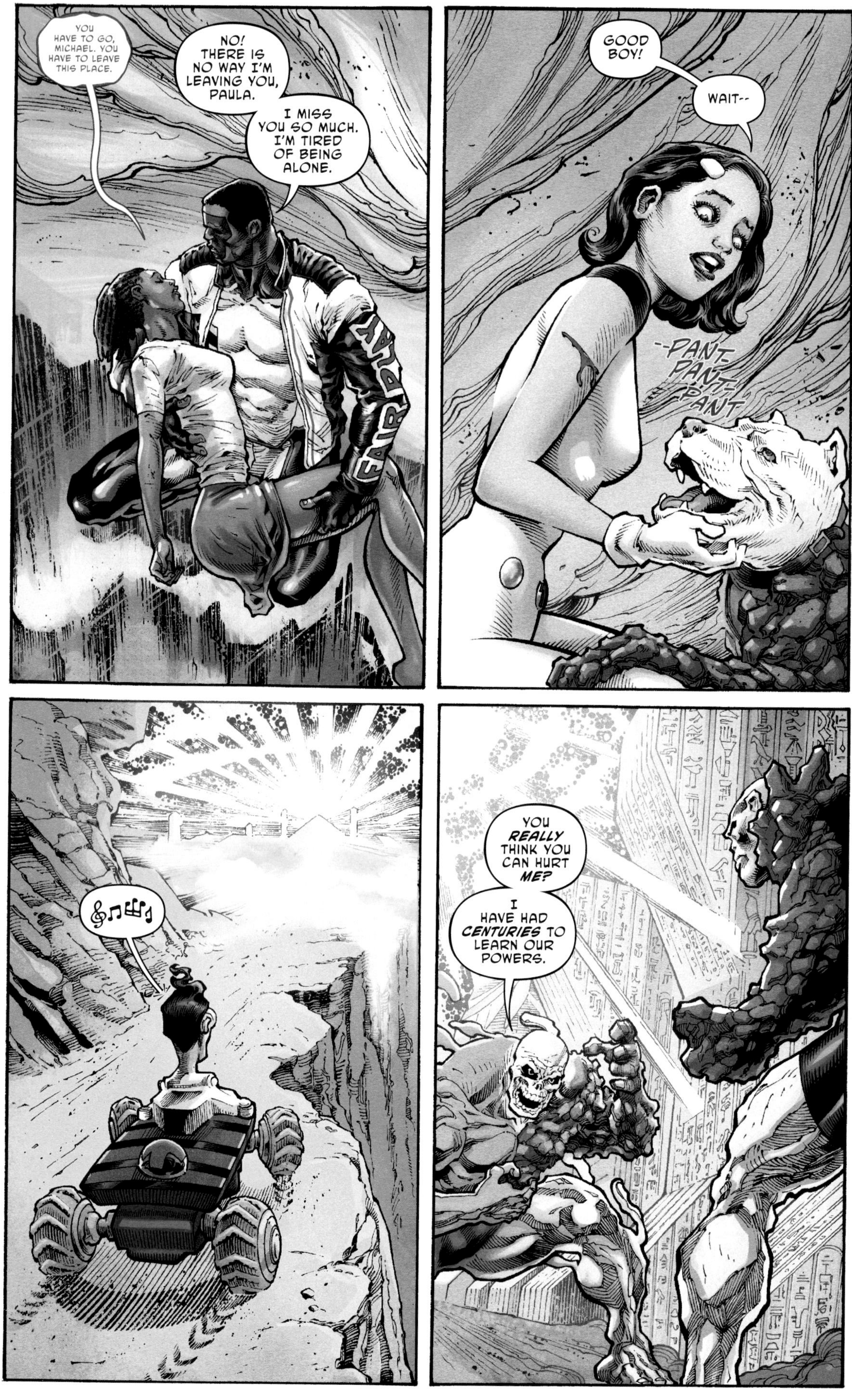
YOU HAVE TO GO, MICHAEL. YOU HAVE TO LEAVE THIS PLACE.
NO! THERE IS NO WAY I'M LEAVING YOU, PAULA.
I MISS YOU SO MUCH. I'M TIRED OF BEING ALONE.
GOOD BOY!
WAIT--
--PANT-PANT-PANT-PANT
YOU REALLY THINK YOU CAN HURT ME?
I HAVE HAD CENTURIES TO LEARN OUR POWERS.

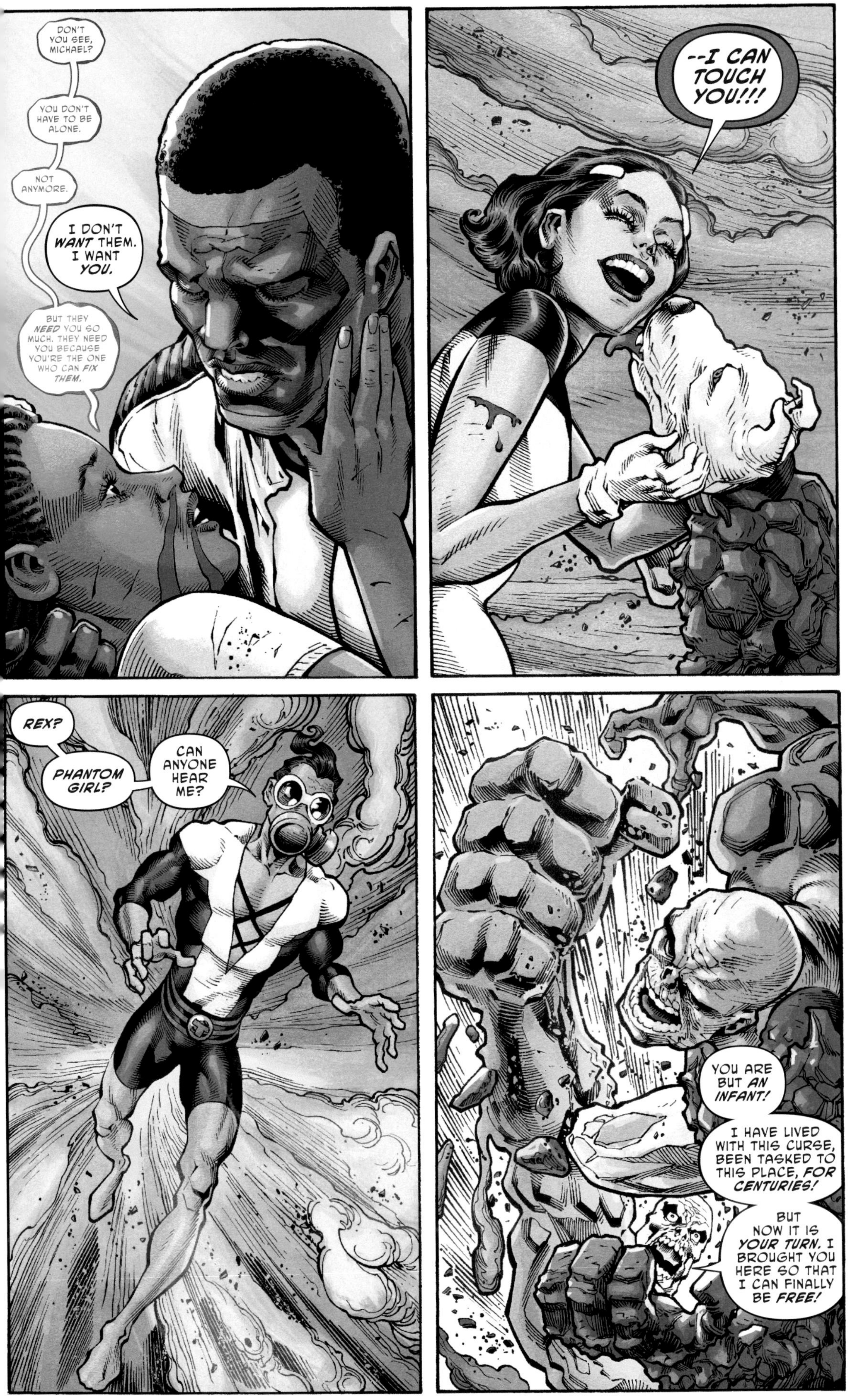
DON'T YOU SEE, MICHAEL?
YOU DON'T HAVE TO BE ALONE.
NOT ANYMORE.
I DON'T WANT THEM. I WANT YOU.
BUT THEY NEED YOU SO MUCH. THEY NEED YOU BECAUSE YOU'RE THE ONE WHO CAN FIX THEM.
--I CAN TOUCH YOU!!!
REX?
PHANTOM GIRL?
CAN ANYONE HEAR ME?
YOU ARE BUT AN INFANT!
I HAVE LIVED WITH THIS CURSE, BEEN TASKED TO THIS PLACE, FOR CENTURIES!
BUT NOW IT IS YOUR TURN. I BROUGHT YOU HERE SO THAT I CAN FINALLY BE FREE!

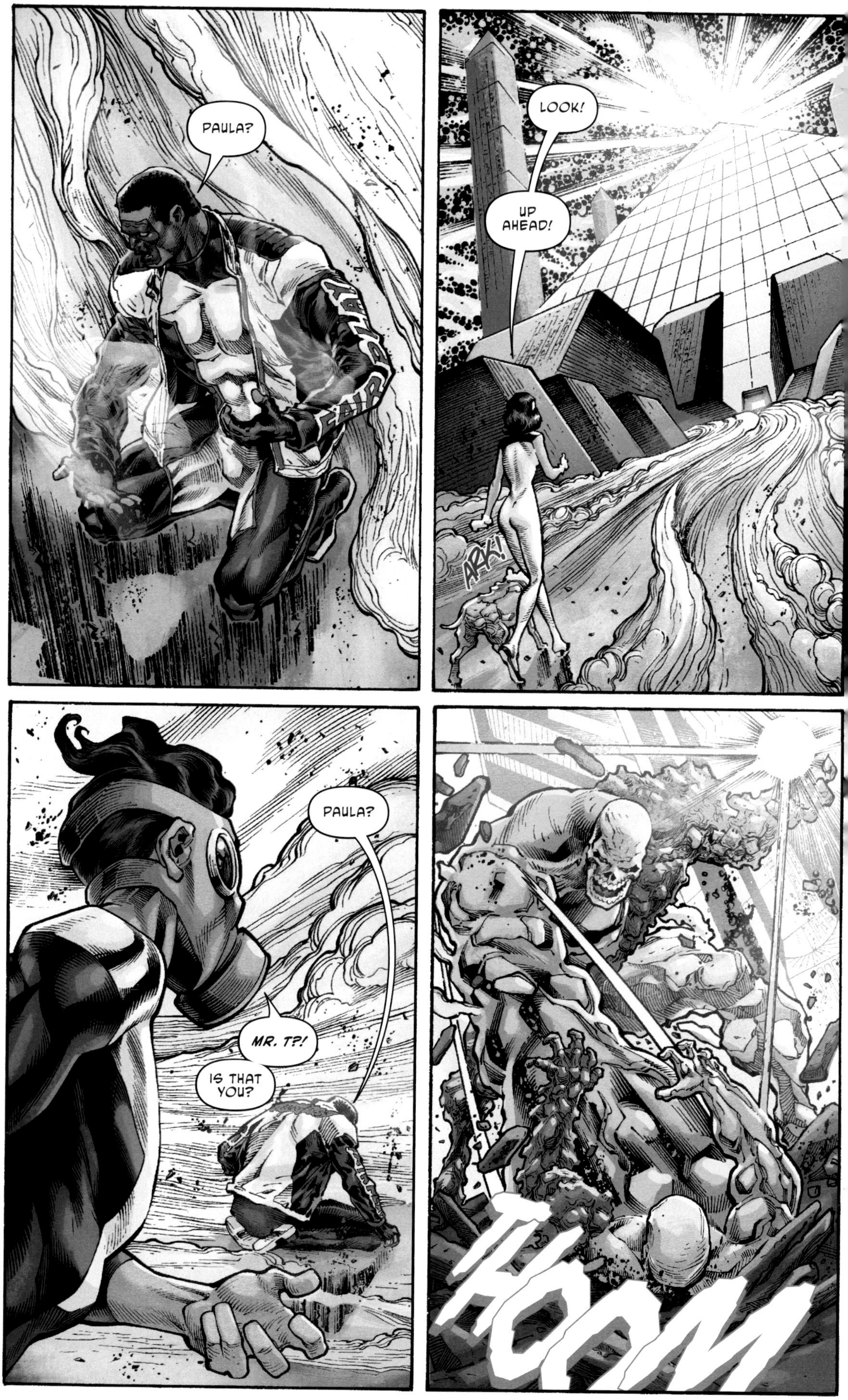
PAULA?
FAIR PLAY
LOOK!
UP AHEAD!
ARK!
PAULA?
MR. T?!
IS THAT YOU?
THOOM

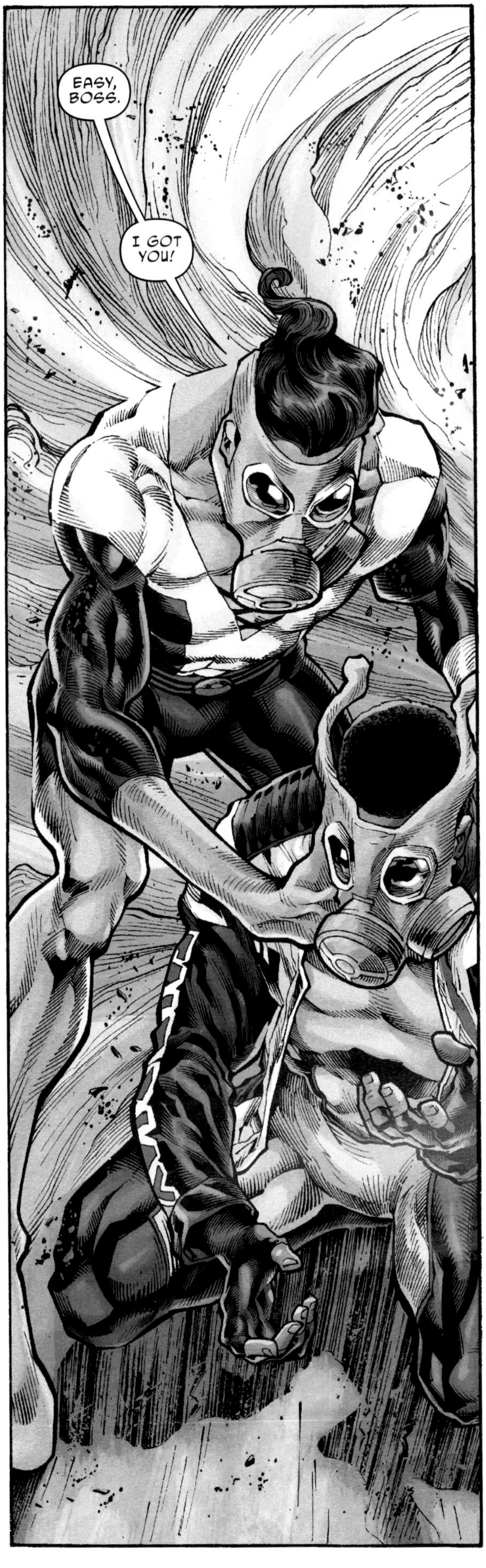
EASY, BOSS.
I GOT YOU!

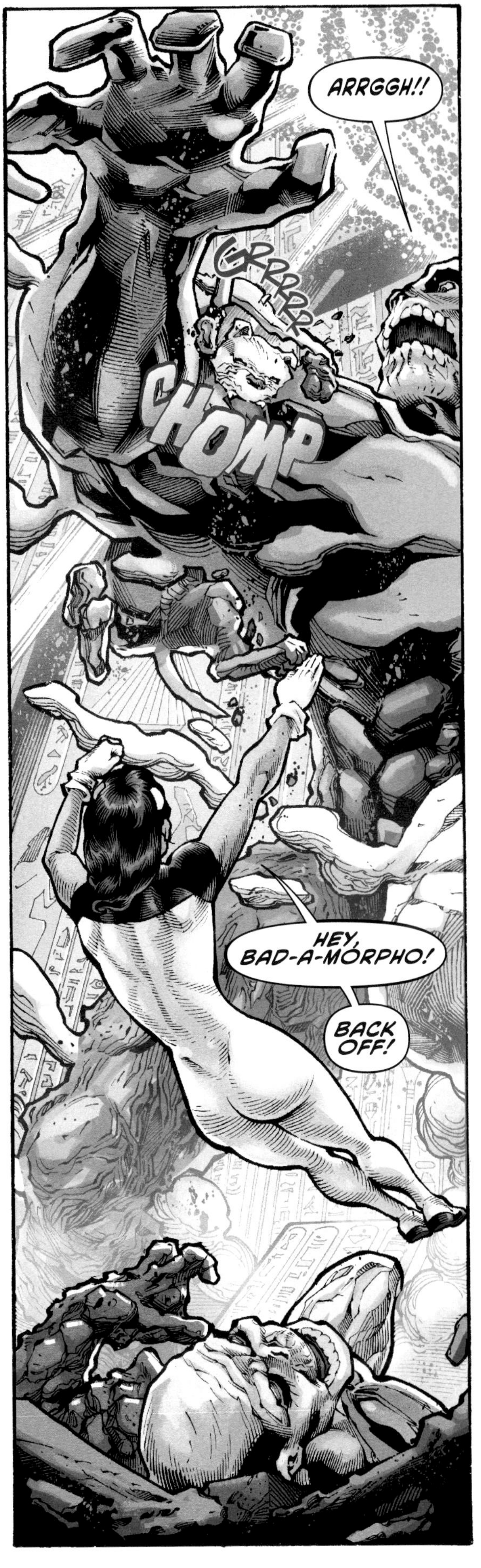
ARRGGH!!
CHOMP
HEY, BAD-A-MORPHO!
BACK OFF!

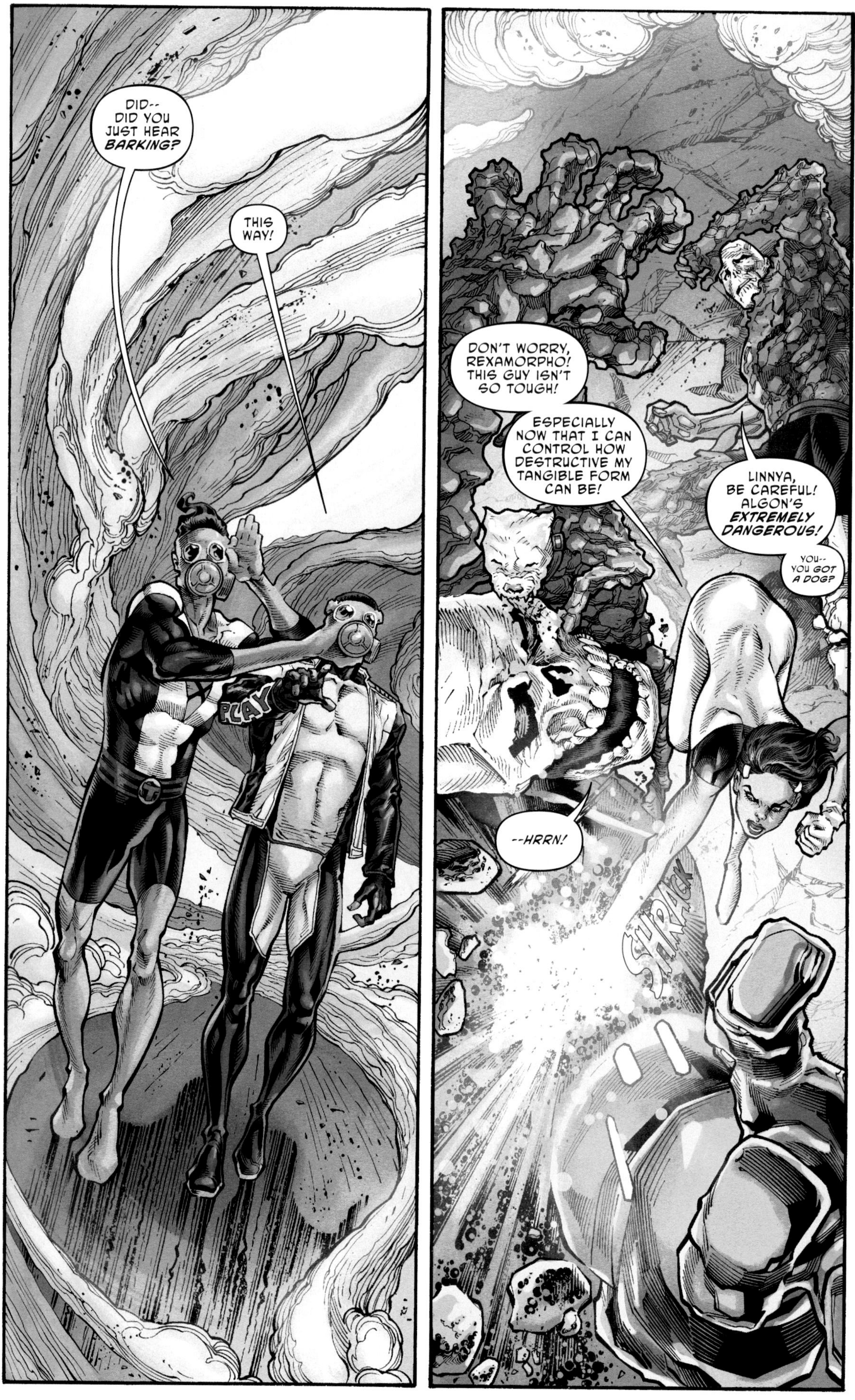
DID--
DID YOU JUST HEAR *BARKING?*
THIS WAY!
DON'T WORRY, REXAMORPHO! THIS GUY ISN'T SO TOUGH!
ESPECIALLY NOW THAT I CAN CONTROL HOW DESTRUCTIVE MY TANGIBLE FORM CAN BE!
LINNYA, BE CAREFUL! ALGON'S ***EXTREMELY DANGEROUS!***
YOU-- YOU GOT A DOG?
--HRRN!
SHRACK

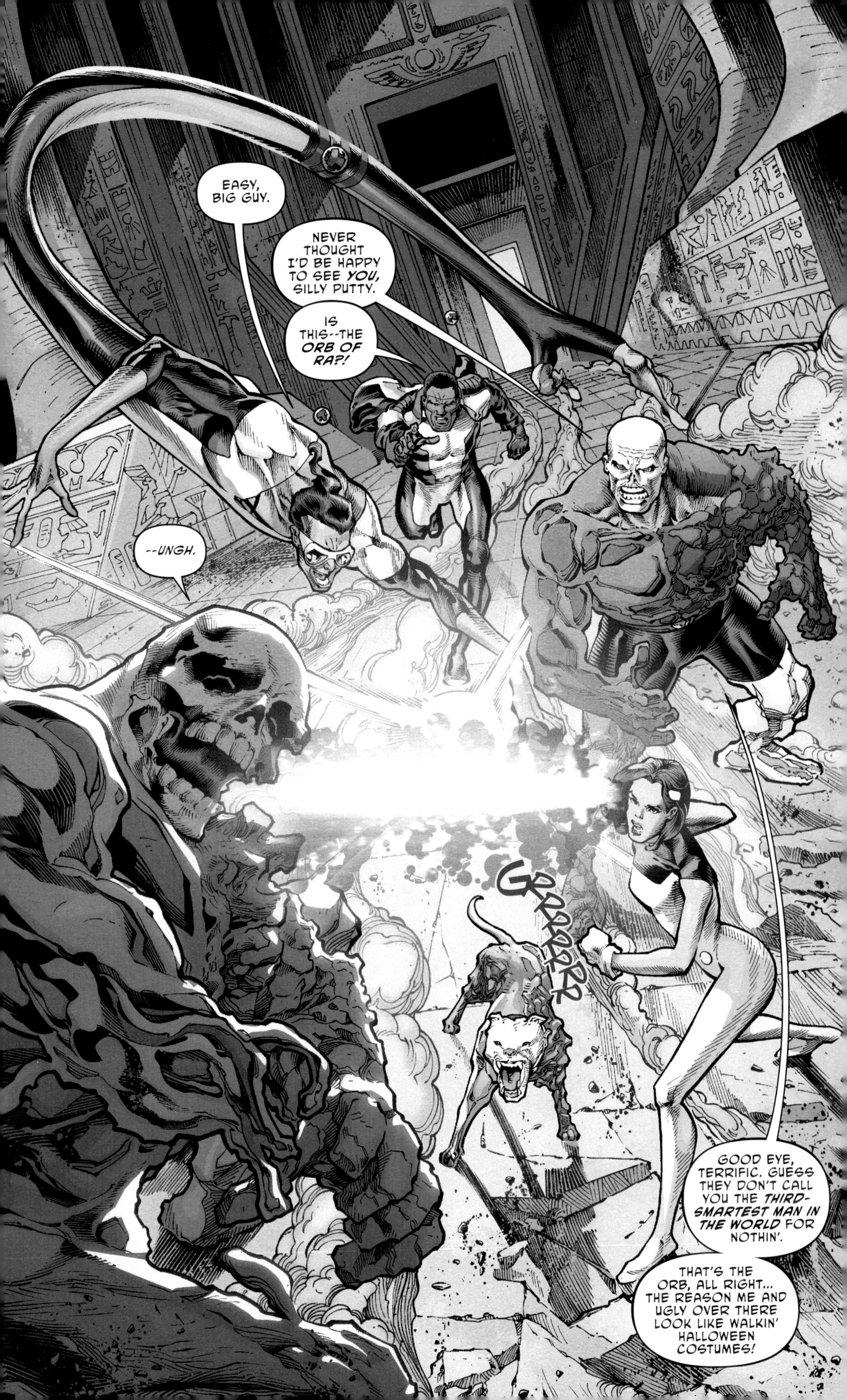
EASY, BIG GUY.
NEVER THOUGHT I'D BE HAPPY TO SEE *YOU*, SILLY PUTTY.
IS THIS--THE *ORB OF RA?!*
--UNGH.
GRRRRRRR
GOOD EYE, TERRIFIC. GUESS THEY DON'T CALL YOU THE *THIRD-SMARTEST MAN IN THE WORLD* FOR NOTHIN'.
THAT'S THE ORB, ALL RIGHT... THE REASON ME AND UGLY OVER THERE LOOK LIKE WALKIN' HALLOWEEN COSTUMES!

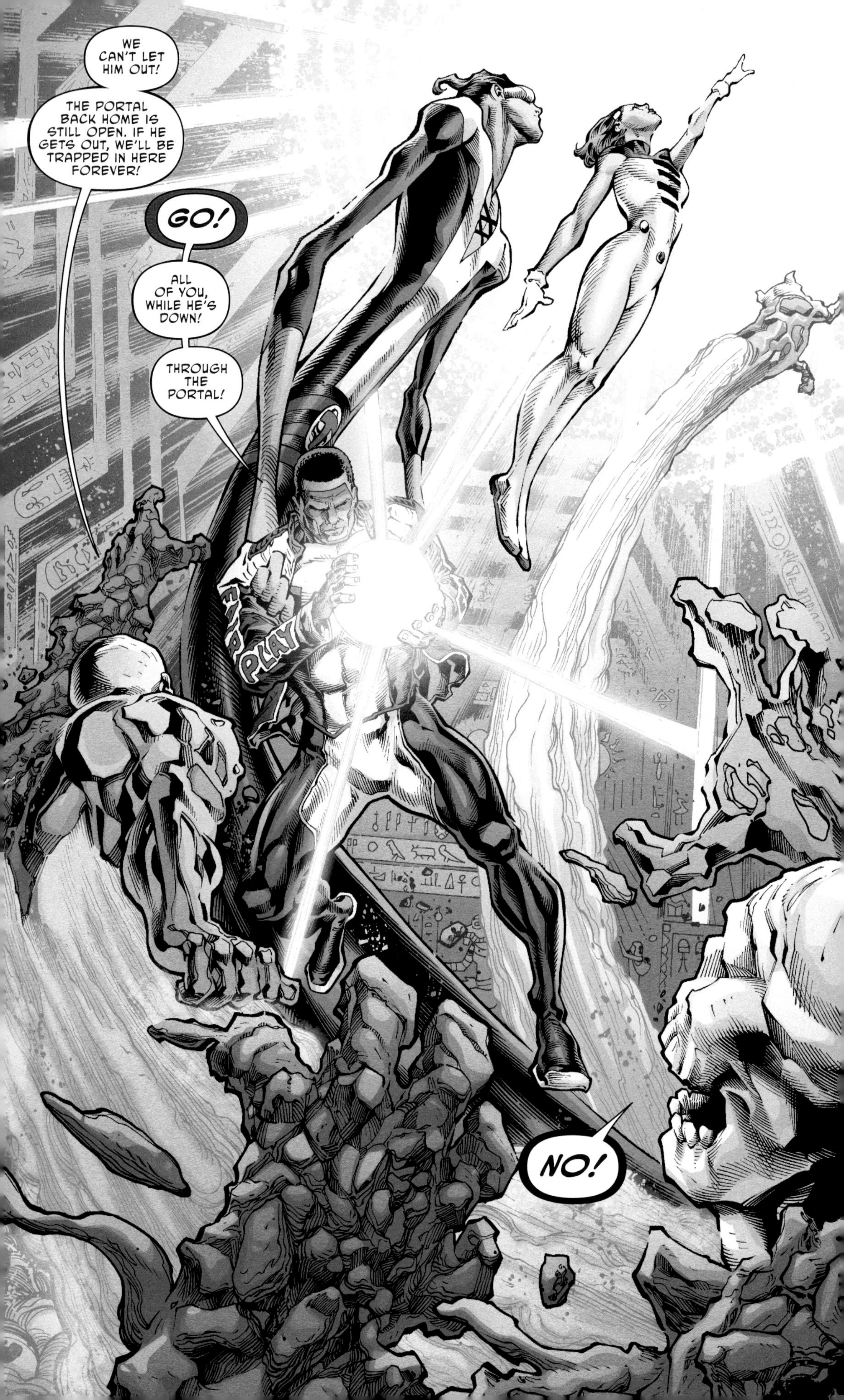
WE CAN'T LET HIM OUT!
THE PORTAL BACK HOME IS STILL OPEN. IF HE GETS OUT, WE'LL BE TRAPPED IN HERE FOREVER!
GO!
ALL OF YOU, WHILE HE'S DOWN!
THROUGH THE PORTAL!
FAIR PLAY
NO!

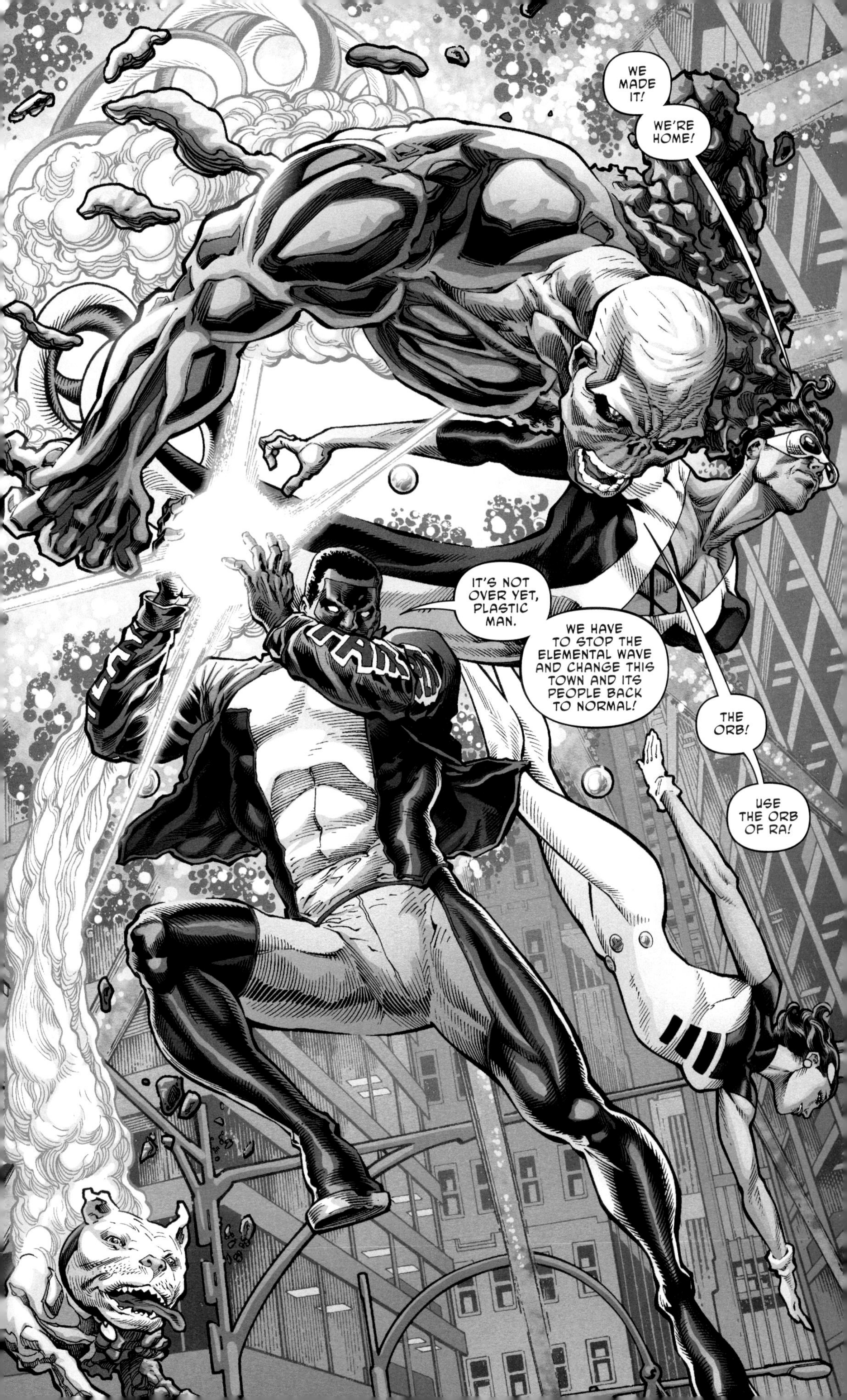
WE MADE IT!
WE'RE HOME!
IT'S NOT OVER YET, PLASTIC MAN.
WE HAVE TO STOP THE ELEMENTAL WAVE AND CHANGE THIS TOWN AND ITS PEOPLE BACK TO NORMAL!
THE ORB!
USE THE ORB OF RA!

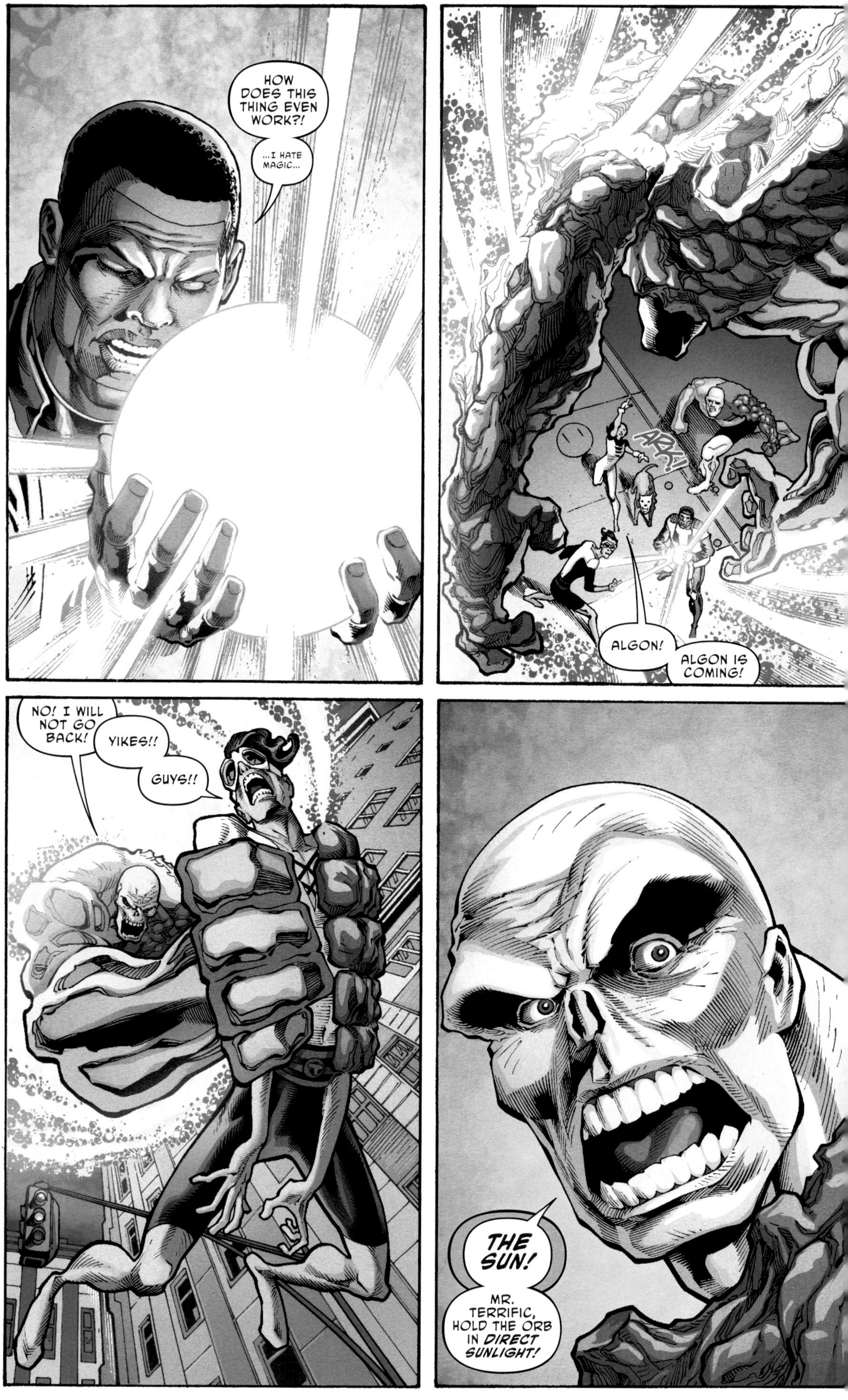
HOW DOES THIS THING EVEN WORK?!
...I HATE MAGIC...
ARK?!
ALGON!
ALGON IS COMING!
NO! I WILL NOT GO BACK!
YIKES!!
GUYS!!
THE SUN!
MR. TERRIFIC, HOLD THE ORB IN DIRECT SUNLIGHT!

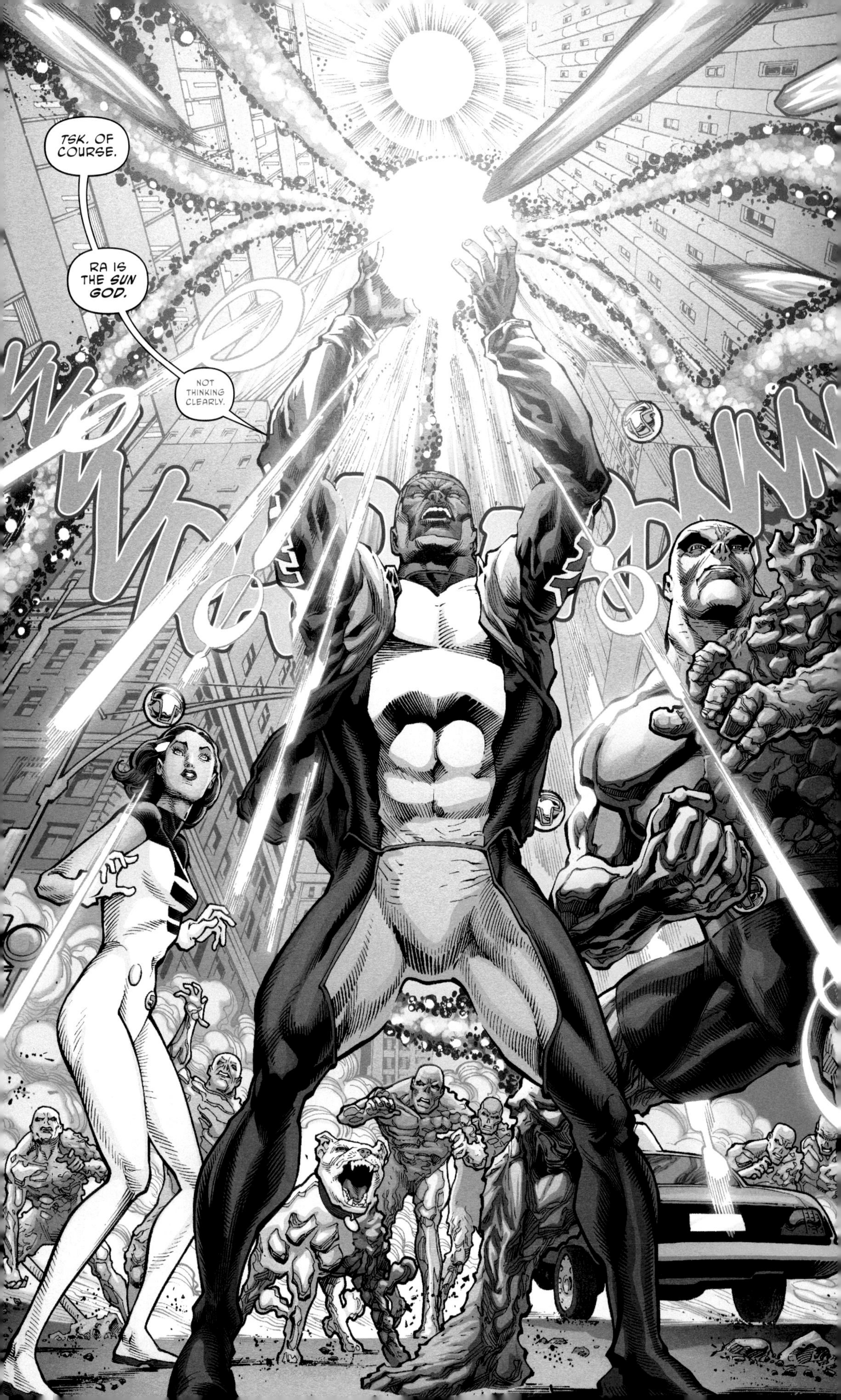
TSK. OF COURSE.
RA IS THE SUN GOD.
NOT THINKING CLEARLY.

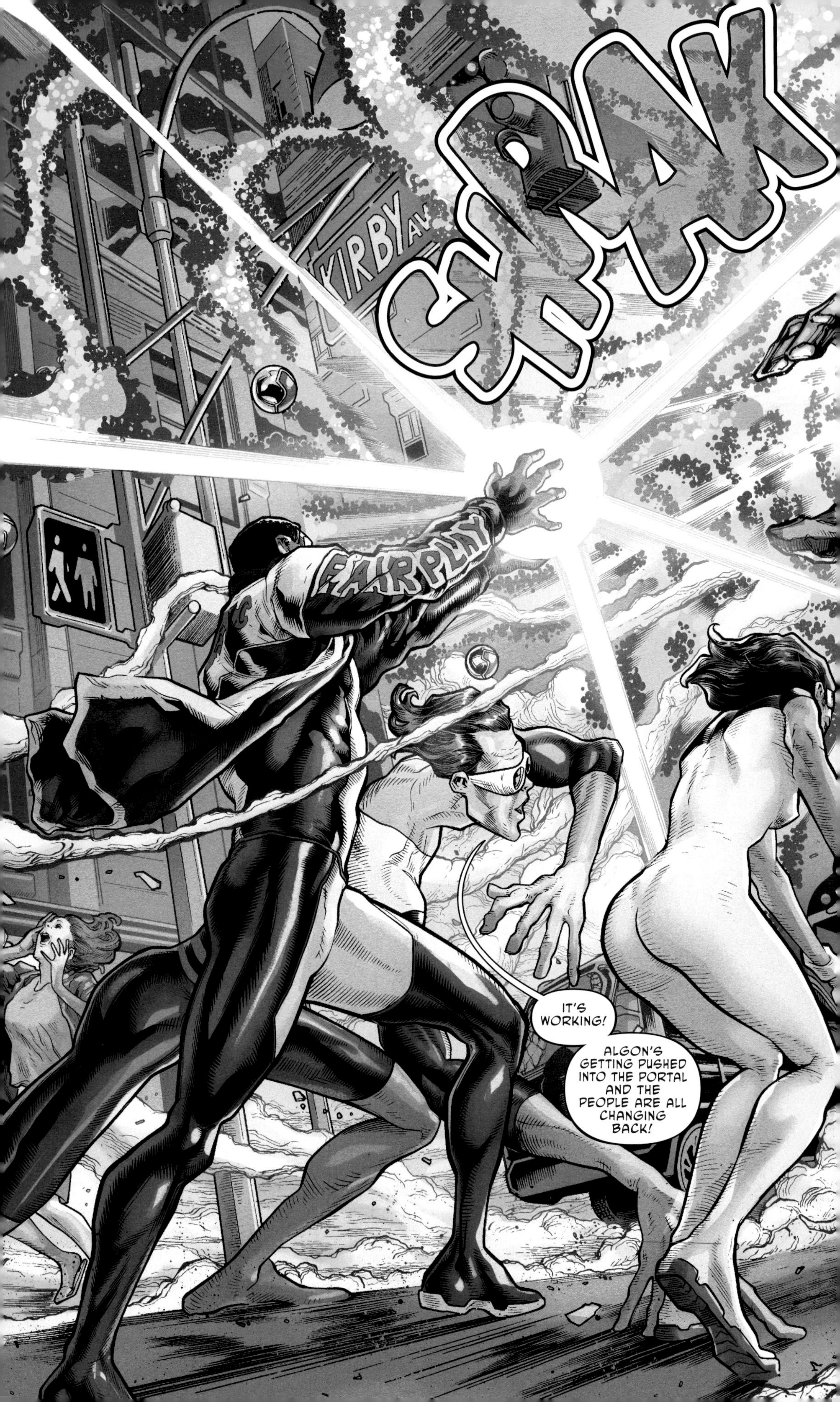
KIRBY AV
CHRAK
FAIR PLAY
IT'S WORKING!
ALGON'S GETTING PUSHED INTO THE PORTAL AND THE PEOPLE ARE ALL CHANGING BACK!

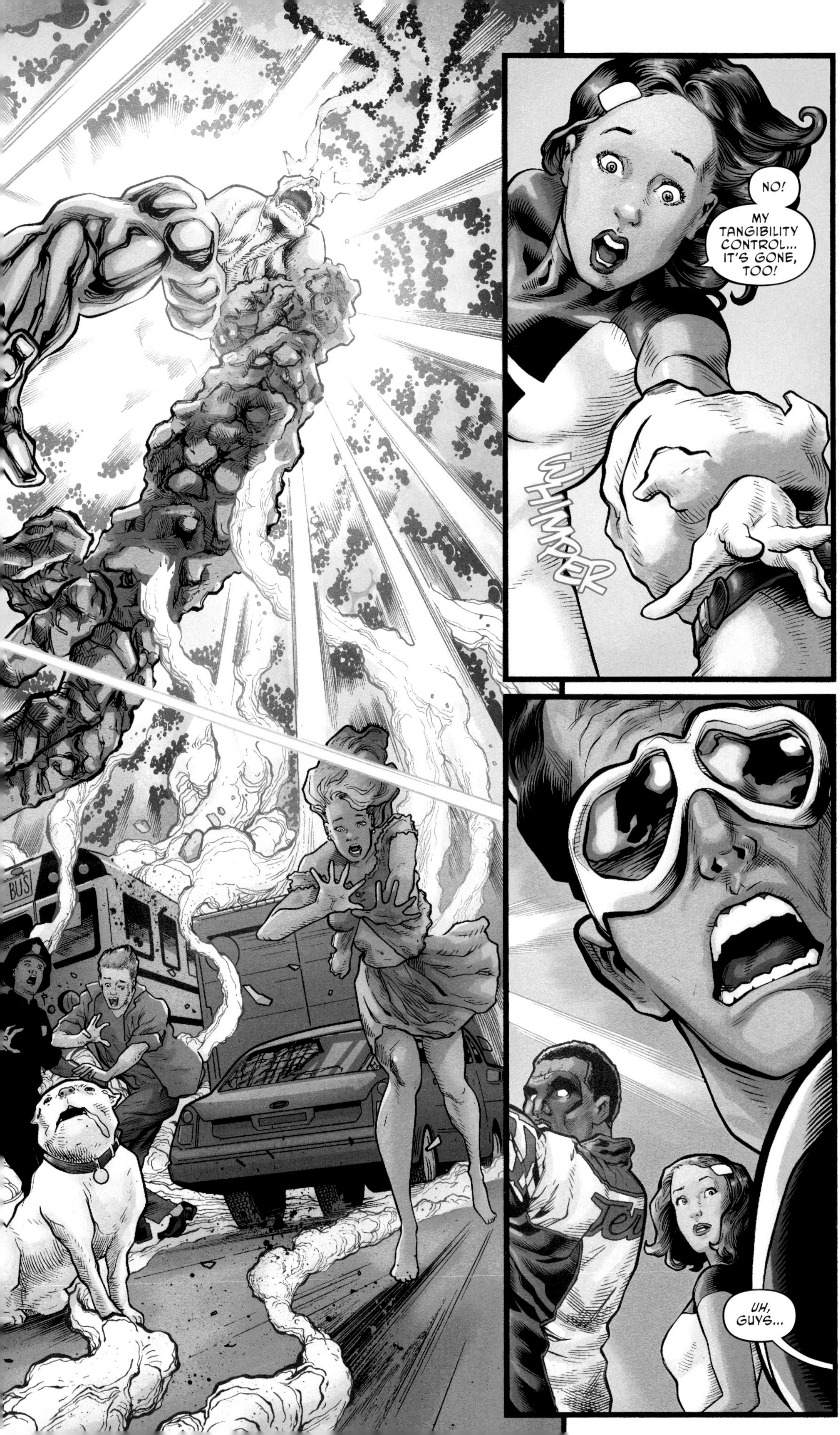

BUS
NO!
MY TANGIBILITY CONTROL... IT'S GONE, TOO!
WHIMPER
UH, GUYS...

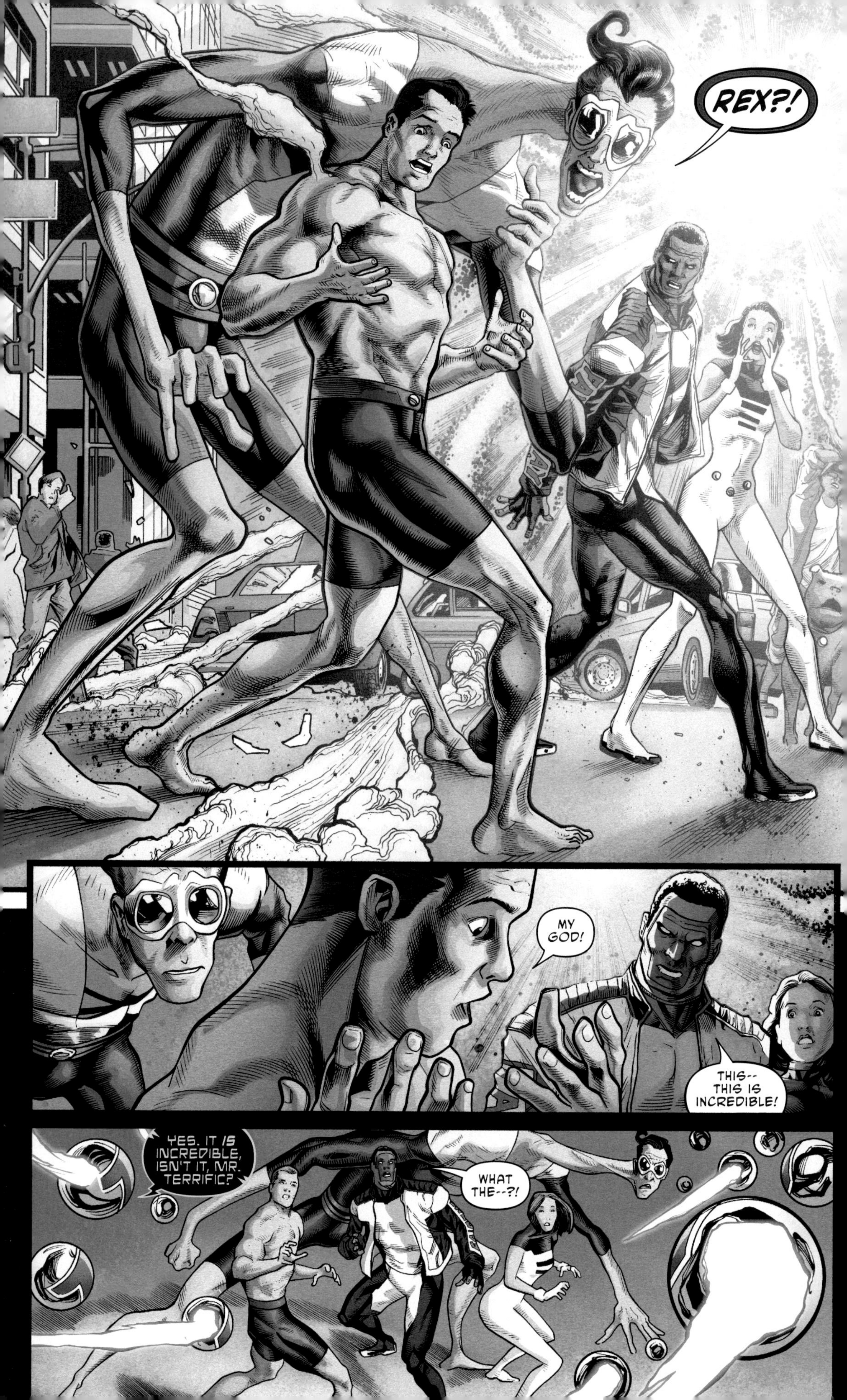
REX?!
MY GOD!
THIS-- THIS IS INCREDIBLE!
YES. IT IS INCREDIBLE, ISN'T IT, MR. TERRIFIC?
WHAT THE--?!

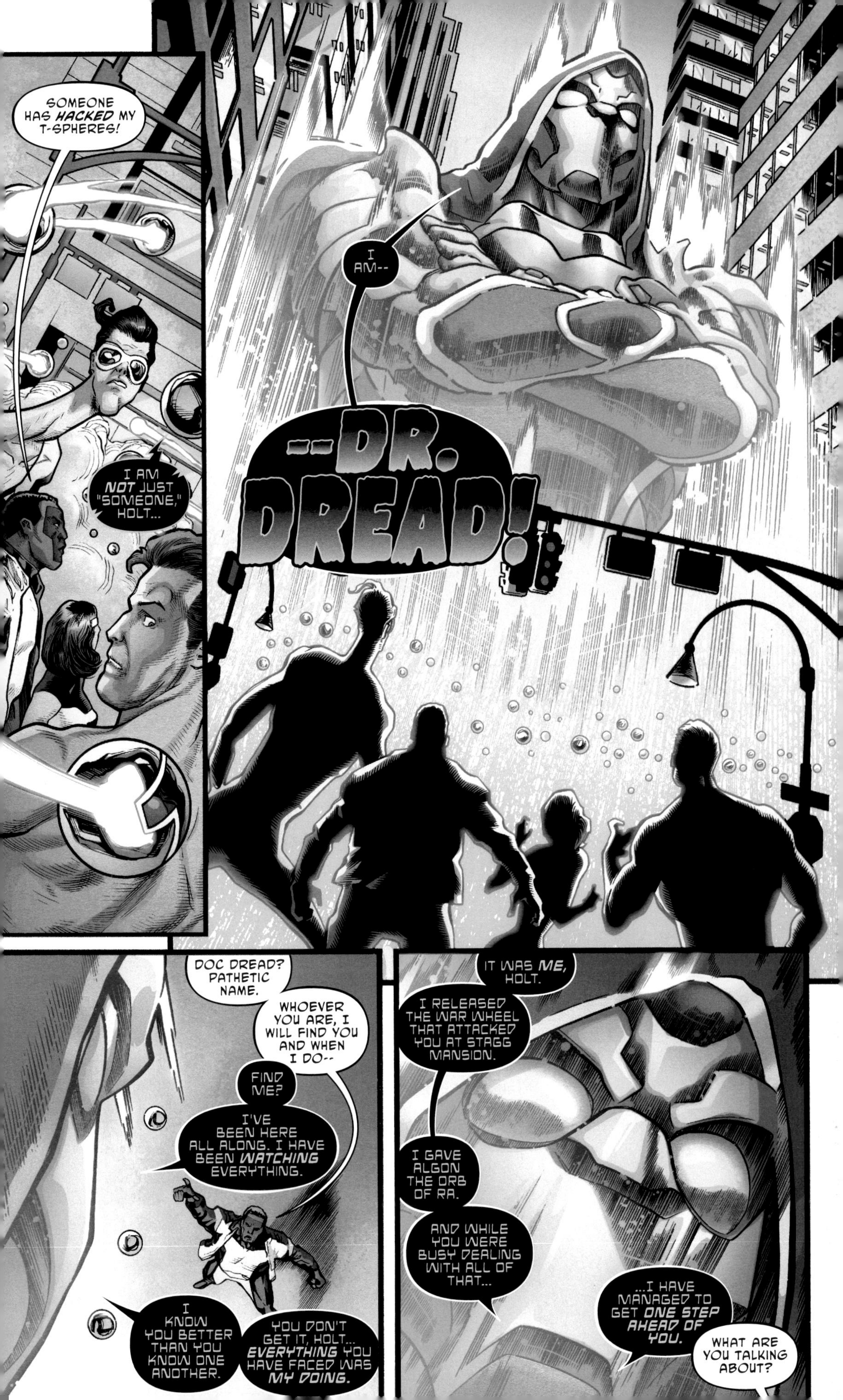
SOMEONE HAS HACKED MY T-SPHERES!
I AM NOT JUST "SOMEONE," HOLT...
I AM--
--DR. DREAD!
DOC DREAD? PATHETIC NAME.
WHOEVER YOU ARE, I WILL FIND YOU AND WHEN I DO--
FIND ME?
I'VE BEEN HERE ALL ALONG. I HAVE BEEN WATCHING EVERYTHING.
I KNOW YOU BETTER THAN YOU KNOW ONE ANOTHER.
YOU DON'T GET IT, HOLT... EVERYTHING YOU HAVE FACED WAS MY DOING.
IT WAS ME, HOLT.
I RELEASED THE WAR WHEEL THAT ATTACKED YOU AT STAGG MANSION.
I GAVE ALGON THE ORB OF RA.
AND WHILE YOU WERE BUSY DEALING WITH ALL OF THAT...
...I HAVE MANAGED TO GET ONE STEP AHEAD OF YOU.
WHAT ARE YOU TALKING ABOUT?

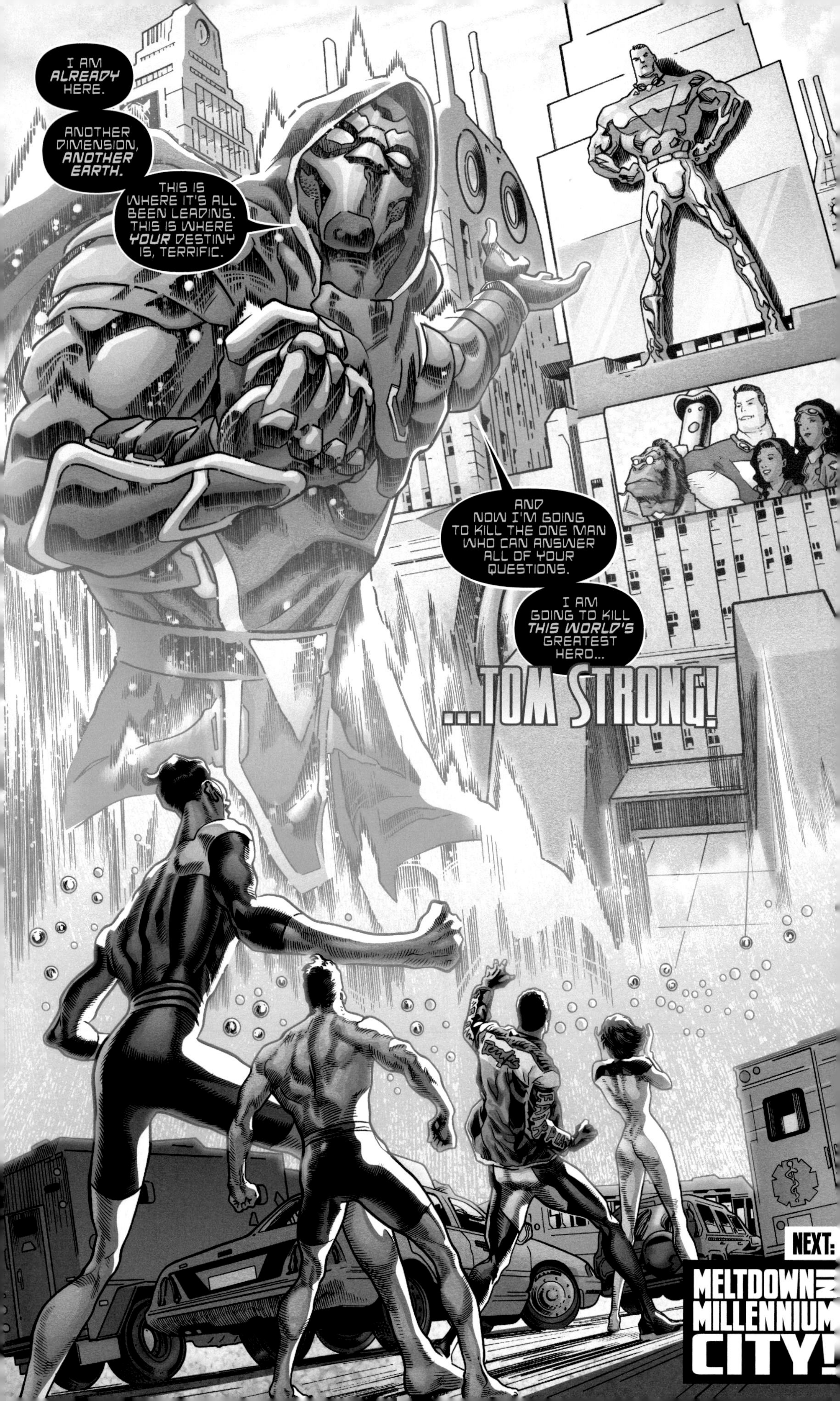

I AM *ALREADY* HERE.
ANOTHER DIMENSION, *ANOTHER EARTH.*
THIS IS WHERE IT'S ALL BEEN LEADING. THIS IS WHERE *YOUR* DESTINY IS, TERRIFIC.
AND NOW I'M GOING TO KILL THE ONE MAN WHO CAN ANSWER ALL OF YOUR QUESTIONS.
I AM GOING TO KILL *THIS WORLD'S* GREATEST HERO...
...TOM STRONG!
NEXT:
MELTDOWN IN MILLENNIUM CITY!

THE TERRIFICS #1 FOLD-OUT COVER

ARTWORK BY IVAN REIS WITH MARCELO MAIOLO

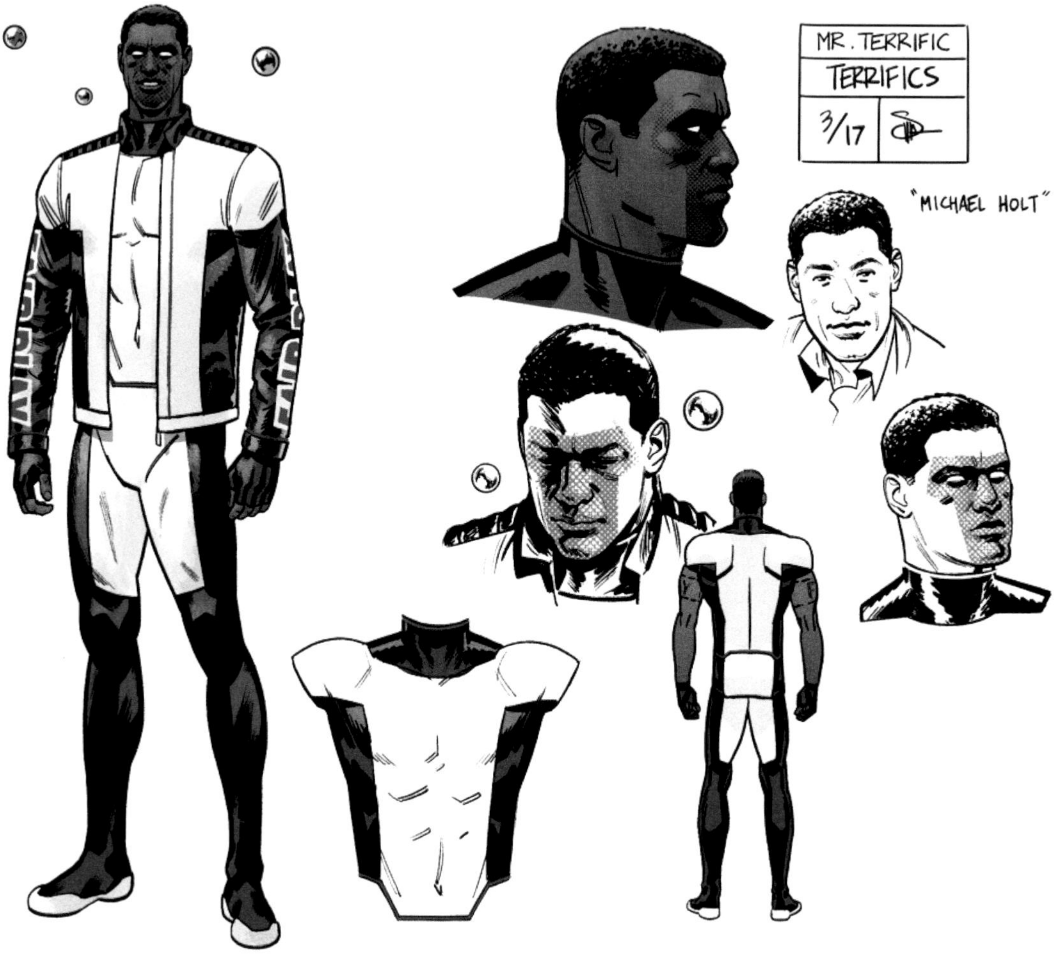
MR. TERRIFIC
TERRIFICS
3/17
"MICHAEL HOLT"

CHARACTER SKETCHES BY EVAN "DOC" SHANER | **MR. TERRIFIC**

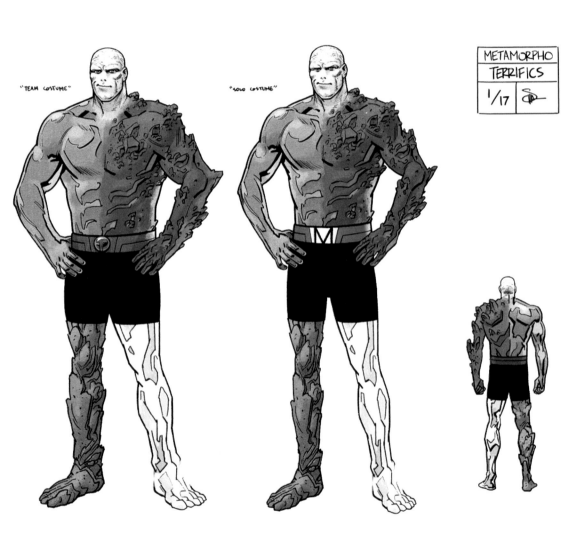

"TEAM COSTUME"

"SOLO COSTUME"

METAMORPHO
TERRIFICS
1/17

EVOCATIVE OF
DAVE COCKRUM'S
DESIGN FOR
TINYA.

PHANTOM GIRL
TERRIFICS
3/17

"LINYN WAZZO"

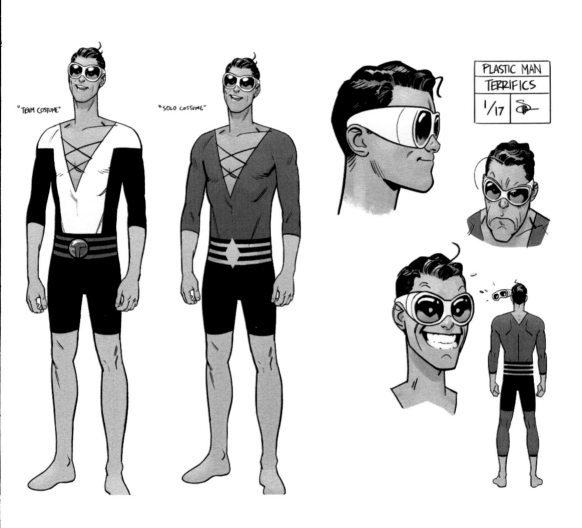

"TEAM COSTUME"

"SOLO COSTUME"

PLASTIC MAN
TERRIFICS
1/17

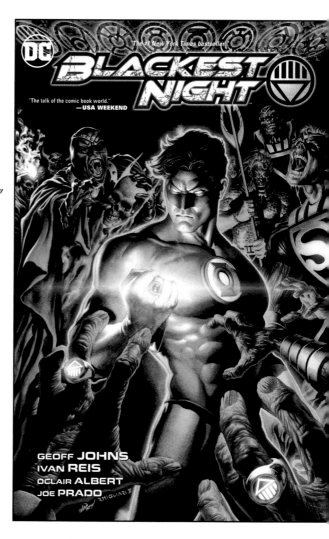

JUSTICE LEAGUE OF AMERICA
VOL. 1 THE EXTREMISTS
STEVE ORLANDO and IVAN REIS

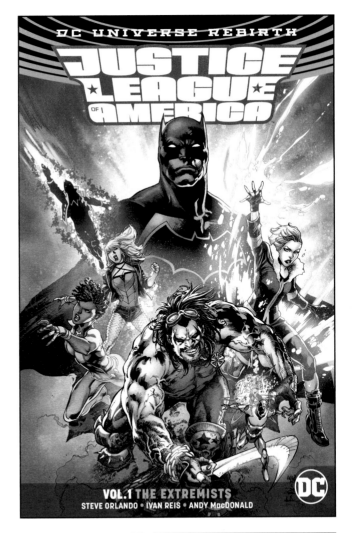

**JUSTICE LEAGUE OF AMERICA
VOL. 2: CURSE OF THE KINGBUTCHER**

**JUSTICE LEAGUE OF AMERICA
VOL. 3: PANIC IN THE MICROVERSE**

**JUSTICE LEAGUE OF AMERICA:
THE ROAD TO REBIRTH**

JUSTICE LEAGUE

VOL. 1: ORIGIN
GEOFF JOHNS
and JIM LEE

JUSTICE LEAGUE
VOL. 2: THE VILLAIN'S JOURNEY

JUSTICE LEAGUE
VOL. 3: THRONE OF ATLANTIS

READ THE ENTIRE EPIC